OXFORD HISTORICAL SERIES

Editors

N. GIBBS R. W. SOUTHERN J. S. WATSON
R. B. WERNHAM

SECOND SERIES

NOTE

*This series comprises carefully selected studies which have been submitted,
or are based upon theses submitted, for higher degrees in this University.
The works listed below are those still in print*

THE
RADICAL DUKE

Career and Correspondence of
Charles Lennox
third Duke of Richmond

BY

ALISON GILBERT OLSON

OXFORD UNIVERSITY PRESS

1961

Oxford University Press, Amen House, London E.C.4

GLASGOW NEW YORK TORONTO MELBOURNE WELLINGTON
BOMBAY CALCUTTA MADRAS KARACHI KUALA LUMPUR
CAPE TOWN IBADAN NAIROBI ACCRA

© *Oxford University Press 1961*

PRINTED IN GREAT BRITAIN

TO MY
MOTHER AND FATHER

PREFACE

IN preparing this study it was my good fortune to have worked with Miss L. S. Sutherland, the Principal, Lady Margaret Hall; to her criticism and encouragement I owe the greatest thanks. Professor Max Beloff and Mr. Steven Watson have offered extremely useful points of information and suggestions on general organization, and I am grateful to Sir Lewis Namier and to Mr. Jack Brooke of the History of Parliament Trust for their help and for permission to use their typescripts and microfilm copies of manuscripts I could never otherwise have read. Professor Thomas Copeland, editor-in-chief of the Burke Correspondence, has given me many hours of his time, particularly in answering my repeated questions about references in the Fitzwilliam manuscripts at Sheffield. I am also grateful to Professor G. H. Guttridge of the University of California for his advice and for his permission to use a letter of Richmond's now in his private possession. To Mr. John Woods and Miss Patricia Whitehead I owe thanks for respectively calling my attention to material concerning Richmond in the manuscripts of Granville Sharp and the Earl of Bathurst. The Earl of Bathurst and the Duke of Richmond have kindly allowed me to inspect manuscripts in their homes. The Keeper of the Brotherton Manuscripts has allowed me to print letters from that collection, and the Duke of Portland, the Marquis of Lansdowne, the Marquis of Camden, the Earl Fitzwilliam, the Earl of Albemarle, and the Earl of Stanhope have kindly allowed me to print letters from their private collections. Needless to add, no study of this kind could have been prepared without the countless favours of people like the librarian who spent hours of time tracing references, arranging for use of a microfilm reader, or obtaining a typist to copy library manuscripts, or like the county record officer who collected out-of-the-way manuscripts in his own car or made special arrangements for my own transportation to the Record Office.

1961.   A. G. O.

CONTENTS

ABBREVIATIONS FOR THE
CHIEF PRINTED SOURCES USED

Albemarle, *Rockingham*: *Memoirs of the Marquis of Rockingham and his Contemporaries*, ed. The Earl of Albemarle, 1852.

Burke Correspondence: *Correspondence of the Right Honourable Edmund Burke, 1744–1797*, ed. Charles, Earl Fitzwilliam and Sir Richard Bourke, 1844.

Chatham Correspondence: *Correspondence of William Pitt, Earl of Chatham*, ed. W. S. Taylor and Captain J. H. Pringle, 1839.

Corr. Geo. III: *Correspondence of King George III, 1760 to 1783*, ed. Sir John Fortescue, 1927.

Walpole Memoirs: Walpole, Horace. *Memoirs of the Reign of King George III*, ed. G. F. Russell Barker, 1894.

Walpole Last Journals: *The Last Journals of Horace Walpole from 1771 to 1783*, ed. Dr. Doran with notes by A. F. Stewart, 1910.

Parl. Hist.: *Cobbett's Parliamentary History*. London, 1765–85.

I

PERSONALITY, PATRONAGE, AND THE KING

IN 1751 Charles Lennox, a fifteen-year-old student in Geneva, succeeded his father as third Duke of Richmond and Lennox and Duc d'Aubigny in France.[1] He also inherited a small estate in Aubigny and two-thirds of the total returns from the duty of one shilling on every chaldron of coal exported from Newcastle, a duty originally granted to the Dukes of Richmond by Charles II and valued at £15,000–£17,000 a year.[2] Six months later, on the death of his mother, the young Duke inherited a house in Privy Gardens, the family estate at Goodwood (worth about £1,000 a year), and the rest of the revenue from the coal duty.[3] After the payment of his father's debts and mortgages and his own living expenses during his minority, Richmond reached the age of twenty-one with an accumulated fortune of nearly £19,000.[4]

[1] In 1734 the second Duke of Richmond had inherited the Dukedom of Aubigny at the death of his grandmother, Louise de Keroualle, Duchess of Portsmouth and Aubigny. The title had been given by letter patent in 1684 but had never been registered with the Parlement of Paris (see Le Chenaye—Des Bois et Badier, *Dictionnaire de la noblesse*, 3rd ed., 1863, i. 953–5). Richmond first tried to obtain the registration in 1769, but was convinced it was impossible (at least during the lifetime of Louis XV) because he was not a Catholic (Madame du Deffand to Horace Walpole, 6 June 1770, *Walpole Correspondence*, ed. W. S. Lewis, 1939, iv. 417–18). In 1777, three years after the accession of Louis XVI, Richmond was finally successful (Douzieme volume des Ordonnances du Roy Louis Seize, 15 May to 31 July 1777, X I H 8819, ff. 237–40, 'Lettres de Surannation, (sur) erection de la terre d'Aubigny en Duche pairie et Confirmation', Archives Nationales, Paris).

[2] The tax was originally agreed to by the burgesses of Newcastle as a substitute for paying the arrears of an ancient duty of 2*d.* per chaldron due to the crown on all coal sold to persons not franchised in the port of Newcastle. In 1677 Charles II granted the profits to his illegitimate son, the Duke of Richmond, and his heirs. From 1751 to 1756 the returns ranged from £14,000 to £16,000; by the period 1789 to 1799 they had risen to an average of £21,000. Fearing that poor rates would be levied on the returns, Richmond sold his grant to the government for £728,333 in 1800. The tax was abolished in 1831 (see J. U. Nef, *Rise of the British Coal Industry*, 1932, ii. 306–7; Matthias Dunn, *An Historical, Geological, and Descriptive View of the Coal Trade of the North of England*, 1844, p. 88; John Sykes, *Local Records . . . in Newcastle upon Tyne*, 1866, i. 117; and R. L. Galloway, *A History of Coal Mining in Great Britain*, 1822, pp. 30–32). [3] Add. MS. 32,722, f. 94.

[4] See Add. MS. 32,889, ff. 195–6, for the financial accounts of the trustees of Richmond's estate. Over the 4½ years from Aug. 1751 to Feb. 1756 Richmond's

Originally Richmond planned a military career. He enlisted in the Army at seventeen, was highly regarded by Wolfe,[1] rose to the rank of Colonel in four years, and emerged from the Seven Years War as a Major-General, having distinguished himself for bravery and leadership at the battle of Minden in 1759. As Lord Lieutenant of Sussex in 1763, he assumed active leadership of the Sussex militia.

After the war he left the military life for a political career, for which he was suited by the possession of both fortunate connexions and exceptional talents. The second Duke, an amiable nonentity in politics, had been a supporter of the Duke of Newcastle. Newcastle, along with Henry Fox, Richmond's brother-in-law, and the Earl of Albemarle, his uncle, had been a guardian of Richmond during his minority, and had probably intended to make him a political protégé. Two of Richmond's sisters, Emily, Duchess of Leinster, and Lady Louisa Conolly, married 'the first peer and first commoner' of Ireland[2] respectively; in 1757 Richmond himself married the beautiful Lady Mary Bruce, daughter of the Countess of Aylesbury and step-daughter of H. S. Conway.[3]

Richmond was commanding in appearance, dignified, above average in intelligence (if poorly educated), and capable of intense work. He spoke well if not brilliantly in Parliament, put careful efforts into rehearsing his delivery, and sought practice at public gatherings in Chichester. By 1765, when Richmond accepted his first major political appointment—the French embassy—his fortune, ability, and personal reputation gave every promise that he would become one of the most influential statesmen of his time.

And yet, in spite of his initial promise, Richmond remained only a minor politician. In one way or another nearly

---

total estate amounted to £68,000, of which £49,000 was paid out, the major expenses being roughly £17,000 for payment of the second Duke's bills and mortgages, £14,700 for Richmond's expenses abroad, £1,650 for his expenses in England, and £4,000 for upkeep of Goodwood. Of the £18,412 clear at Richmond's majority, £14,112 was invested in South Sea annuities and £4,300 in 3½ per cent. bank annuities.

[1] A bundle of fifteen letters from Wolfe, from 1755 to 1757, is among the Goodwood MSS. (Box 29, Bundle IX).

[2] Burke to Richmond, 26 Sept. 1775, *Burke Correspondence*, ii. 75.

[3] Richmond's request and Conway's response are in the Goodwood MSS. See Richmond to Lord George Lennox, 25 Jan. and 12 Feb. 1757, *H.M.C. Bathurst*, pp. 676–9.

every one of his assets dwindled into a liability by the end of his career. Despite his bravery as a military officer he never worked well with troops, often quarrelled with subordinates, and in 1795 was dismissed from the post of Master-General of the Ordnance in near disgrace partly because he had been held responsible for the failure of military expeditions to the Continent. Despite his immense inheritance and frugal personal expenditure he was £95,000 in debt by 1799 and paying £700 interest per quarter.[1]

Despite close family ties he had broken politically with every member of his family by 1786 except his brother, Lord George Lennox, and possibly his father-in-law, H. S. Conway. Despite his intelligence, hard work, and speaking ability he never became a parliamentary orator of the first rank; he was so disliked that the defeat of his Fortifications Bill in 1786 was regarded primarily as the result of his own unpopularity, and faithful government supporters opposed the bill out of personal hatred for Richmond.[2]

Why did Richmond's career prove so disappointing? A

[1] Richmond's major account books consist of Goodwood household accounts, 1762–1806 (A2–6), his quarterly expense accounts, 1775–1805 (B1–3), a list of expenses, 1756–61 (Ae1), and one of travel expenses in 1759 (Ae2), a book giving servants' wages (A4a), a bank account book of 1794 (E5), farm accounts, 1781–3 (MS. K), and a miscellaneous account book covering roughly 1798–1806, now in the personal possession of the present Duke of Richmond. It would appear from these very incomplete records that Richmond's enormous annual income varied from approximately £17,000 in 1756 to about £23,000 immediately before he sold his right to the coal duties in 1800. His figures for the period 1775 to 1792 indicate that he spent roughly £4,000 annually for the upkeep of Goodwood House and its plantations, and £400 each for the upkeep of Richmond House, care of his own sloop, his militia, and hunting. By 1798–9 he was spending £8,600 for interest and taxes alone (£3,300 for interest, £2,300 for poor rates, and £3,000 for taxes). The remainder of his money, and the £95,000 he borrowed, seems to have been spent primarily on extending the Goodwood estate, adding two new wings to Goodwood House, and building at least two new houses, new dog kennels, and a race track on the estate (see John Kent, *Records and Reminiscences of Goodwood*, 1896). He sustained a heavy financial loss when his uninsured house in Privy Gardens burned down in 1792. In order to reduce his taxes Richmond sold his coal duties to the government in 1800 and in 1802 disposed of £6,000 of 5 per cent. bank stock and 3 per cent. consols. He thus hoped to save nearly £6,000 a year on taxes, to be applied to the principal of his debts, but by 1805, probably because of the building of the Goodwood race track, his debts had increased still further.

[2] Daniel Pulteney to Duke of Rutland, 28 Feb. 1786, *H.M.C. Rutland*, iii. 285. 'The fact is—what his Grace might have discovered long ago—the House of Commons here has no opinion of his candour or of his judgement . . .'; George III to Pitt, 28 Feb. 1786, P.R.O. 30/8/103.

major reason was that nearly every one of Richmond's assets was counter-balanced by a serious political handicap. For eighteenth-century parliamentary leaders wealth, connexions, and speaking ability were of use only if accompanied by the King's favour, patronage control, and an agreeable personality, none of which Richmond possessed.

First, he lacked the King's support. In 1760 he rashly resigned the Bedchamber because Harvey and Lords Fitzmaurice and Downe received army promotions over the head of his brother, Lord George Lennox.[1] In two days he repented the incident; the King never forgot it. When Richmond was appointed Secretary of State, the King, having suggested other alternatives, told both Newcastle and Hardwicke, 'I have done all I could to avoid this.'[2] If anything, relations between Richmond and the King deteriorated during Richmond's short term of office in 1766.

Second, Richmond influenced the return of only three members of the Commons at most, and except for the election of 1790, when he wanted to extend the electoral influence of the Ordnance, he was not interested in returning more. Unlike Rockingham, Newcastle, or the Cavendishes, he did not have a pocket borough. He was offered the borough of Haslemere in 1778, but turned the offer over to Portland because 'I have no money and am not particularly desirous of that sort of interest.'[3]

[1] At least twelve contemporary sources cover the incident in some detail, and valuable unprinted letters to and from Richmond are in the Bute MSS., Goodwood MSS. (Box 29, Bundle 3), and Egerton MSS. (1862, f. 86). For an adequate discussion in a published source see 'Memoir on Events attending the Death of George II and the Accession of George III', by Henry Fox, in *Life and Letters of Lady Sarah Lennox*, ed. the Countess of Ilchester and Lord Stavordale, 1901, i. 20–24.

[2] Newcastle Memorandum, 24 May 1766, printed in the Duke of Newcastle's *Narrative of Events attending the Changes in Government, 1765–67*, ed. M. Bateson, 1898, p. 66. 'His Majesty . . . has never once failed to express his own disapprobation of the Duke of Richmond.' See also Hardwicke to C. Yorke, 17 May 1766, Albemarle, *Rockingham*, i. 331–3. In 1767 the King held Richmond particularly responsible for the opposition to civil list grants for the royal brothers (George III to Grafton, 7 Apr. 1767, *Corr. Geo. III*, i. 499). When Richmond took up opposition to the government in the General Court of the East India Company, the King wrote that 'it showed blackness if it wanted any elucidation, and that his whole conduct is dictated by malevolence'; George III to Lord North, 12 June 1773, ibid. ii. 504.

[3] Richmond to Portland, 3 June 1778, Nottingham MSS. By 1780 the borough had been sold to Sir James Lowther.

With one exception,[1] the most he ever spent from his own income for an election was £800, and his average election expenditure did not exceed £300. Of the three members whose return he did influence, one was for Sussex, chosen with Newcastle's support until 1768. From 1767 until Richmond's death the representatives were first his brother, Lord George Lennox,[2] and then his nephew, Charles Lennox, more able than Lord George, and also more independent of Richmond. Whereas Lord George had consistently echoed his brother's opinions, Charles Lennox supported Pitt long after Richmond's dismissal from the Ordnance and subsequent entrance into opposition councils. In 1804 when Richmond intended to oppose Pitt's Additional Force Bill in the Lords he reprimanded his nephew for supporting the bill in the Commons without consulting him: 'I cannot help thinking that going to or returning from the House you might as well have taken the trouble of enquiring, and at all events not have left me to pick up from common report that you was come to Town on Purpose to vote differently from what you knew would be my wishes.'[3]

The other two members were returned by Richmond

[1] The county election of 1774 (Richmond's Account Book, Box 47, A2, Goodwood). Lord George Lennox's return for one seat was not in doubt, but there was a contest for the other seat between Sir James Peachy, candidate of the Pelhams, and Thomas Spencer Wilson, an independent candidate who ultimately won the election. Hence Richmond had to spend money getting voters to the polls even though he was unquestionably neutral in the contest between Peachy and Wilson.

[2] Lord George Lennox (1737–1805) entered the Army in 1751, was appointed Brevet Colonel and A.D.C. to the King in Feb. 1762, Colonel of the 25th Foot in Dec. 1762, Major-General in 1772, Lt.-General in 1777, and General in 1793. He served as Richmond's secretary at the Paris embassy, 1765–6, and as Minister Plenipotentiary during Richmond's extended absence in 1766; in 1784 Pitt appointed Lord George Constable of the Tower and later Governor of Plymouth. He rarely, if ever, spoke in Parliament, disliked attendance there, and in 1790 refused to run again. Despite Lord George's small inheritance—an estate on the Isle of Wight and a negligible investment in a French construction concern—Richmond was at least £1,000 in debt to him by 1798.

[3] Richmond to Charles Lennox, 6 June 1804 (see Selected Letters), Richmond Papers, Dublin, no. 1274. Charles Lennox (1764–1819), fourth Duke of Richmond, was Richmond's secretary at the Ordnance, 1784–95. He entered the Army in 1785, serving in Scotland, became A.D.C. to the King, 1795–8, Major-General, 1798, Lt.-General, 1805, and General, 1814, having been Colonel of the 35th Foot, 1803–19. He was M.P. for Chichester, 1790–1806, High Steward of Chichester, 1807, Lord Lieutenant of Ireland, 1807–13, P.C., Apr. 1807, K.G., 1812, Governor of Hull, 1813–14, and Plymouth, 1814–19, Lord Lieutenant of Sussex, 1816–19, Governor-General of Canada, 1818–19.

for Chichester, one with considerable uncertainty. Until 1768 one seat in Parliament was held by Richmond's personal enemy, John Page, who considered himself an independent, although he was backed by Newcastle.[1] Page was succeeded by Richmond's brother-in-law, Thomas Conolly, whom Richmond hoped to make his spokesman in the Commons. But Conolly, who was concurrently serving in the Irish Commons as M.P. for Londonderry, was often absent from England, and in 1780 retired to Ireland, primarily to concentrate on Irish politics, but also because he disagreed with Richmond on parliamentary reform.[2] After that he and Richmond were usually on opposite political sides: Conolly supported the Fox–North Coalition, opposed Pitt's revised commercial bill for Ireland, and in 1788 was one of the members of the Irish House of Commons deputed to offer the regency to the Prince of Wales. Conolly was succeeded as M.P. by two supporters of parliamentary reform—Thomas Steele[3] and, in 1784, an opponent of Richmond's, G. W. Thomas, Page's son-in-law.[4] The other Chichester seat was held by General William Keppel,[5]

[1] When Page retired he published a manifesto attacking aristocratic influences (Richmond to Newcastle, 27 and 29 Sept. 1767, and Newcastle to Richmond, 28 and 30 Sept. 1767, Add. MS. 33,985, ff. 245, 255, 288). See particularly Sir Lewis Namier, The Structure of Politics at the Accession of George III, 1929, pp. 153–5. Page's manifesto was referred to in James Burgh's Political Disquisitions, 1775, iii. 273.

[2] Thomas Conolly (1738–1803) was M.P. (England) for Malmesbury, 1759 to 1768, M.P. (England) for Chichester (1768–80), although he was in the country only during February and March each year. Conolly was also M.P. (Ireland) for Londonderry, 1761–1800, and held various Irish offices, as Lord of the Treasury, Commissioner of Trade, Lord Lieutenant of Londonderry county, P.C. (1784). Conolly was a bad speaker, but great wealth gave him considerable influence.

[3] Thomas Steele (1753–1823) of Chichester, was a scholar of Trinity College, Cambridge, 1772, Richmond's secretary at the Ordnance, 1782, joint Secretary to the Treasury from Dec. 1783 to Feb. 1791, joint Paymaster-General of the Forces from Mar. 1791 to June 1804, P.C., Mar. 1791, Commissioner of the Board of Control, 1791–3, King's Remembrancer in the Court of Exchequer from 1797. Steele represented Chichester from 1780 to 1807.

[4] George White-Thomas (1750–1821), M.P. for Chichester, 1784 to 1812, had taken the name of Thomas in 1778 on inheriting an estate at Yapton in Sussex from his grandfather, Sir George Thomas, first Bart.

[5] The Hon. William Keppel (1727–82), a military officer with little interest in politics, rose from Ensign (2nd Foot Guards) in 1744 to Lt.-General in May 1772. He had served with Albemarle and Augustus Keppel in the taking of Havana in 1762, was appointed Commander-in-Chief of the Forces in Ireland in Dec. 1773, and was Colonel of the 12th Regiment of Dragoons from 1775 until he resigned from the staff before his brother's court martial in Jan. 1779.

brother of the Admiral and guided by him rather than by Richmond. After Keppel's death in 1782 Percy Wyndham,[1] younger son of the Earl of Egremont, served two years and was succeeded by Thomas Steele, for many years Richmond's personal friend, but as a member of the Treasury Board, politically more responsible to Pitt than to Richmond.

Richmond had little parliamentary support from family connexions. His eldest sister, Lady Caroline, married Henry Fox, Lord Holland, whose political influence was dead after May 1765. Holland then retired from Parliament and afterwards looked hopefully for Richmond's support to win him an earldom. Lady Sarah Lennox married first Sir Charles Bunbury, a Bedfordite,[2] and second the Hon. George Napier,[3] a military officer of no political influence. Lady Emily's first husband, the Marquis of Kildare, ceased nearly all political activity after being created Duke of Leinster in 1767; besides, he was too outstanding a figure in his own right to come under the influence of Richmond in Ireland, and had no influence at all in England.[4] The first Duke of Leinster died in 1773; the second Duke,[5] who controlled

---

[1] The Hon. Percy Wyndham (1757–1833), second son of the second Earl of Egremont, was Chancery Registrar in Jamaica and secretary and Clerk of the Courts and Prothonotary of the Court of Common Pleas in Barbados before serving as M.P. for Chichester, from 1782 to 1784. He later represented Midhurst from 1790 to 1796.

[2] Sir Thomas Charles Bunbury, Bart. (1740–1822), was M.P. for Suffolk, 1761–84 and 1790–1812, and Sheriff of Suffolk 1788–9. See Lady Sarah to Lady Susan Fox-Strangways, 12 July 1765, *Life and Letters of Lady Sarah Lennox*, i. 173.

[3] The Hon. George Napier (d. 1804), second son of Francis, fifth Baron Napier, had emerged from the American War as only a Captain; Richmond, who was Napier's only 'connexion', disapproved Lady Sarah's second marriage and refused to help him with a promotion. Ultimately Richmond must have softened, for in 1794 Napier was appointed Deputy Quartermaster-General to Lord Moira's army in Holland. Later Napier was given command of the Londonderry Regiment, and in 1799 he was appointed by Cornwallis to be Controller of Army Accounts in Ireland.

[4] James Fitzgerald (1722–73), first Duke of Leinster, was M.P. for Athy from 1741 to 1744, when he became twentieth Earl of Kildare. In 1746 he was appointed to the Irish P.C., and in 1747 created Viscount Leinster in the English peerage. Leinster led the moderate party in Irish politics and in 1754 gained immense personal popularity by his successful protest to the King against the nomination of the Archbishop of Dublin, leader of the ministerial party, to be Lord Deputy during the Lord Lieutenant's absence. Thereafter Leinster tended towards increasing support of the English government. He was created Marquis of Kildare in 1761, and Duke of Leinster in 1766.

[5] William Fitzgerald (1749–1804), second Duke of Leinster, was relatively inactive in politics. He was M.P. for Dublin, 1769–73, High Sheriff of Kildare,

seven seats in the Irish Commons and was for a time head
of the Volunteers, apparently co-operated with Richmond
until 1780, when he and Thomas Conolly, husband of Lady
Louisa, began to drift towards support of the Lord Lieutenant, Lord Buckinghamshire, Conolly's brother-in-law.
Leinster, with Conolly, opposed Richmond and the Pitt
ministry during the regency crisis of 1788–9. Lady Emily's
second husband was William Ogilvie,[1] her children's tutor,
a non-influential figure for whom Richmond attempted to
find a place or pension. Apparently the only family relations
directly under Richmond's wing, besides his brother, were
his cousins, Lord Berkeley and Lord Craven.[2]

In local patronage Richmond was slightly stronger. As
Lord Lieutenant and Custos Rotulorum of Sussex, he
appointed military and legal officers—particularly coroners
and J.P.s. In Chichester he managed to retain his father's
right to Custom House appointments when he was with the
government,[3] and Chichester Common Council members
were selected with his approval. But his influence over the
city seems to have been nothing like that of Newcastle over
Lewes or Rockingham over York, and in church patronage
he was successfully limited by the Pelhams of Lewes. Since
Sussex was divided administratively into semi-autonomous
halves, the Pelhams by tacit agreement kept out of Chichester
political patronage. But the county's church administration
was not divided, and a vacancy among the canons residentiary
at Chichester cathedral inevitably meant a drawn battle until

1772, Knight of the Order of St. Patrick, 1783, Master of the Rolls, 1788, and was
best known for his support of the Act of Union, 1801.

    1 William Ogilvie (1740–1832), a classical scholar originally from Edinburgh,
had migrated to Ireland as an impoverished school teacher and later turned to private
tutoring. In 1774, less than a year after the death of the first Duke of Leinster,
Ogilvie married the Duchess and retired with her in social exile to Richmond's
estate in Aubigny. Six years later Thomas Conolly returned him to the Irish
Commons. Ogilvie never made a major speech until 1786, when he opposed Pitt's
commercial treaty. In 1782, attempting to win both recognition and an office, he
put forth an idealistic scheme for reform of the Irish government; two years later
Richmond (who first met him in France in 1777) introduced Ogilvie to Pitt, but
made no further effort to obtain the sinecure office he wanted. Ogilvie remained
without employment other than the management of his wife's estates.
    2 Richmond to Newcastle [23 May 1767], Add. MS. 32,982, f. 101.
    3 Richmond to Newcastle, 26 Aug. 1757, Add. MS. 32,873, f. 293; Richmond to
Grenville, 14 Apr. 1764, Grenville MSS.; Richmond Memorandum, 26 July 1764,
Goodwood Small Libr. MS. E.

the death of a second residentiary enabled Richmond and Pelham each to nominate one new residentiary.[1]

A more serious handicap than lack of the King's favour or political patronage was a difficult personality. Richmond was considered generous and affectionate by close relatives, but there is no question that he was extremely unpopular with most of his political associates. Walpole thought his appointment as Secretary of State in the Rockingham ministry was 'a mighty ingredient towards the fall of that Administration' in 1766;[2] Jenkinson despised 'that plagueing fellow, the Duke of Richmond';[3] and even Burke, in the height of friendship, described him sympathetically as being 'of little management with the world'.[4]

Basically Richmond was intensely nervous, driven by an immense energy. He worked hard—his London day began at 8 a.m.—dressed plainly, checked his account books to the penny, and rarely drank, entertained, or joined late parties. He found close companionship first with Burke, then with Shelburne—both of whom shared his regular hours.

To his other colleagues he seemed unsociable, ostentatiously upright, and a little too ambitious. To the public, who would have considered uprightness a virtue, he instead appeared miserly.[5] Both reputations were partially justified.

What none of his friends realized was that Richmond was essentially an introvert. After an irresponsible youth in Geneva and then in the Army, he had settled down at about the age of twenty-five, and from that time he and the Duchess had tended to retire more and more from society.[6] Part of

---

[1] Chichester Cathedral Chapter Account Books D and E, County Record Office, Chichester; Richmond to Duchess of Newcastle, 22 Apr. 1772, Add. MS. 33,082, f. 152; Richmond to Pelham, 22 Apr. 1772, Add. MS. 33,089, f. 273.

[2] 7 July 1766, *Walpole Memoirs*, ii. 239–40.

[3] 'I was brought to town today . . . by that plagueing fellow, the Duke of Richmond. If there were two Dukes of Richmond in this country I would not live in it.' Jenkinson to John Robinson, 21 July 1780, *H.M.C. Abergavenny*, p. 31.

[4] Burke to Chas. O'Hara, *c.* 11 July 1771, Burke Corr. Book (Sheffield), ii. 205. 'His brother has got into difficulties by being too like himself . . . very full of rectitude, zealous against abuses, a little teizing in his disposition, and of little management with the world.'

[5] He was ridiculed by the Rolliad in 1794 (quoted in W. S. Sichell, *Sheridan*, 1909, ii. 91). 'Hail thou for either talent justly known, to spend the nation's cash or save thine own.'

[6] For example, Lady Caroline Fox wrote Emily, Marchioness of Kildare, 30 Oct.

Richmond's love of Goodwood came from his enjoyment of farming; a larger part came from his desire for seclusion and his abhorrence of London.

What the public did not know was that frugality alternated with impetuous generosity. When Richmond disapproved of Lady Sarah's marriage to Sir Charles Bunbury, he cut her off from the family money and refused even to buy her wedding dress,[1] but when she returned from her scandalous elopement with Lord William Gordon, he built a house near Goodwood for her and her daughter.[2] He provided free beer for Chichester road workers[3] but was up at 7 a.m. to see that his own estate workers were on time.[4] He censured John Caryll, to whom he had leased part of the Goodwood estate, for being dilatory in the payment of debts,[5] but he bailed Chichester debtors out of jail.[6] He spent as much money on the arts as on politics, a claim few of his associates could make: he built a theatre in Richmond House, subsidized several Chichester landscape painters, set up a free studio for artists in Richmond House,[7] and personally patronized a young portrait painter whose work at this studio drew early approval—George Romney.[8] It was not until 1792, when Richmond House burned down and the Duke feared being unable to pay off his debts, that his frugality became accentuated.

1760. 'The world soon grows shy of those who despise them.' *Correspondence of Emily, Duchess of Leinster*, ed. Brian Fitzgerald, 1949–53, i. 301.

[1] Lady Caroline Fox to Emily, Marchioness of Kildare, 9 Mar. 1762, *Correspondence of Emily, Duchess of Leinster*, i. 320.

[2] E. R. Curtis, *Lady Sarah Lennox*, 1948, ch. xiv.

[3] May 1761, Richmond's Diary of 1761, at Goodwood.

[4] Kent, *Records and Reminiscences of Goodwood*, pp. 26–33.

[5] Richmond to J. Caryll, 4 June 1765, Add. MS. 28,235, ff. 259–60.

[6] Lady Holland to Marchioness of Kildare, 9 June 1766, *Correspondence of Emily, Duchess of Leinster*, i. 453–4.

[7] In 1759 when Richmond was serving with the Army on the Continent, he failed to offer the annual prize which he had previously promised. The artists posted placards of complaint which so enraged the Duke that he shut down the studio the following year. Arthur Chamberlain, *George Romney*, 1910, p. 43.

[8] For the best description of Richmond's assistance to Romney see Chamberlain, *George Romney*, pp. 43, 71, 83, 216, 341, and Richmond's letters to Burke and Rockingham in 1776 asking them to sit for Romney. Humphrey Ward and W. Roberts, *George Romney, a Biographical and Critical Essay*, 1904, gives a list of Richmond's sittings. Articles on the Richmond House theatre and programmes presented there appeared frequently in the papers from 1788 to 1792.

Nervous energy may have made Richmond capable of intense work, but he worked in spurts and not always effectively. At the Ordnance he was several times called 'The most industrious man in Europe' and even compared to Frederick the Great.[1] Unlike most of his contemporaries, he was able to arrive in town on the morning of a debate and master the issues quickly enough to speak effectively in the afternoon. In January 1773 he suddenly became interested in the politics of the East India Company General Court: within two weeks he had grasped company politics entirely and was the most formidable court speaker. But the result of inspired concentration (and to some extent of thwarted ambition) was extended periods of depression. When Richmond was defeated in the East India Company in February 1774, he wrote Rockingham, 'Indeed the Fate of this Day will be decisive as to the Company, and (but that is of infinitely less consequence) of your humble Servant as a political Man.'[2] After the defeat of his bill for parliamentary reform he lamented: 'I mean to go no more to London this year, and probably never to Parliament again',[3] and in 1782 he attempted to bind Rockingham to set up a committee for investigating plans of parliamentary reform: 'I believe no man can say with greater Truth than I, that he should prefer a retired Life; I am daily sacrificing my Health and the Comforts of my Life for the Public and should be happy to retire and see Things go on well in other Hands than mine.'[4] Between 1774 and 1790 he made at least five threats to retire from politics altogether. In 1769 he dismissed five months of parliamentary absence with the explanation that 'I must for some time at least indulge myself in my present disposition which I will give no name to.'[5]

When he did work, the love of detail displayed in his financial accounts sometimes led him to waste time on

---

[1] For example, *Public Advertiser*, 3 Apr., 6 and 20 July 1782.

[2] 15 Jan. 1774, Fitzwilliam MS. R1–824. See Selected Letters.

[3] Richmond to Rockingham, 12 June 1780, Fitzwilliam MS. R1–1066. Printed in Albemarle, *Rockingham*, ii. 418–20.

[4] 11 May 1782, Fitzwilliam MS. R1–1168, printed in Albemarle, *Rockingham*, ii. 481–3.

[5] Richmond to Rockingham, 10 Mar. 1769, Fitzwilliam MS. R1–650. See Selected Letters.

irrelevant trivia. He dragged the committee investigating fortifications at Portsmouth and Plymouth through ten-hour days for two weeks, but the work, according to Cornwallis, was 'sheer torture' because Richmond inserted so much useless material.[1]

His committee work was further impeded by tactlessness and excitability. He knew himself that 'I pass in the world for very obstinate, wrong-headed, and tenacious of my opinions.'[2] On guard he could delight Newcastle, disarm Chatham, and write Rockingham 'the prettiest letter I ever read'.[3] But he could be 'tenacious' when his close friend Edward Sedgwick refused to serve as his private secretary in France,[4] and with no finesse at all he could lecture Rockingham on Lady Rockingham's tea parties and the Marquis's fetishes about health, and at one time it was even rumoured that he had called the King a liar.[5] Once, when Rockingham was ill, Richmond wrote a letter of condolence beginning,

My Dear Lord,

You are so often ill without being dangerously so, and are so often doctoring yourself that when I first heard you was not well I concluded it was only a surfeit of Phisick and I am told that it might possibly be owing to your not letting yourself alone that you have been ill but that your disorder has not been a slight one.[6]

In the House of Lords he repeatedly made personal attacks which were taken far more seriously than he intended. Between 1780 and 1792 he made six such attacks[7] and alienated a seventh individual, Lord Pembroke, by rudely haranguing him for accepting the governorship of Portsmouth which had been coveted by Lord George Lennox. When he was dismissed from the Ordnance in 1795, largely because of his inability to get along with the Duke of York and Henry

[1] Cornwallis to Lt.-Colonel Ross, 3 May 1785, *Correspondence of Charles, First Marquis Cornwallis*, ed. Charles Ross, 1859, i. 189.

[2] Richmond to Burke, 15 Nov. 1772, *Burke Correspondence*, i. 370.

[3] Lady Rockingham to Newcastle, 20 May 1766, Add. MS. 32,975, f. 766.

[4] Edw. Sedgwick to Edw. Weston, 13 Aug. 1765, *H.M.C. Eglintoun*, p. 394.

[5] A 'reminiscing' anecdote quoted in C. C. F. Greville, *A Journal of the Reigns of King George IV and King William IV*, ed. H. Reeve, 1834, iii. 129.

[6] 26 Apr. 1772, Fitzwilliam MS. R1–789. See Selected Letters.

[7] Against Lords Amherst, Rawdon, George Germaine, Loughborough, Thurlow, Lauderdale.

Dundas in particular, not a single cabinet associate was really sorry to see him go.

In part his tactlessness stemmed from lack of respect for the limited abilities of his associates. In part it stemmed from a quick temper. It was hard to convince Richmond he was wrong; he would yield one day, then come calling the next with new arguments.[1] Then he would lose his temper, quarrel, and quickly repent. When Conway stayed on with Pitt in July 1766, Richmond was furious for several days and then wrote a letter of reconciliation;[2] when he thought Rockingham did not intend opposition to Pitt in November of the same year, he threatened to leave town, then yielded ungraciously to the Marquis's entreaties to stay with the explanation that, 'if I open my Lips I shall unavoidably fall into some matter in which I differ from you.'[3] A week later he had reconsidered and was back in party councils.

'Some day', wrote Cornwallis, 'Charles Lennox [Richmond's nephew] will be a popular Duke of Richmond'— implying that his uncle was not. Few contemporaries challenged the implication.

[1] Thus in July 1767 he wrote Rockingham asking him to join the existing ministry even after the Marquis had firmly refused to enter government along with Grafton (Rockingham Memorandum, 23 July 1767, Fitzwilliam MS. R1–537). On 7 July 1766 Horace Walpole talked Richmond and Conway into resigning. Richmond returned to Walpole the following day, again unconvinced. *Walpole Memoirs*, ii. 238–9.

[2] Ibid. 249. Conway's acknowledgement of the letters, probably written on 19 July 1766, is untrue. Goodwood MSS., Box 29, no. 3d.

[3] [12 Nov. 1766], Fitzwilliam MS. R1–217–10.

II

1765 TO 1770
A SHORT TERM IN OFFICE AND A
LONG TRUANCY IN OPPOSITION

IN the decade following the accession of George III political factions developed around six individuals who held office at one time or another during the period. Pitt and Newcastle, in power when the young King came to the throne, were followed in office first by the Earl of Bute and eleven months later by the Duke of Bedford and George Grenville. When Grenville, whom the King personally disliked, mistakenly advised him on the Regency Bill in May 1765, George III authorized the Duke of Cumberland to sound Pitt about taking office. Pitt refused, and Grenville was recalled until 30 June, when Cumberland was finally able to collect a new ministry under the nominal leadership of the Marquis of Rockingham. The ministry consisted of two groups, loosely united by the common experience of opposition to the Regency Bill: the Duke of Newcastle's 'Old Whigs', most of whom had left office in the 'rout' of 1763, and the Marquis of Rockingham's young Ascot friends brought together by family connexions and the geographical proximity of their estates.

During this period the Duke of Richmond was looking about for advantageous political connexions. In May he offered himself to Cumberland,[1] and in July he wrote to the Earl of Albemarle, one of Rockingham's principal advisers, virtually asking to be included in any government formed by Albemarle and the Duke of Cumberland and setting forth with some modesty his 'influence over some friends' and talents in debate.[2] During July he was considered for Constable of the Tower, Cofferer, Chamberlain of the Household, and Groom of the Stole, all minor 'places of honour';[3]

[1] Horace Walpole to Lord Holland, 28 May 1765, *Letters to Henry Fox, Lord Holland*, ed. Earl of Ilchester, 1915, p. 218.

[2] Richmond to Albemarle, 4 July 1765, Albemarle MS. L1/1/13(9). See Selected Letters.

[3] See *Walpole Memoirs*, ii. 204; George III Memorandum, 2 July 1765, *Corr. Geo. III*, i. 132; *St. James' Chronicle*, 7–8 July 1765; Lady Sarah Bunbury to Lady Susan Fox-Strangways, 10 July 1765, *Life and Letters of Lady Sarah Lennox*, i. 173.

ultimately through the influence of Albemarle and H. S.
Conway he was offered the Paris embassy. He did not want
the embassy, as it would keep him out of the new parliamentary session, and refused the first offer.[1] By August, Richmond realized an embassy was the best position for which
he could hope.

But his heart was never in his work. Before he even
reached Paris he had alienated the French by an ostentatious
visit to Dunkirk in October to publicize their failure to
demolish the jetties there as agreed at the conclusion of the
Seven Years War. Unquestionably he was efficient, handling
firmly and even tactfully the final settlement of reparations
still owed to British merchants from the war. But his aloofness on social occasions when he and the Duchess cloistered
themselves only with other English couples never ingratiated him with French society. Less than four months after
crossing the Channel, he rushed back to England again,
leaving the embassy in charge of his brother, who had
originally gone over as his secretary. Ostensibly Richmond
asked for leave to clear up Sussex affairs;[2] actually he returned in much-ridiculed haste to bolster a weak ministerial
team in debate on the repeal of the stamp tax.[3]

At the end of April the Duke of Grafton announced his
intention of resigning as Secretary of State. Richmond virtually offered his services to Rockingham through Conway
early in May, then waited hopefully off the scene at Goodwood. But at first he was considered only for Groom of the
Stole while Hardwicke and Egmont were sounded for Grafton's position.[4] Only when both refused did Conway and
Rockingham put up Richmond's name as a last resort during
a cabinet meeting on 14 May. Newcastle ardently opposed
the nomination but when Egmont and Winchelsea gave it
lukewarm support Rockingham convinced the King that
there was no alternative.

[1] C. Fox to Lord Holland, 13 July 1765, *Letters to Henry Fox*, p. 233.
[2] Richmond to Conway, 19 Jan. 1766, S.P. 78/269.
[3] De Guerchy wrote that Richmond was so eager to witness the Commons'
debates that he took a fishing boat across the channel and left the Duchess behind to
await better winds for a calmer crossing (De Guerchy to De Praslin, 23 Feb. 1766,
F.F.O. Corr. Pol. Ang. 469, f. 174).
[4] Rockingham to Newcastle, 14 May 1766, Add. MS. 32,975, ff. 178-80.

Newcastle then carried his opposition to a private audience with the King on 22 May,[1] details of which he publicized himself in order to magnify the appearance of his own entrenchment in the royal favour. The King suggested unkindly that Newcastle opposed Richmond because of political conflict in West Sussex, a charge Newcastle denied. Instead, as he explained to Richmond himself, he based his opinion on the inexperience of the young Duke in handling foreign policy debates in the House of Lords.[2]

What he implied was that Richmond was as yet generally considered by his contemporaries to be a man of no personal stature. 'The Seals of State having gone abegging, sometime, the Duke of Richmond Begged them', wrote Chesterfield.[3] 'The Duke of Richmond . . . will not change many opinions', added the French ambassador.[4]

Egmont consoled the King that Richmond's appointment was a temporary expedient and that he could not be thought likely to continue very long.[5] And indeed, as Egmont predicted, the King had to put up with the Duke for only seven weeks until Rockingham's dismissal—so short a time that Horace Walpole worried that the appointment hastened the fall of the ministry.[6]

When Rockingham was replaced by Pitt in July 1766 Richmond was quite willing to stay on in the same position, but Pitt dismissed him for Shelburne, and Richmond was cast into involuntary opposition with the Rockingham Whigs, with whom there seemed very little chance he would ever get on.

For the Rockingham group in particular Richmond had two handicaps—his geographical situation and his background under the political tutelage of Lord Holland. When Parliament adjourned in summer, the Rockingham party scattered to their country homes. Rockingham himself, at his best in personal relations and management of individuals

---

[1] See Add. MS. 35,975, ff. 187, 203, 225, 254-7.
[2] 23 May 1766, Add. MS. 32,975, f. 244.
[3] Chesterfield to his son, May 1776, *The Letters of the Earl of Chesterfield*, ed. C. Strachey, 1904, xi. 2741.
[4] De Guerchy to Choisseul, 27 May 1766, F.F.O. 470, f. 76.
[5] Egmont to George III, 18 May 1776, *Corr. Geo. III*, i. 308-9.
[6] 7 July 1776, *Walpole Memoirs*, ii. 239-40.

during session, was a lazy letter-writer, and allowed the fringe of the party to be cut off during vacations. For nearly five months every year Richmond thus lost contact with the rest of the party.

For three of his first four summers in the group he was in France. In 1766 he left England immediately after the dissolution of the ministry and did not return until one week before Parliament opened. Even his close friend Horace Walpole wrote Lady Louisa Conolly, who was travelling with Richmond, 'What have you done with the Duke and Duchess? . . . not a soul has heard a word of them.'[1] That year Newcastle wrote him local news; in 1768 he apparently received none, and in 1769 a single letter from Burke arrived two months late.[2] When Richmond was not on the Continent, he was engrossed on his farm or in local government. At most he seems to have come to London once or twice in a summer, and from 1766 to 1769 he never attended a party meeting before the opening of Parliament.

At Goodwood there were few visitors to bring news. Richmond's closest friends, the Cavendishes, visited for hunting parties in July 1765, December 1766, and March and September 1767.[3] The Duke of Devonshire and Lord Carlisle came for a hunting party in March 1767;[4] Burke, Rockingham, and Bessborough came down in August and October of the same year.[5] Richmond repeatedly asked Rockingham to visit Goodwood again; but the Marquis came only once after 1767. For three summers at least— 1766, 1768, 1769—Richmond seems to have had no visitors at all.

[1] Walpole to Lady Louisa Conolly, 8 Sept. 1766, *H.M.C. Bathurst*, pp. 693–4. Richmond apparently also received a letter from Walpole.

[2] Burke to Rockingham, 9 July 1769, *Burke Correspondence*, i. 175–6; Richmond to Burke, 2 Sept. 1769, Fitzwilliam MS. R8–2. Richmond may also have received news from Horace Walpole.

[3] Richmond to Albemarle, 4 July 1765, Albemarle MSS. L1/1/13(9), see Selected Letters; Newcastle to Lord George Cavendish, 29 Dec. 1766, Add. MS. 32,980, f. 366; Lord Fred Cavendish to Newcastle, 19 Sept. 1767, Add. MS. 32,985, f. 136.

[4] Richmond to Newcastle (22 Mar. 1767), Add. MS. 32,980, f. 366. See Selected Letters.

[5] Newcastle to Bessborough, 28 Sept. 1767, Add. MS. 32,985, f. 218; Newcastle to Keppel, 8 Oct. 1767, Add. MS. 32,985, f. 398; Burke to Rockingham, 18 Aug. 1767, *Burke Correspondence*, i. 138.

While Richmond remained out of touch in the south, a clique of friends was developing in the north—the younger and middle generations of the party, and generally the weaker minds—consisting of Rockingham, Portland, Albemarle, Keppel, possibly Savile, and later Devonshire, Fitzwilliam, and Fred Montagu. Visits were frequently exchanged during vacations. Rockingham visited Albemarle in July 1767, Portland and Savile in the Christmas holidays of the same year, and Portland again in August 1768.[1] Savile and Scarbrough came to Wentworth in November 1769,[2] and on the way to Newmarket Rockingham travelled the 'circuit'—Albemarle, Savile, Portland, Keppel, Saunders, Bessborough.[3] As early as 1772 Burke referred to Rockingham's northern friends as a thinking unit[4] on the issue of secession.

Burke and Dowdeswell, who also suffered from not living in the north, overcame the problem by travelling there. There is no evidence that Richmond ever travelled north after 1761. Burke, Dowdeswell, and Newcastle made an effort to see Rockingham when he visited London, usually once during the summer. But Goodwood was eight hours away, and when Richmond did come up, his visits never seem to have coincided with those of the Marquis.

Richmond's other handicap was his connexion with Lord Holland, to whom he had been particularly obliged since 1763, when Holland had obtained for him the lord lieutenancy of Sussex.[5]

In April 1765, when Holland was dismissed from office, he employed Richmond to scout further the reasons for his dismissal.[6] The following year Richmond sought his brother-in-law's advice on bringing the King's Men into Rockingham's government: in April when Grafton had announced his

---

[1] Rockingham to Dowdeswell, 11 Aug. 1768, Fitzwilliam MS. R1–617.

[2] Savile to Rockingham, 7 Nov. 1767, Fitzwilliam MS. R2–75.

[3] Rockingham to Dowdeswell, 11 Oct. 1769, Fitzwilliam MS. R1–686; *Public Advertiser*, 13 Oct. 1767.

[4] Burke to Rockingham, 11 Nov. 1772, *Burke Correspondence*, i. 367.

[5] Sandwich to Holland, 14 and 18 Oct. 1763, *Letters to Henry Fox*, pp. 189, 195. Richmond was appointed Lord Lieutenant in October but had expected the appointment since January.

[6] Richmond to Lord Holland, 23 May and 8 June 1765, *Letters to Henry Fox*, pp. 214–16, 222–3.

resignation and two other members of the cabinet were
expected to resign before the end of the parliamentary
session, Richmond had discussed with Rockingham the possibility of overtures to the King's Men. At that time Rockingham, Winchelsea, Conway, and Newcastle believed that
support of the King's Men might be obtained by the single
concession of a place for James Stewart Mackenzie, only
brother of the Earl of Bute. But Richmond was so doubtful
that he wrote Holland early in May, naïvely asking what
terms Bute's followers would demand.[1] Holland urgently
suggested seven followers—Sir Fletcher Norton, Dr. George
Hay, Welbore Ellis, Robert Nugent, Hans Stanley, and
Lords Northumberland and Despencer—who should be
offered employment. On 6 or 7 June, only two weeks after
his appointment, Richmond relayed Holland's suggestions
to the Marquis, with a renewed plea for union with Bute to
give the appearance of royal support.[2]

Unknown to Richmond a cabinet meeting in May had
terminated in ill feeling after Egmont, himself a King's
Man, had insisted that only a group offer facilitated by the
removal of some of Rockingham's personal friends would
suffice to establish a coalition.[3] Also unknown to the Duke,
Mackenzie had been dissuaded by Egmont from accepting
the offer Rockingham actually did make to him in May;[4]
hence Richmond's critical comment:

It was evident we could gett no strength while it was seen that we
had not the King's good will, & were unwilling to take the necessary
steps to obtain it, and had not spirit enough to resign when we could
not gett it. I represented all this very strongly, and finding could not
succeed to bring any thing about of any kind, I told them that when
the turning out came I was persuaded I should repine as little as they,
that by the methods they pursued I thought they were drawing it
on a pace, and that I should only now think of picking up as much
knowledge as possible in the office during the short time I had to stay
there.[5]

[1] Lord Holland to Richmond, 4 and 26 May 1766, Ilchester, *Life of Henry Fox*,
ii. 308–9.
[2] Richmond Memorandum (1–7 July 1766), Goodwood Small Libr. MS. E.
[3] *Newcastle's Narrative of Changes in the Government*, pp. 60–62.
[4] Egmont to George III, 4 May 1766, *Corr. Geo. III*, i. 305.
[5] Richmond Memorandum (1–7 July 1766), Goodwood Small Libr. MS. E.

At least a day before the conference the King had already decided that Rockingham's ministry was too weak to continue in office.[1] Because Richmond never knew when the King's decision was made, he blamed 'Lord Rockingham's disposition . . . always to defer'[2] for not rebuilding the ministry's prestige in June; and he openly criticized the Marquis for preferring procrastination to decision, speculation to action, and rationalization to realistic appraisal.[3]

On 2 June 1767 Richmond's motion of censure on the Chatham ministry was defeated 73–61 in the Lords despite the united backing of Grenville, Bedford, and Rockingham.[4] The defeat convinced Richmond that the Bedford and Grenville parties were not numerically essential to a stable government and, if anything, renewed his inclination to alliance with Bute.[5] Thus the following month when Rockingham was asked by Conway to draw up a plan of government Richmond advocated a coalition with the existing ministry, fortified if possible by the assistance of the King's Men. Since Newcastle and Rockingham still favoured a coalition with Bedford and Grenville strong enough to displace the ministry, Richmond conceded at a meeting on 7 July that Bedford might be sounded, particularly to see how far he was willing to go without Grenville. After promising preliminaries a meeting between leaders of the Bedford and Rockingham parties on 20 July broke up over Bedford's insistence on two points—a declaration that British supremacy over the American colonies be asserted and maintained, and Conway's removal as Secretary of State. During the meeting Richmond lost his temper over Bedford's objection to Conway's remaining in office; a second meeting was

---

[1] Northington to George III, 5 June (1766), *Corr. Geo. III*, i, p. 536.

[2] Richmond Memorandum (1–7 July 1766), Goodwood Small Libr. MS. E.

[3] W. G. Hamilton to Earl Temple, 1 July 1766, *The Grenville Papers*, ed. J. Smith, 1853, iii. 257.

[4] See J. Brooke, *The Chatham Administration*, 1956, p. 153.

[5] See H. Walpole to Grafton, 7 June 1767, Grafton MS. 777. Holland, who was in London during July, may have counselled Richmond before the negotiations but there is no evidence on this point. Richmond was certainly influenced by Conway, who had been dismissed from his army rank in 1764 for voting against the government in the House of Commons. At the time Richmond had warmly taken Conway's part in private discussions with Grenville (memorandum inserted in Goodwood Small Libr. MS. E).

called by Newcastle for the following evening, to which Richmond was not invited.[1]

When the Bedford negotiations collapsed some of the party held Richmond responsible for their failure. In August Burke even admonished Rockingham that only the Marquis's personal attention would counterbalance Holland's influence over Richmond.[2] As Richmond explained his own worry to Newcastle,

I who am reckon'd warm and hot, think you all in extremes, and could have wished that we had all gone a little farther to meet. I mean the Marquis and the Duke of Grafton etc.[3]

Newcastle's admonition was tempered by his gratification with Richmond's confidence:

I shall only make One Observation upon These Affairs. The Miscarriage of the late Negotiation for a Comprehensive Plan, which had all the good Appearances possible, has evidently flung every Thing, The New Administration &c., as appears by the Arrangements already made, and to be made, into the Hands of *a Certain Quarter*;[4] and indeed My Dear Lord, would have done so Equally, if our Friend had agreed to come in; Which I hope, He will not, at any time, without the Duke of Bedford and His Friends; and such a support, as may make him and His Friends Independent of that Influence which we have been endeavouring to free this Country from, now for many years. I can't avoid saying thus much to a Friend who has open'd Himself with so much Friendship and Freedom to Me; and I say no more.[5]

When Richmond continued to press his point in October Rockingham was so disgusted that he neglected to ask the Duke to attend a party meeting before Parliament opened; for his part, Richmond was so demoralized that he refused to come to London early for a conference with the Marquis.[6]

In two ways Richmond was at odds with the Rockingham party for his support of alliance with the King's Men. He

---

[1] For a full discussion of the negotiations see Brooke, *Chatham Administration*, esp. pp. 203–10.

[2] Burke to Rockingham, 18 Aug. 1767, *Burke Correspondence*, i. 140.

[3] Richmond to Newcastle, 7 Aug. 1767, Add. MS. 32,984, ff. 208–9. See Selected Letters.   [4] The Earl of Bute.

[5] Newcastle to Richmond, 10 Aug. 1767, Add. MS. 32,984, ff. 239–40.

[6] Lord Fred Cavendish to Rockingham, 12 Nov. 1767, Fitzwilliam MS. R5–34; *Public Advertiser*, 27 Nov. 1767.

was personally at odds with Newcastle and Bessborough—
the 'old guard' who had left office in 1762—with Rockingham's uncle, Winchelsea, and with Albemarle. He also
differed with Rockingham, who had been attempting since
January 1766 to negotiate an alliance strong enough to 'tie
the King's hands'. To Richmond such an alliance seemed
unnecessary, for the King's desire for a stable government
would lead him to give unreserved support to any mode-
rately co-operative, efficient ministry. Richmond was out of
town during the King's attempt to replace the Rockingham
ministry in January 1766. He overestimated the permanency of three successive ministries—those of Grenville,
Rockingham, and Pitt. Until 1768, his thinking about any
limitation of the King's use of his powers was distinctly
more conservative than that of Rockingham.

Rockingham himself disliked Chatham, inclined to alliance with Bedford, and thought that any advantages in
royal favour gained by alliance with the King's Men would
be more than offset by the unpopularity of such a union.
But Rockingham was primarily concerned with holding the
balance between party extremes. On major issues he usually
sounded the party, then took a middle ground, with particular attention to advice from Albemarle.[1]

Richmond, with very little understanding of the group,
considered Newcastle the sole dominating force. In June
1765 he referred to the future ministers as 'Newcastle's
party'; in November 1766 he came up to Parliament, found
Newcastle lukewarm on opposition to Pitt, and assumed
that all the party agreed. Yet until the last six months before
Newcastle's death Richmond and he were on terms of
suspicion and jealousy. Richmond scoffed at Newcastle's
jealous complaints;[2] Newcastle indeed envied Richmond's
supposed influence with Rockingham and bewailed the
young Duke's ingratitude for his help in Sussex politics. In
the autumn of 1767 when Newcastle was not invited to a number of social events at Goodwood, his tortured imagination

---

[1] He did so in May 1766, over bringing some King's Men into the ministry, in
Nov. 1766, over Edgecumbe's dismissal from the Bedchamber, and in July 1767,
in the Bedford negotiations.

[2] Richmond to Rockingham, 4 Oct. 1767, Fitzwilliam MS. R1–557. Quoted in
Albemarle, *Rockingham*, ii. 59–62.

led him even to suspect that a Goodwood 'cabal' was plotting
to join the government without him. Only a personal visit
from Rockingham dispelled his fears.[1]

Richmond thus remained a minor member of the party until
1770. As a minister, Richmond had reached Rockingham's
private councils; after the ministry fell he was included
only in general meetings and occasional social gatherings.
In July 1766 Richmond, Newcastle, Dowdeswell, and
Winchelsea were turned out of office with Rockingham,
but several members of the Rockingham ministry, such as
Keppel and Portland, remained with Pitt in minor positions.
Richmond was the only one of the dismissed ministers whom
Rockingham did not consult about the advisability of communication with their former associates. When Rockingham
corresponded with Albemarle, Hardwicke, and Newcastle,
his principal advisers, Richmond's views were never mentioned. In November, when Rockingham conferred with
Bessborough, Dowdeswell, Albemarle, and Newcastle,[2]
Richmond was not invited to the conference, nor did he
attend the party meeting before Parliament. Apparently he
never learned the Marquis's full opinions on opposition until
a large party meeting was held on 19 November, to discuss
Pitt's dismissal of Lord Edgecumbe from the treasurership
of the Household.[3]

When Grafton asked Rockingham to draw up terms for a
coalition ministry in July 1767, Rockingham and Newcastle
held meetings on 3 and 5 July.[4] With haste Richmond could
have come from Goodwood to reach the second, but he was
never asked; he was finally summoned to town two days
later by Conway, not Rockingham.[5] With Rockingham,
Dowdeswell, and Newcastle he did attend a private conference with Bedford on 20 July, to iron out policy differences
and settle upon major offices; but when he warmly defended
Rockingham's insistence on Conway as House of Commons

[1] Lord Fred Cavendish to Newcastle, 19 Sept. 1767, Add. MS. 32,985, ff. 136–7.

[2] Newcastle to Rockingham, 8 Nov. 1766, Add. MS. 32,977, f. 350.

[3] Rockingham to Scarbrough, 20 Nov. 1766, Albemarle, *Rockingham*, ii. 19;
Newcastle Memorandum, 21 Nov. 1766, Add. MS. 32,978, f. 1.

[4] Rockingham to Newcastle, 4 July 1767, *Newcastle's Narrative of Changes in
the Government*, p. 105; *Public Advertiser*, 8 July 1767.

[5] 6–7 July 1767, *Walpole Memoirs*, iii. 47.

leader, the jealous Albemarle was astonished that 'the Duke of Richmond affected to take a considerable lead'.[1] Had the negotiations succeeded, Richmond expected the lord lieutenancy of Ireland[2]—recognition that he had no bargaining power for a position inside the country—but even that expectation may have been too hopeful: the *Public Advertiser* did not mention him for any office in a speculative list of a coalition ministry.[3]

Burke and the Cavendishes warned Rockingham in the autumn of 1767 that Richmond was wavering and in vain exhorted the Marquis to get Richmond up to a pre-Parliament meeting in November.[4] But Albemarle and Newcastle, far more influential advisers, never mentioned him. Despite spurts of parliamentary leadership Richmond remained so insignificant that as late as the summer of 1769, when Rockingham consulted Burke, Bessborough, Keppel, and Albemarle on the phraseology of county petitions against Wilkes's expulsion, Richmond (again in France) did not even know how fully Rockingham supported the petitioning movement.[5] In the spring he had missed five months of Parliament: no one, least of all Rockingham, had urged him to return.

Richmond, for his part, did not think himself particularly bound to Rockingham. His initial loyalty was weakened by constant misunderstandings that only aggravated his tendencies to obstinacy and temper. For example, at a stormy meeting on 1 May 1766, the Rockingham ministry—still under the stigma of a rumoured association with Bute—finally decided not to offer places to the King's Men as a group. Had Richmond been told of the decision, he might not have been so exasperated with Rockingham's rejection of his own similar suggestion in June. In autumn of the same year Rockingham was anxious to bring his former associates

[1] Albemarle to Rockingham, 22 July 1767, Fitzwilliam MS. R1–533.
[2] Lady Holland wrote to the Duchess of Leinster on 11 Aug. 1767 (*Correspondence of Emily, Duchess of Leinster*, i. 516), 'I don't know if my brother wishes to go to Ireland.' She may have been referring to vacation plans; more likely she was thinking of the lord lieutenancy.
[3] *Public Advertiser*, 24 July 1767.
[4] Burke to Rockingham, 18 Aug. 1767, *Burke Correspondence*, i, p. 138; Lord Fred Cavendish to Rockingham, 12 Nov. 1767, Fitzwilliam MS. R5–34.
[5] *Walpole Memoirs*, iii. 259.

out of Pitt's ministry but desperately feared 'real disunion among our group' if he chose the wrong time to do it.[1] Had Richmond understood Rockingham's predicament, he would never have accused the Marquis of personal support for Pitt. When the dismissal of Lord Edgecumbe from the Bedchamber in November finally gave Rockingham a pretext for reuniting his party in opposition, Conway remained in office—though he still kept up his former connexion with the Rockingham party. At best Conway was an embarrassment to Rockingham; at worst he was a threat to the party unity the Marquis had been striving to obtain. But despite his growing annoyance with Conway's continual absence from party ranks, Rockingham returned the social call which Conway paid in December 1767. Had Richmond known either Rockingham's attitude to Conway or his immediate response to the minister's call, he would never have reprimanded Rockingham for failing to keep up the appearance of friendly association with Conway and thus exposed himself to the sarcasm of the Marquis's reply: 'Alas that that person should attend more to such trifling outward appearances than to all the former proofs I had given of regard and friendship.'[2]

In 1766 Richmond was uncertain about his future political affiliation;[3] in August 1767 Burke was doubtful what the Duke would do in the next session of Parliament.[4] When Richmond was finally reconciled with Newcastle in 1768, he paid the usual price for friendship with the old Duke by receiving unrequested advice:

But Lord Rockingham told Me, that you were very unwilling to leave your Hunting, to come to Town, to consider with our Friends the Plan of Conduct to be held by them, any considerable Time before the Meeting. Your Grace must forgive Me, if I press you very strongly, upon that Subject and I have a Right to do it, from the Respect and Affection which I have for you, and the Cause; and from My Knowledge of your right way of Thinking upon the Subject, and of the Ability with which you support your Opinion, which made so much Impression upon Charles Yorke. For God sake, My Dear Lord,

1 Rockingham to Newcastle, 29 Aug. 1766, Albemarle, *Rockingham*, ii. 12.
2 (Rockingham to Richmond), 14 Dec. 1767, Fitzwilliam MS. R9–8.
3 Walpole to Lord Holland, 2 Aug. 1766, *Letters to Henry Fox*, pp. 266–7.
4 Burke to Rockingham, 18 Aug. 1767, *Burke Correspondence*, i. 140.

Don't let it be said that upon Points of this Infinite Consequence to this Nation, Your Grace had suffer'd Your Fox Hunting to deprive the Cause, and your Friends, of the Advantage of your Assistance, and most Material Support, and for the sake of a Fox Chace. *That* is not an Object for the Duke of Richmond, who deservedly stands in the Light He is now. Let me therefore conjure you, My Dear Lord, as a most Faithful Friend and Servant (as I most undoubtedly am) to let My Lord Rockingham, the Duke of Portland and our friends know, that you will certainly meet them in Town, the last Day of this Month (which is the Day they all propose to be in Town) to concert with them the Conduct to be held by you, at this Time.[1]

Even as late as the spring of 1769 Richmond seems to have considered himself on the fringe of the Rockingham party.

Very likely he would have remained there had it not been for three simultaneous political developments: the four factions with whom different elements within the Rockingham party had favoured conflicting alliances, were replaced by one faction whose alliance the whole Rockingham party was willing to seek, Richmond himself abandoned his support for union with the King's Men, and the elements within the Rockingham party who had opposed Richmond's influence retired from political life. The most obvious change was the elimination of the disputed possibilities for alliance over which Richmond, Conway, and the Cavendishes had quarrelled with the rest of the party. In 1767 the choice of allies lay among Bedford, the King's Men, Grenville, and Grafton. In December 1767 Bedford's followers joined the government. By 1768, when they realized that Bute no longer had influence at court, the King's Men had disintegrated as a unified force. In November 1770 Grenville died, and two months later his followers joined the government. Meanwhile Chatham, largely recovered from his illness, took offence at promotions Grafton had made during his absence and resigned in October 1768. Temporarily reunited with Grenville and seeking an alliance with Rockingham, Chatham proved extremely tractable: in 1770, with the prospect of renewed ministerial offers after Grafton's resignation and

[1] Newcastle to Richmond, Oct. 1768, Add. MS. 32,991, ff. 264-5.

with two issues—Wilkes and the Falkland Islands—on which easy agreement was possible, the entire Rockingham party, including Richmond, supported a superficial union of opposition forces.

Even had the possibilities for alliance remained unchanged, it is unlikely that Richmond would have continued to support union with the King's Men, for two reasons. The first was his break with Lord Holland, which occurred in 1768–9 over the issues of Wilkes's expulsion from Parliament and Lady Sarah Bunbury's elopement. In the Middlesex elections of 1768 Richmond supported Wilkes, while Holland opposed him, perhaps to regain the King's attention. Later in the same season, Lady Holland with some justification accused the Duchess of encouraging Lady Sarah's elopement with Lord William Gordon.[1] On 6 December 1768 Lady Holland hinted at an 'awkwardness between Lord Holland and the Duke of Richmond';[2] on 10 March 1769 Richmond wrote Rockingham abjectly confessing the juvenility of his previous attachment.[3]

A family quarrel alone was insufficient cause for Richmond's political change of heart; added to it, however, was the pressure of effective protests from the Rockingham circle that alliance with royal favourites was useless in soliciting the King's voluntary support. Three ministries had been overturned in three years; was this not sufficient proof that the King considered ministers merely as tools, and that no ministry could trust the King unless it was willing to be entirely subservient to every royal wish? By July 1768 Richmond was convinced: 'they [the administration] are never changed but when they are getting strong enough to do the country some real service'.[4]

Richmond held the King partly to blame for the unheralded removal in August 1768 of Jeffery Amherst, whom the Duke considered to be an able colonial administrator,

---

[1] Lady Holland to Duchess of Leinster, 13 Mar. 1769, *Correspondence of Emily, Duchess of Leinster*, i. 568.
[2] Lady Holland to Duchess of Leinster, 6 Dec. 1768, Fitzgerald MSS., Dublin, C. Fox III.
[3] Fitzwilliam MS. R1–650. See Selected Letters.
[4] Richmond to Newcastle, 20 July 1766, Add. MS. 32,990, f. 322.

for the resignation of Conway to give the Bedfords an additional place in December 1767, and for the bribery of members of Parliament. By 1769, when he condemned a government bill because it allowed the King to distribute larger bribes[1] he was completely in line with Rockingham's views of seeking an alliance strong enough to come into office on its own terms.

Not only did Richmond's political thinking catch up with Rockingham's, but also the men with whom he had most often been at odds—the 'old guard' of Rockingham's party —died or withdrew from active political life. Newcastle formally retired in 1767, although his personal influence over Rockingham ended only with his death in November 1768. Winchelsea died (at 81) in August 1769. Albemarle's influence declined after his severe illnesses in 1767 and 1768, though he lived until 1772 and attended the Lords until the spring of 1770. Hardwicke, by far the youngest, gradually retired from active politics after a serious illness in 1767. He was still corresponding with Rockingham in 1770, but after the death of his brother the same year Hardwicke went over to the court. The only one of the 'old guard' who remained active into the 1770's was the Earl of Bessborough, uncle and political supporter of Richmond's reliable friends the Cavendishes.

The retirement of the 'old guard' was a triple blessing; it eliminated Richmond's worst antagonists within the party, it established Rockingham's single direction of his own party (for he was no longer obliged to consult and compromise with four diverging minds and at least two groups of satellites[2]), and it made way for the two men whom Richmond respected most—Burke and Dowdeswell. Dowdeswell became important about 1767, Burke not until 1769, just before the circulation of the *Present Discontents*. Dowdeswell was included in major discussions in 1765–6 by virtue of being Chancellor of the Exchequer and was then drafting the major ministerial bills and addresses, but he was out of town for the critical discussions about the King's Men and

---

[1] Richmond to Rockingham, 10 Mar. 1769, Fitzwilliam MS. R1–650. See Selected Letters.

[2] To some extent Portland and Montagu, for example, were early followers of Newcastle, and Keppel and Saunders of Albemarle.

Grafton's replacement in May 1766,[1] and was included, as was Burke, only in the general group discussions on Pitt's ministry in July and November. Not until the summer of 1767 did Dowdeswell visit Rockingham at Wentworth[2] and begin vacation correspondence[3]—indications of increasing friendship; by 1769 he visited Wentworth again,[4] and his correspondence with the Marquis became more frequent. Burke toured Yorkshire with Rockingham in 1767 and corresponded often with the Marquis. Not until 1769 was Burke influential on major policies. The rise of Dowdeswell was significant for the parliamentary organization of the Rockingham party; the rise of Burke was significant for Richmond's own prestige.

On 11 March 1766, after hearing Richmond's speech on the stamp tax repeal, Burke prognosticated, 'I think the Duke of Richmond will become a considerable man'[5]—the first prediction of Richmond's political ability. In 1767 Burke urged Rockingham to use Richmond.[6] Burke respected Richmond's energies, put up with his personality, and for more than a decade was his strongest supporter in the party.

The ability Burke first recognized in Richmond was his debating, which Richmond had himself early discovered to be his forte. He objected to the ambassadorship in 1765 because it would keep him from Parliament;[7] when the stamp tax repeal came up to the Lords, Richmond took the first available boat home from France to debate the issue.[8] Rockingham still thought him a mediocre speaker, and praised him only mildly after the window tax debates in May 1766.[9] Apparently his first effective oration was

---

[1] Dowdeswell to Rockingham, 19 May 1766, Dowdeswell MSS.

[2] Dowdeswell Memoir, Sept. 1767. Printed in *Sir Henry Cavendish's Debates,* ed. John Wright, 1840–3, i. 585.

[3] See Rockingham to Dowdeswell, 14 Sept. and 24 Nov. 1767, Fitzwilliam MS. R1–556, 559; Rockingham to Dowdeswell, 20 Oct. 1767, *Cavendish Debates,* i. 585.

[4] Rockingham to Dowdeswell, 20 Oct. 1769, Fitzwilliam MS. R1–687; Dowdeswell to Rockingham, 24 Oct. 1769, Fitzwilliam MS. R8–5.

[5] Burke to Arthur Blennerhasset, 11 Mar. 1766, Burke Corr. Book, i. 262.

[6] Burke to Rockingham, 18 Aug. 1767, *Burke Correspondence,* i. 140.

[7] C. J. Fox to Lord Holland, 13 July 1765, *Letters to Henry Fox,* p. 233.

[8] De Guerchy to Praslin, 23 Feb. 1766, F.F.O. 469, f. 174.

[9] Rockingham to George III, 28 May 1766, *Corr. Geo. III,* i. 342.

against Chatham's corn embargo on 6 December 1766, concluding with the well-known challenge, 'Nobility will not be browbeaten by an insolent minister.' Contemporaries extolled it as a powerful, if exaggerated attack. Rockingham recognized Richmond's usefulness as a speaker and thereafter he was given the opposition leadership for nearly all debates in the Lords. Few records of the Lords' debates survive; but Richmond certainly was the principal speaker on the East India and Canada Bills (May–June 1767), the presentation of the East India Company's petition against the Dividend Bill (February 1768), the King's Brothers' Annuities Bill (March 1768), and the debate on the Earl of Sandwich's subpoena by the House of Commons (December 1768). The development of Richmond's reputation as a speaker led directly to his rise in the party.

In the decade 1770–80 Richmond was considered one of the foremost Rockingham Whigs. But his reputation as a parliamentary speaker and his ability to understand and co-operate with his associates had developed slowly; he thus was only on the periphery of the Rockingham party during the five years before 1770, and showed no sign of being drawn to the centre.

III

1770 TO 1780

THE PARTY'S SHARP DECLINE AND RICHMOND'S GRADUAL DEFECTION

EARLY in 1771 Richmond advised Chatham 'to reunite in Party, to hold steadily together, and by acting upon true Whig principles to recover the weight and Party of the Whigs'.[1] By June 1780 he was advising the Lords that 'Party is the enemy of the Constitution'. In 1770 Richmond had exulted over Burke's defence of party in the *Present Discontents*; ten years later the Rockingham party was recovering from near collapse and Richmond was alienated from Burke and his friends.

The decade began with deceptive promise both for Richmond and for the Rockingham party, now the largest single faction in Parliament. Grafton resigned in January 1770 and his successor, the phlegmatic Lord North, was not expected to remain long in office. Opposition was divided only two ways—between Rockingham and Chatham; when ministerial offers appeared imminent and two plausible opposition issues were found in the Middlesex election and the Falkland Islands, the two opposition leaders reached the apex of co-operation. Within the Rockingham party a workable parliamentary arrangement was evolved so that Dowdeswell generally drew up motions, Richmond, Burke, and Dowdeswell debated them and prepared protests, and Rockingham personally extracted co-operation from recalcitrant elements in the party. After the disappearance of the 'old Whigs', Rockingham assumed an extensive, unquestioned leadership of his own party. Burke waited for him to call party meetings; Dowdeswell considered the Marquis's support alone sufficient to maintain his own prestige and occasionally even deferred to Rockingham's judgement on financial questions; and Richmond looked to him to suggest ideas for motions and to 'keep people together, particularly the H. of Commons

---

[1] Richmond to Rockingham, 12 Feb. 1771, Fitzwilliam MS. R158-44. See Selected Letters.

gentlemen . . . for I do not know $\frac{1}{2}$ of them, and the Thing
that influences them is the personal Regard they have for you
which will make them do for your speaking what they will
not for another man's'.[1] The normally taciturn parliamentarian
had even made efforts to debate in the House of Lords.[2]

At the same time Richmond's own antagonists in the
party had been replaced by men with whom he worked well.
With Dowdeswell Richmond enjoyed mutual respect, with
Burke and Rockingham a companionship promising to be
lifelong. So well settled was Richmond in the party that in
January 1771, when Lady Rockingham was too ill to allow
the Marquis to leave her, and Portland, the Marquis's first
choice as a substitute leader, was too ill himself to conduct
meetings, a not-very-reluctant Richmond was drafted temporarily to take the Marquis's place.

Several factors were responsible for the party's decline
and near disintegration. One of the lesser factors was lack of
communication during the summer. Richmond was particularly cut off, but by 1777 even Burke and Rockingham evidently went several months without writing. There were no
visitors of political importance to Goodwood after 1775: in
1776 Richmond was in France 'a long time'[3] until October,
in 1777 he spent June and July in France registering his
Dukedom of Aubigny,[4] and in 1778 and 1779 he was occupied all summer with the Sussex militia. He corresponded with
Burke over secession in 1772, with Rockingham over the
East India Court and Irish absentee land tax in 1773, and
apparently did not correspond at all in 1774. From 1775
to 1779 he exchanged at most one letter with Burke or
Rockingham each summer, the only exception being in 1778
after Keppel's encounter at Ushant.

A party could get along without correspondence in the

---

[1] Richmond to Rockingham, 16 Feb. 1771, Fitzwilliam MS. 158-45-1. See
Selected Letters.

[2] On 2 Mar. 1769, opposing a ministerial address which stated the willingness of
the Lords to pay the King's debts (£513,000), 'even Lord Rockingham attempted,
though under great perturbation, to open his mouth; and, being very civil and very
gentle, he was well heard' (Walpole Memoirs, iii. 228). See Richmond to Rockingham, 10 Mar. 1769 (Fitzwilliam MS. R1–650), in Selected Letters.

[3] Lady Charlotte Fitzgerald to Emily, Duchess of Leinster, 29 Oct. 1776, Fitzgerald MSS., Dublin, Duchess of Leinster II.

[4] See Burke to Richard Brocklesby, 21 July 1777, Burke Correspondence, ii. 170.

early summer months, even overlooking events like the American Declaration of Independence, news of which must have reached England in August 1776. But when communication did count was immediately before the opening of Parliament, usually in November. For the entire period from 1773 to 1779 there were possibly three party meetings before Parliament; in 1773, 1776, 1777, and 1778 there definitely were none. Even the Newmarket meetings ceased. In the four years in which no meeting was held, only one amendment was prepared for the address of thanks at the opening of Parliament.[1]

In part, the absence of communication resulted from Rockingham's laziness and the characteristic absorption of Whig lords in the running of their country estates. In larger part it resulted from the absence of news which would logically have been the subject of correspondence—ministerial changes and offers. Both parties were so certain of ministerial offers in 1770 that they discussed the allocation of offices. But no offer was extended for six years: Fox, who was just entering the Rockingham party, received overtures in May 1776,[2] Chatham in early spring 1778,[3] and Fox again in May 1778;[4] and even these later soundings were for reinforcement rather than replacement of the existing ministry. Six years without office meant inevitably the loss of the party's less loyal adherents.

The rest of the party was so apathetic, discouraged, or ill-disciplined that full party representation could not be obtained on measures like the New Shoreham Elections Bill or Dowdeswell's Enacting Bill. A stalwart like Sir George Savile originally declined to stand for Parliament in 1774.[5] The House of Lords minority dropped from 35 to 25,[6] and the House of Commons minority from 120 to 60,[7] over the first six years of the decade.

---

[1] On 27 Nov. 1778 an amendment was presented urging the King to take most speedy and effectual measures to restore peace in America.

[2] Portland to Rockingham, 29 May 1776, Fitzwilliam MS. R1–986.

[3] Christopher Hobhouse, *Fox*, 1947, pp. 84–85.

[4] Loc. cit., and Portland to Rockingham, 29 May 1778, Albemarle, *Rockingham*, ii. 353.   [5] Rockingham to Savile, 9 Aug. 1774, Fitzwilliam MS. R1–834.

[6] An average compiled from extant records of votes, largely collected in Thorold Rogers, *A Complete Collection of the Protests of the House of Lords*, 1875.

[7] Richmond to Rockingham, 25 Nov. 1775, Fitzwilliam MS. R2–146.

Just at the time when minority numbers were dwindling, the party lost Dowdeswell, its most capable parliamentary organizer. Dowdeswell's death in 1775 was a disaster often underestimated, partly because to people who knew him only slightly, 'honest Dowdeswell' appeared not only stolid but dull. But it was Dowdeswell who drew up most opposition motions: he initiated or prepared motions on the stamp tax repeal in 1766, land tax reductions in 1767, 'Expulsion does not create incapacitation' in April 1770, ministerial inactivity on the Falkland Islands' crisis in November 1770 and February 1771, and the 'recovery of lost powers of juries to determine libels' in February 1771. Dowdeswell wrote at least two pamphlets defending the party (1769 and 1772),[1] and occasionally collaborated with Burke on the formulation of protests. Richmond thought Rockingham and Dowdeswell the two men besides himself who 'would take the pains of getting people together'.[2] Rockingham thought so highly of Dowdeswell that he was willing to come to London in the midst of Lady Rockingham's serious illness in February 1771 to support Dowdeswell's Enacting Bill if it met with any opposition in party councils.[3] The opposition was half expected from Richmond, whose efforts at parliamentary union with Chatham were being impeded by Chatham's antagonism to the Enacting Bill; but from personal regard for Dowdeswell Richmond supported the bill at the cost of his hopes for a unified opposition. Dowdeswell, for his part, thought Richmond impractical but well-meaning, urged the party leadership on him during Rockingham's absence in 1771, and consulted Richmond on the party's contemplated secession from Parliament in the spring of 1773 before putting forth his own opinion.

In 1772 and again in 1776 the Rockingham party, discouraged by diminishing minorities, did attempt mass secessions from Parliament. No agreement was ever reached on the purpose or the procedure of either secession, and both attempts were failures which nearly broke up the party. In

---

[1] The pamphlets are referred to in correspondence, but probably they were published anonymously or circulated among the party in manuscript form.

[2] Richmond to Burke, 25 Nov. 1772, *Burke Correspondence*, i. 392.

[3] Dowdeswell to Rockingham, 8 Feb. 1771, Fitzwilliam MS. R126-14; Rockingham to Dowdeswell, 11 Feb. 1771, Fitzwilliam MS. R1-770.

the first secession Rockingham and Richmond wanted in-
definite absence from Parliament with reasons explained
after secession had taken place.[1] Richmond wanted regular
party meetings in London during the secession.[2] Dowdeswell wanted only two weeks' absence (from London) with
reasons presented beforehand.[3] Burke originally agreed with
Rockingham but grew discouraged before secession ever
began (November 1772) and attended the opening of Parliament.[4] Chatham's followers, along with Portland, Saunders, Lord George Germaine, Lord Fred Cavendish, and
others of Rockingham's 'northern friends', never sanctioned
secession at all.[5] Less than two weeks after secession was
decided upon, Richmond conceded to Burke that demon-
strating the party's want of discipline and unanimity in
such a way was worse than any possible performance in
Parliament.[6]

By spring 1773 the whole party had drifted back. In the
aftermath Burke admonished, 'Our own corps . . . appears
to me in great danger of dissolution.'[7] Richmond challenged
'the pride of the individuals which unfortunately . . . hinders
us from acting like men of sense',[8] and significantly began
questioning the purposes of party.

The second secession was determined upon in November
1776; the party was to be in London, attend private business,
and be absent for public business. But Richmond took
secession as an excuse to remain at Goodwood, while Rockingham occasionally attended public business, and Portland,
Savile, and Lord John Cavendish soon drifted back to regular attendance after only a token absence. In February 1777
—the same month in which Cartwright's pamphlet on
political reform was published—Richmond sympathized
with Rockingham:

The only comfort is, that as it seem'd almost impossible to do *any*

1 Burke to Dowdeswell, 7 Nov. 1772, *Burke Correspondence*, i. 359.
2 Richmond to Burke, 15 Nov. 1772, ibid. 371.
3 Dowdeswell to Burke, 8 Nov. 1772, Dowdeswell MSS.
4 Burke to Rockingham, 11 Nov. 1772, *Burke Correspondence*, i. 365–7.
5 Ibid. 367.
6 Richmond to Burke, 15 Nov. 1772, *Burke Correspondence*, i. 71.
7 Burke to Dowdeswell, 10 Jan. 1773, ibid. 422.
8 Richmond to Burke, 15 Nov. 1772, ibid. 71.

good, any way, tis to be hoped *no great Harm* has been done. We are but where we were; that is, as far as ever from seeing affairs grow better.[1]

By the middle of April the divided party had all drifted back: Richmond 'said no more of public affairs than just what was sufficient to express something very like . . . his entire despondency over them'.[2] In November 1777, when secession was again being discussed, Richmond urgently reminded Rockingham of the previous winter's disaster: total secession of all members of the Opposition might promise some useful publicity; further betrayal of disorganization might bring about the party's dissolution.[3]

What divided the party even further was the American revolution. From its administration of 1766 the party inherited the Declaratory Act, formalizing Parliament's right to legislate for the American colonies. Opposition to North's colonial policies was feasible on questions of administrative expediency but not of right; balking on expediency looked suspiciously like obstructionism, even though the party as a whole was motivated by a genuine desire to avert war.

In Parliament adherence to the Declaratory Act meant that alliance with Chatham could be formed only on negative or futile motions—for information on supplies,[4] or censure on the ministry.[5] On all major bills—for removal of troops from North America,[6] or repeal of laws by which the Americans felt themselves aggrieved[7]—the Opposition was divided and so was the Rockingham party itself. The Cavendishes and Portland supported the Declaratory Act entirely, to the point of supporting the government's coercive measures. Burke never formally repudiated the act, but his own bill for conciliation with the colonies virtually did so.[8] Richmond

---

1 Richmond to Rockingham, 19 Feb. 1777, Fitzwilliam MS. R1–946, printed in Albemarle, *Rockingham*, ii. 308–9.
2 Burke to Wm. Baker, 12 Oct. 1777, Burke Corr. Book, iii. 697.
3 Richmond to Rockingham, 2 Nov. 1777, Fitzwilliam MS. R1–968–1, printed in Albemarle, *Rockingham*, ii. 315–19.
4 For example, Nov. 1774; Nov. 1775; Dec. 1777; Jan.–Mar. (Committee on the State of the Nation) 1778.
5 Oct. 1775.   6 20 Jan. 1775; 5 Mar. 1776; Mar. 1778.
7 May 1775 (repeal of Quebec Act); Nov. 1776 (acts by which Americans felt themselves aggrieved).
8 Burke's resolutions presented in Mar. 1775 demanded the repeal of coercive

was the earliest to oppose the act: in a parliamentary debate in January 1775 he openly deplored it as anachronistic and impractical.[1] Rockingham hedged: had the colonists ever actually demanded repeal?

I cannot feel easy till I have voted for a Repeal of the declaratory act [Richmond repeated]. Burke has defended it with his usual Ingenuity, but long ago my own feelings and the bad use that has been made of that act have convinced me that it is indefensible.[2]

It was only one more step to the urging of recognition of American independence after the signing of the Franco-American treaty of alliance in March 1778:

This Event makes it the more necessary to come out with the Proposition of declaring the Independency of America. This being done instantly, and publickly, declaring against a War with France notwithstanding this Treaty, is the only means to keep America from joining France as allies. It is the only Chance we have for preventing such a Measure which must be our Ruin.[3]

So little common ground had the party for discussion that many abortive bills were prepared but never even discussed. Richmond drew up unnoticed bills in the spring of 1776[4] and in November 1777;[5] a motion of indirect censure on the ministry was prepared in vain in January 1775;[6] Portland wrote a paper on the American revolution which was never published.[7] The level of speaking in Parliament was poor, and few of the party stalwarts cared whether they attended or not. Formal secession lasted less than two months in 1776; but the idea of secession was under constant discussion from 1775 to 1777. With minorities diminishing and the party nucleus divided the prospects looked so hopeless

acts and the substitution of voluntary grants of revenue for taxes on the American colonies.

[1] Burke to Committee at Bristol, 20 Jan. 1775, Burke Corr. Book, iii. 160; *Parl. Hist.*, xviii. 198.

[2] Richmond to Rockingham, 2 Nov. 1777, Fitzwilliam MS. R1–968–1. Printed in Albemarle, *Rockingham*, ii. 315–19.

[3] Richmond to Rockingham, 15 Mar. 1778, Fitzwilliam MS. R1–983.

[4] Richmond to Portland, [2 Mar. 1776], Nottingham MSS.

[5] Richmond to Rockingham, 2 Nov. 1777, Albemarle, *Rockingham*, ii. 315; Shelburne to Chatham, 27 Nov. 1777, *Chatham Correspondence*, iv. 461–2.

[6] Shelburne to Chatham, 31 Jan. 1775, P.R.O. 30/8/54–162.

[7] Burke to Rockingham, 6 Jan. 1777, Burke Corr. Book, ii. 25–83.

that in 1778 Richmond had reached the first stage in repudiating the *Present Discontents* and was willing to consider a ministerial compromise with North.[1]

The second stage was Richmond's personal alienation from the Rockingham party, largely because of personality clashes with its leaders, aggravated by the party's failure to give him more than lukewarm support in the East India Company in 1773–4 and later in several of his parliamentary motions such as the inquiry into Greenwich Hospital in 1778, or the reduction of civil list expenditure in December 1779.

In October 1772 the East India Company asked the government for permission to suspend its quarterly payment since overspending in India had put the company in debt. At the end of November the government successfully moved two bills—for a secret committee to examine the books of the company and for a restraint on the company's sending out supervisors to India—indicating that the company was not to be allowed to clean up its own finances and that more drastic measures were to follow upon the recommendations of the secret committee. At first Richmond was so indifferent to the company's fate that he refused even to leave Goodwood to discuss the subject with Burke in December,[2] but after studying the government proposals cursorily the next month he decided that the issue was one of government invasion of the company's chartered rights. As a £500 shareholder in East India stock, Richmond impetuously transferred his energies from Parliament to the General Court of Proprietors. He first unwisely persuaded the General Court that by rejecting co-operation with the government and forcing the ministry to take the offensive the company would rally sympathy for its chartered rights, at least from other chartered institutions like the Bank of England. But when no other corporations supported the company except the city of London,[3] the government easily passed a regulating bill far stiffer than the company had

---

[1] Richmond to Rockingham, 31 May 1778, Albemarle, *Rockingham*, ii. 354.

[2] Richmond to Portland, 2 Dec. 1772, Nottingham MSS.; Richmond to Burke, 2 Dec. 1772, *Burke Correspondence*, i. 395–9.

[3] *Gentlemen's Magazine*, 1773, p. 252; *Annual Register*, 1773, p. 104 (Eur. Hist.); Richmond to Burke (27 May 1773), Burke Corr. Book, ii. 372.

expected and without checking with the company beforehand.[1]

Subsequently the East India directors drew up a set of
instructions to company servants in India, to implement the
Regulating Act, while Richmond gathered support for an
alternative set of instructions in hopes of proving the Regulating Act unworkable. In the voting for instructions at the
General Court in January 1774, 'The sudden appearance of
many courtiers as proprietors'[2] defeated Richmond's hopes;
three months later, when all his personal nominees were
defeated in the company elections for the board of directors,
Richmond retired from the General Court for good.

For a time Richmond considered success in East India
politics essential to his political future; the rest of the party
was more concerned for the effect on public opinion of
Richmond's defence of the rights of an avowedly corrupt
company. Keppel admitted the accounts of Richmond's
activity in the company made him laugh.[3] Burke urged the
party members who owned company stock to join Richmond
in the General Court[4] and in November 1773 discussed possible alternatives to the directors' instructions with Richmond;[5] he could do little else and gave up hope by January
1774.[6] Lord John Cavendish came up to the General Court
in January 1774, but only because Richmond 'makes it so
much a personal matter'.[7] Rockingham thought his efforts
largely futile: there is only slight evidence that Rockingham
ever urged his friends to buy up £1,000 shares of stock, as
Richmond pleaded in the autumn of 1773, probably because
Rockingham was currently more interested in the Irish
absentee land tax.

[1] For passage of the Regulating Bill see Sutherland, *East India Company*, ch. ix.
[2] Walpole, *Last Journals*, i. 286. See also Richmond to Rockingham, 10 Sept.
1773, Fitzwilliam MS. R158–53; Richmond to James Adair, 1 Dec. 1773, Burke
MS. 4a; Richmond to Rockingham, 2 and 15 Jan. (9 Feb.) 1774, Fitzwilliam
MS. R2–145, R1–824, and R1–127–29.
[3] Keppel to Rockingham, 15 Mar. 1773, The Hon. Thomas Keppel, *Life of
Augustus, Viscount Keppel*, 1842, i. 411.
[4] Burke Memorandum to Gentlemen of the Opposition in Parliament, 1773,
Burke Correspondence, i. 427–9.
[5] Burke dined with Richmond, 15 Nov. 1773, when he probably discussed the
instructions.
[6] Burke to Rockingham, 2 Feb. 1774, *Burke Correspondence*, i. 451.
[7] Lord John Cavendish to Rockingham, 7 Jan. 1774, Fitzwilliam MS. R1–823.

Inevitably Richmond took indifference as personal affront. It was all the easier to do so since his two friendships which had seemed most promising in 1770—with Burke and Rockingham—were proving disappointments. Possibly because the Marquis was jealous, more probably because he could not put up with Richmond's eccentricities and nagging personality, Richmond never received Rockingham's affection or even his relaxed companionship. He was omitted from the Rockingham–Burke–Dowdeswell correspondence (1770–4) and often learned the Marquis's thoughts only from Burke. No summer visits were exchanged with Rockingham except possibly in 1771. In 1772 Burke told Richmond he was well thought of by Lord Rockingham[1]— hardly an indication that Richmond knew Rockingham very well. When Richmond wrote to Rockingham that his future career depended upon the outcome of a vote in the East India Company Court, Rockingham wrote to Burke that the outcome was not decisive.[2] Undoubtedly Richmond was kept in the party from 1778 to 1782 primarily by devotion to Rockingham, but Rockingham was not nearly as devoted to Richmond as to his northern friends.

The friendship with Burke, on the other hand, grew for a time, through frequent visits, correspondence, and private consultations; Burke, for example, came to Goodwood to ask Richmond's advice about taking a supervisorship in India in August 1772.[3] But by 1777 each man had begun to think the other ambitious, irresponsible, and prone to wild ideas. Burke visited Goodwood only once after 1775; by 1776 his correspondence with Richmond had begun to taper. Although he was still full of praise for Richmond in writing to Dr. Brocklesby in 1777[4] he rarely again mentioned Richmond in his letters, until in May 1780 even the remnants of their friendship were destroyed in a quarrel. When Burke spoke against Alderman Sawbridge's motion for annual parliaments, Richmond, then in the midst of preparing his own motion on parliamentary reform, foolishly asked

1 Burke to Richmond, 17 Nov. 1772, draft, *Burke Correspondence*, i. 372–82.
2 Rockingham to Burke, 30 Jan. 1774, Burke MS. 312.
3 Burke to Richmond, [21 Aug. 1772], *Burke Correspondence*, i. 339–42.
4 Burke to Dr. Richard Brocklesby, 21 July 1777, ibid., p. 170.

Burke for a copy of his speech in order to refute his arguments. With neither taste nor tact he threatened Burke not to refuse for he was determined to answer him point by point. But Burke did refuse, sarcastically referring Richmond to the *Causes of the Present Discontents* for his political principles.[1]

It was no coincidence that Burke's friendship with Charles James Fox increased as that with Richmond declined. Throughout his life there was probably no man Richmond detested more than his nephew Fox, son of Lord Holland with whom Richmond had split in 1768. Richmond may have objected to his nephew's wild reputation; more important, he considered him a rival for the family affections. Fox was more popular with the rest of the Lennox relatives, some of whom looked to him as head of the family instead of Richmond. Fox delighted the Irish relatives on his visits; he was probably far more tolerant than Richmond of the second marriages of Lady Emily and Lady Sarah. When Richmond declined to join the Fox–North coalition Lady Sarah queried how he could possibly be of service to the country without Fox.[2] In 1787 William Ogilvie visited Richmond and Fox and was far more impressed with the latter;[3] in the regency crisis two years later all of the Irish members of the family supported Fox and the Prince, though Richmond was in Pitt's cabinet.

Fox was dismissed from the Treasury in 1774; thereafter he made a determined effort to break into the Rockingham party leadership. He early ingratiated himself with the northern clique, particularly Devonshire and Portland, systematically sought political advice of Rockingham and Burke, and gave it, often unsolicited, in return. In October 1776 he wrote to Rockingham urging a party manifesto on the American revolution.[4] In 1778, 'desperately keen for

---

[1] Burke to Richmond, [10 May 1780], Burke MS. Northants. Rec. Soc. A. II. 71.

[2] Lady Sarah Napier to Lady Susan O'Brien, 25 Mar. 1783, *Life and Letters of Lady Sarah Lennox*, ii. 33.

[3] Wm. Ogilvie to Emily, Duchess of Leinster, 1 Apr. 1787, Fitzgerald MS. Ogilvie III.

[4] Fox to Rockingham, 13 Oct. 1776, Albemarle, *Rockingham*, ii. 297. Fox mentioned 'the conduct . . . projected at Wentworth', indicating that he had visited Rockingham earlier in the summer.

office',[1] he advised Rockingham to enter the ministry with North.[2] Burke had to admonish him not to appear too eager about politics.[3] He was not considered for a major office by Rockingham until June 1780, but long before then he had been particularly useful to the party as a parliamentary speaker and as a channel through which ministerial offers were relayed from his close friend Lord Weymouth. In May 1776[4] and May 1778[5] Fox had sounded Rockingham for the King. As early as 1776 Fox was well into the centre of the party.

Disappointed by Rockingham, disaffected from Burke, Richmond looked elsewhere for political friendship and found it, after Chatham's death, in Shelburne.

With Chatham, personal co-operation had been extremely difficult. Richmond had been willing to stay on with Chatham in 1766; when Chatham made the insulting offer of an embassy[6] Richmond went into violent opposition. After Chatham's resignation in October 1768, Richmond was torn between personal hatred of Chatham and idealistic support of a union of opposition factions.

He opposed an alliance with Chatham, Grenville, and Temple in 1769.[7] But in 1771 Burke wrote, 'Indeed the Duke of Richmond is very attentive to any method . . . of connecting us with the high and mighty allies.'[8]

The apex of Rockingham–Chatham co-operation had been reached in 1770: news and visits were regularly exchanged, and measures were postponed or reworded for mutual convenience.[9] After 1770 relations deteriorated as the possibility of ministerial offers declined. There were vitriolic words and ridiculous personal quarrels about credit for the presentation of Dowdeswell's Enacting Bill in 1771.

---

[1] Hobhouse, *Fox*, p. 99.

[2] Fox to Rockingham, 24 Jan. 1779, Albemarle, *Rockingham*, ii. 371–5.

[3] Burke to C. Fox, 8 Oct. 1776, Lord John Russell, *Life and Times of Charles James Fox*, 1859, i. 52.

[4] Portland to Rockingham, 29 May 1776, Fitzwilliam MS. R1–986.

[5] Portland to Rockingham, 29 May 1778, Albemarle, *Rockingham*, ii. 353.

[6] Random paper inserted in Richmond's Journal, 1766, Goodwood, Small Libr. MS. E.

[7] Burke to Rockingham, 5 Dec. 1769, *Burke Correspondence*, i. 218.

[8] Burke to Rockingham, 16 Feb. 1771, Burke Corr. Book, ii. 171.

[9] See Fitzwilliam MSS. and P.R.O. 30/8/54.

During the trial of William Woodfall, publisher of the *Public Advertiser*, for libel in June 1770, Lord Mansfield had instructed the jury to determine only upon the fact of publication and not upon the criminality of the libel. At the end of the year Dowdeswell drew up a bill which would have made such a limitation upon the jury illegal for the future. Meanwhile Chatham had Camden draw up a resolution declaring that Mansfield had acted illegally.[1] Followers of both Chatham and Rockingham, convinced that a union of opposition factions was not essential since immediate ministerial offers were unlikely, magnified the trivial difference in order to vent personal animosities—Chatham called the bill a 'compound of connection, tyranny, and absurdity';[2] and Burke, sermonizing on the strength of Chatham's feelings, warned Dowdeswell that 'The great aim of that party is that you should do nothing that is useful. This will be a trial of firmness between Mr. Dowdeswell and Ld. Chatham.'[3]

Richmond, who was in charge of the party during the Marquis's absence with Lady Rockingham in Bath, was virtually the only party member besides Manchester to desire a union of opposition factions. To achieve this end he was neither above appropriate flattery to the great Earl's vanity nor afraid to scold him for lack of communication. Richmond reported both sides of the quarrel to Rockingham with such relative objectivity that both Rockingham and Dowdeswell feared his taking Chatham's side in a joint party meeting. Chatham he criticized for unnecessarily bringing into the open his disapproval of Dowdeswell's bill, but he added in a letter to Rockingham that 'Dowdeswell was devilish sulky at Lord Chatham already, and Burke is all combustible.'[4]

Realizing the impossibility of compromise between the infuriated Dowdeswell and the intractable Chatham, Richmond

---

[1] For background see Basil Williams, *The Life of William Pitt, Earl of Chatham*, 1913, ii. 275–7 and W. S. Holdsworth, *A History of English Law*, 1903, vii. 342–5.

[2] Chatham to Barre, 21 Feb. 1771, *Chatham Correspondence*, iv. 100.

[3] Burke to Dowdeswell, n.d. (about 2 Feb. 1771), Burke Corr. Book, ii. 183.

[4] Richmond to Rockingham, 12 Feb. 1771, Fitzwilliam MS. R158–44. See Selected Letters.

tried to divert the energies of the two parties to an attack
on the government's handling of the Falkland Islands' crisis.
In June 1770 the Governor of Buenos Aires had occupied
Port Egmont on the Falkland Islands and held a British
ship captive. War was averted by the negotiations of Lord
Rochford leading to a Spanish disavowal of the attack and
restitution of the *status quo* before the attack.[1] On 25 January
the Rockingham and Chatham parties combined to move for
papers concerning the negotiations; but when the papers
were presented a motion to amend the address of thanks by
omitting a paragraph thanking the King for defending the
honour of Great Britain and securing the peace was defeated,
and four additional motions suggested by Richmond to
Chatham later in the month generally met with so little
enthusiasm that they were never presented.[2] Ill feeling still
unhealed, Dowdeswell was overwhelmingly defeated on the
presentation of his Enacting Bill in March, Chatham's followers gloatingly supporting the government. Two years
later, when Chatham and Shelburne thought the East India
Bill 'an honest attempt',[3] Rockingham and Richmond
accused them of wanting to throw increased patronage to the
government.[4] Of all the Rockingham party only Richmond
took an interest in a bill warmly supported by Chatham;
and Shelburne, an Irish landowner, joined Rockingham
in opposing a tax on absentee landowners which threatened
to pass the Irish Parliament, but changed his mind after
consulting Chatham, who upheld the tax as being within the
right of the Irish legislature to determine.[5]

Over the American colonies there could be no agreement
between Rockingham and Chatham as long as the Declaratory Act existed. Attempts at conciliation—Keppel's visit to
Shelburne in 1776,[6] Grafton's attempt at mediation in

---

[1] See Julius Goebel, *The Struggle for the Falkland Islands*, 1927, chs. vi and vii;
J. F. Ramsay, *Anglo-French Relations, 1763–70*, University of California Publications in History, xxvii, no. 3, 1939, chs. iv, v, viii–x.

[2] Richmond to Chatham, 19 Feb. 1771, P.R.O. Chatham Papers, 1/54/54.

[3] Lord Fitzmaurice, *Life of William, Earl of Shelburne*, 1912, i. 448.

[4] Shelburne to Chatham, 26 June 1773. Quoted ibid., p. 453.

[5] Shelburne to Chatham, 31 Oct. 1773, and Chatham to Shelburne, 4 Nov.
1773, *Chatham Correspondence*, iv. 302, 308.

[6] See Keppel to Rockingham, 5 Jan. 1776, Keppel, *Life of Keppel*, i. 420.

November 1775,[1] Chatham's own overtures in November 1777[2]—were abortive.

In January 1775 Chatham notified opposition lords in general terms of his intention to present a bill for conciliation with the American colonies. Then without warning Rockingham who attended to support the bill, he turned his introductory speech into a caustic attack on the Declaratory Act. After that Rockingham's friends were so sure the Earl could not be trusted that when he circulated vague notice of a motion several days later, intending to present a bill more in line with Rockingham's legislative record, the Marquis advised caution to his friends[3] and Richmond answered Chatham with an undisguised reprimand.

> I wish for communication and consultation between those who mean the same thing, only the better to answer the objects we all have in view: that by talking over business, it may be better understood; that little differences of opinion may be settled by fair discussion, and mutual giving way, or at least that they may not appear in public; and lastly, that those who are to support a question may be prepared to do so. I am not attached to punctilious ceremony, and for my own part would readily forego the most usual attentions; I am only anxious for such as are necessary for carrying on business. The importance of the present object, and the desperate temerity of the Ministry, make it peculiarly necessary at this instant, that all the real friends of England and of America, the true Whigs, should come to a good understanding, and heartily unite to save the Nation. God knows if our utmost efforts can succeed; but I am sure that nothing less than such united efforts can have any chance.[4]

Somewhat mollified by Chatham's second bill, Richmond suggested that Rockingham visit Hayes.[5] Rockingham never met with Chatham, and subsequent meetings with his associates produced no agreements. On all major issues, such as removal of troops from North America and repeal of all acts aggrieving the American colonists—the opposition was

---

[1] Quoted in *Autobiography and Political Correspondence of Augustus Henry, third Duke of Grafton*, ed. Sir William Anson, 1898, p. 277.

[2] See the exchange of correspondence in Albemarle, *Rockingham*, ii. 324 (Chatham to Rockingham, 27 Nov. 1777), and *Chatham Correspondence*, iv. 450–62.

[3] Albemarle, *Rockingham*, ii. 270.

[4] Richmond to Chatham, 1 Feb. 1775, *Chatham Correspondence*, iv. 391–3.

[5] Richmond to Rockingham, 17 Feb. 1775, Fitzwilliam MS. R1–867. See Selected Letters.

divided. Finally, in December 1777, the development of a
future pattern of co-operation seemed possible again when
both parties united behind a motion for a committee on the
state of the nation. To wind up the business of the committee Richmond announced his intention of moving an address
for the removal of troops from America since Chatham's
associates were in sympathy with the spirit of the motion.
Richmond twice postponed it in hopes that Chatham could be
present to give his support. Chatham did come on 8 April,
but not to help. The seizure which took his life occurred as
he characteristically rose to pour invective on Richmond and
his measure.

In opposition Shelburne was a far more agreeable partner.
He was amiable, nearly obsequious: '. . . he emphatically
declared, that where your Grace leads, he will follow'.[1] With
Richmond he shared an unsociably abstemious life, a military background, and ability in parliamentary speaking,
which suited the two men for collaboration on military
debates. In March and April 1780, for example, when
Richmond moved for an inquiry into the defenceless state
of Devon and Cornwall, charging that Lord Amherst, the
Commander-in-Chief and Lieutenant-General of the Ordnance, had been inattentive to the demands of Sir David
Lindsay, military commander at Plymouth, for more adequate
fortifications at the base during the previous summer, he
conferred with Shelburne at each step in preparing the
motion.[2] In December 1779 the two Lords collaborated on
a motion to check increases in military expenditures granted
for extraordinary reasons beyond the supplies voted by Parliament for departmental reasons.

Unlike Chatham, Shelburne temporized with Rockingham on all major disputed issues except parliamentary reform, on which he supported Richmond. Fox claimed that
Shelburne's views on America were irreconcilable with those
of the Rockingham party, but before Chatham's death in
May 1778 Shelburne had approved Richmond's motion to

---

[1] F. D. Cartwright, *Life and Correspondence of Major John Cartwright*, 1826,
i. 142.

[2] Richmond to Shelburne, 15 Mar. and 20 Apr. 1780, Lansdowne MSS. See
Selected Letters.

withdraw troops from America and treat with America as an independent country. As Chatham's successor Shelburne realized that he could not form a successful ministry without Rockingham's superior numbers and borough control, and that Rockingham's price was the Treasury and America. On 2 February 1779 Shelburne let it be known that he would not negotiate without Rockingham,[1] thus tacitly yielding the colonies and the Treasury. Richmond and Rockingham themselves considered American independence only a last resort to obtain peace.[2]

Gratified personally and politically, by 1780 Richmond had virtually switched allegiance from Rockingham to Shelburne. Well before the Yorkshire movement began he was certain that the Rockingham party, even in power, would not remodel government to his liking.

[1] 3 Feb. 1779, *Grafton Autobiography*, pp. 307–8.
[2] Prince Hoare, *Memoirs of Granville Sharpe*, 1820, pp. 195–7.

IV

THE RADICAL DUKE
AND THE MOVEMENT
FOR PARLIAMENTARY REFORM

ETWEEN 1770 and 1775 a wide range of plans for the
reform of Parliament was drawn up by pamphleteers
and parliamentarians, varying from the most conservative programme of economic reform embodied in Dowdeswell's bill for the disfranchisement of revenue officers, to the
most radical scheme for universal suffrage and annual parliaments put forth by pamphleteers like Major Cartwright.
In the spring of 1780, primarily under pressure of economic
distress resulting from the American War, the Yorkshire
Association attempted to unite all reformers into a common
movement for moderate political reform. But before the
Yorkshire Association could gain the adherence of the radicals (particularly the orators and pamphleteers for the city
of London), it had already lost the support of the Conserva-
tives (most of the Rockingham Whigs), and by April all
hope for a unified reform movement had disappeared. At
least three separate campaigns trickled on, to be all but
destroyed by the Gordon Riots which began on 3 June.[1]

On the same day, 3 June, Richmond moved his bill for
parliamentary reform.[2] The bill put forth an elaborate
scheme dividing England, Scotland, and Wales into 558
equally populous electoral districts, and providing for registration of all male inhabitants over eighteen years of age each

[1] See particularly Herbert Butterfield, *George III, Lord North, and the People*,
1952, chs. v–vii: G. S. Veitch, *The Genesis of Parliamentary Reform*, 1913; *London
Chronicle*, 8–11 Jan. 1780; Burke to Richmond, 10 May 1780 (Burke MS. North-
ants. Rec. Soc. A. II. 71); Richmond to Rockingham, 12 June 1780 (Albemarle,
Rockingham, ii. 418–20); Richmond to Shelburne, [20 Apr. 1780] in Selected
Letters.

[2] For the bill itself see *Authentic Copies of a Declaration of the Rights of Englishmen: a Bill for Reform of Parliament; and a Letter to Lieutenant Colonel Sharman by
His Grace, the Duke of Richmond*, 1794, G.P. 1957, Political Tracts 1793–4, Bodleian Library. Since the speech was long, and Richmond expressed his intention of
having it printed, few of the newspapers reported it. The most complete summary
was given by the *Morning Chronicle* on 5 June.

May, and elections every June, with Parliament opening for a two- or three-month session every September. The bill was introduced by a lengthy speech (described as masterful, but probably very dull) embodying two points. The first was that while all men ought to have the right to a share in government and all who paid taxes (presumably everyone, for bread and beer taxes fell on the lowest classes) should have a vote for the legislature, only one Englishman in six actually had a vote in 1730.

The second point—in answer to Burke's defence of the inviolability of the constitution—was that laws of Parliament were not synonymous with constitutional principles, and were therefore alterable, and moreover that existing laws for electing Parliament were at odds with the original purpose of the constitution. Richmond traced the history of English constitutional development from the supposedly open assemblies of the Anglo-Saxons to the Parliament of 1780, corrupted by faction and connexion.

Richmond's receptivity to the idea of political reform can be traced directly to his experiences in the Rockingham party during the previous decade. In 1771, when there had seemed a possibility that the King would be forced to offer the Treasury either to Rockingham or to Chatham, Richmond in a conference with Chatham had expressed hope that a Whig alliance sufficiently strong to enforce its own nomination to the Treasury might under the existing operation of government enter office in a position to dictate its own terms to the King.

. . . the Minister must be from among our Corps, and no one amongst us stood in competition with you. . . . we did not confine our pretensions here, for we should expect to have the Majority of the Cabinet from our Corps and the efficient offices of the Admiralty, Plantations, etc., that in short we meant to be the Ministers to govern the country by the Corps of Whigs, and that having secured this we should leave Ribbons, white sticks, and Court places to any assistants we could meet with.[1]

---

[1] Richmond to Rockingham, 12 Feb. 1771, Fitzwilliam MS. R158–44. See Selected Letters. Cf. Burke's 'Observations on a Late Publication intituled The Present State of the Nation' in *The Works of the Right Honourable Edmund Burke,* 1925, i. 352.

By 1773, when it had become clear that the Rockingham party faced a long exile from office, Richmond had complained that the ministry was kept in office by the influence of the crown, which was steadily corrupting the House of Commons. By this time Richmond had begun looking outside Parliament to organizations like the East India Company and the city of London for means to limit the increasing influence and interference of the crown in Parliament.

Four years later his thinking had developed farther along the same lines. Having despaired that Rockingham could ever return to office except by popular acclaim, he had suggested that the Marquis should therefore consider specific measures for a statutory limitation of the influence of the crown once the party had attained office.

I would also very much wish you to consider of some Plan which you would execute if in Power for reducing the Influence of the Crown within proper Bounds, and when digested to propose it in Parliament. It will certainly be rejected, but it will give the People a more precise Idea of what they may expect from you and may induce them in the Hour of Difficulty to call upon you and give you Powers to execute your Plan. It is very true that after such a Proposal which would bind you not to accept without performing it, no King as they are now taught would send for you as long as he could possibly avoid it, but have you a better have you any Chance any other way? or (which will I am sure be a stronger Reason with you) can you hope to do any good in coming in by any other Means than by a call of the Nation to relieve their Distress? I know you will laugh and say this is Shelburne's language. I know it is, or was for I have not seen him, but be it whose it may, if the Reasoning is good I would adopt it from any Quarter, and I trust it has one advantage more in coming from me than from him, you know it is sincere.[1]

He thus anticipated his concept of the selection of the governor residing with the governed, though the 'people' were to exercise authority on only one particular occasion in order to enable the party—'popular' in the sense that it favoured limiting the authority of the crown—to return to office. From this position it was only one step toward considering the people as the permanent seat of authority and

---

[1] Richmond to Rockingham, 2 Nov. 1777, Fitzwilliam MS. R1-968-1, quoted in Albemarle, *Rockingham*, ii. 315-19.

toward dropping the concept of party government entirely. That Richmond took the step at all was probably due both to his personal quarrels with members of the Rockingham party, and to his reading in political theory.

There is no direct evidence as to the reading he had done for the bill, but three points are certain: Richmond was not very interested in the study of philosophy in general, he was not generally well read, so he had probably not studied widely in political philosophy, and his thinking was usually far from original—his parliamentary motions, for instance, had been based largely on the ideas of Burke and Dowdeswell, or on motions previously presented. For example, not one important idea expressed in his vigorous opposition to the government's handling of the Falkland Islands' crisis had been his own: after the Spanish attack he had waited passively for inspiration from other members of the party. The best suggestion he could make in January 1772 was 'a hash of all our old complaints'.[1]

His ideas on reform, therefore, were most likely culled from a few works and a few conversations, and thrown together not fully assimilated—hence the contradictions among several of his objectives.

Apparently none of his ideas came from America. Like the rest of the Rockingham party he never defended the rights of the colonists either to be represented in Parliament or to be governed by themselves. His sole aim after 1774 had been first to avoid, and then to end, a costly war. He had read few, if any, of the American pamphlets.

He had read and discussed Rousseau[2] and the fashionable French philosophers—certainly Voltaire. He also had a rudimentary knowledge of Greek and Roman political theory, taught to him in a summer by Walker King, an Oxford don he had employed for the purpose.[3]

A study of his bill, however, indicates that his ideas came mainly from contemporary English sources. He had

---

[1] Richmond to Rockingham, 21 Jan. 1771, Fitzwilliam MS. R1–784. Printed in Albemarle, *Rockingham*, ii. 214–15.

[2] De Praslin to De Guerchy, 14 Feb. 1766, F.F.O. 469, f. 133. Most of the Lennox family, including Richmond, accepted Rousseau's views on the education of children.

[3] Burke to Walker King, 21 June 1774, Burke Corr. Book, ii. 472.

certainly discussed politics often with the three other peers—
Manchester, Abingdon, and Effingham[1]—who supported
radical reform, and he was particularly close to Manchester.
In 1774 Granville Sharp had published *The Natural Right
of People to Share in the Legislature*: since Richmond knew
the author well and had discussed politics with him,[2] he had
doubtless read the pamphlet. But he seems to have drawn
far more upon James Burgh's *Political Disquisitions* (1775),
Richard Price's *Nature of Civil Liberty* (1776), and Major
John Cartwright's *Take Your Choice* (1777). Together the
three works contained virtually every point in Richmond's
speech. From Price Richmond took whole the distinction of
four types of liberty—religious, physical, moral, and civil,
with civil liberty being the power of society to govern itself
without being subject to any extraneous will or power.[3]
Burgh, postulating government as a trust and the legislature
as an institution for which all men should have a vote by
virtue of paying taxes, put forth a scheme of proportional
representation dividing the English householders into 513
equal groups (for 558 M.P.s minus 45 Scottish representatives).[4] Cartwright modified Burgh's scheme by dividing the

[1] Thomas Howard (1747–91), third Earl of Effingham, and George Montagu
(1739–88), fourth Duke of Manchester, had both begun their careers in the Army.
Effingham held no office until 1782; Manchester had served as Lord of the Bed-
chamber, 1762–70. From 1770 to 1782 both Lords were on the edge of the Rockingham party, occasionally attending meetings to discuss opposition to the American
War. In the second Rockingham ministry they were respectively Treasurer and
Lord Chamberlain of the Household. At Rockingham's death Manchester followed
Fox (and was Ambassador to Paris during the coalition) while Effingham remained
with Shelburne and later held minor offices under Pitt. Both men, incidentally, were
Grand Masters of the Free Masons. Manchester was connected through friends with
the reform movement in the city as early as 1776 (Nottingham MSS. In that year
he was involved in an attempt of Sayer and Lee, Sheriffs of the city, to organize
a meeting of protest against the American War). Effingham's interest developed
later: he was one of the contributors of a letter to Colonel Sharman in 1783. Of the
three peers Willoughby Bertie (1739–88), fourth Earl of Abingdon, was the least
known to Richmond and the least important politically; he held no office except
the stewardship of Abingdon and Wallingford, rarely spoke in Parliament, and was
considered slightly insane, or at least eccentric, by contemporaries.

[2] *Memoirs of Granville Sharp*, pp. 195–7. Lord Mahon claimed to have written
a similar pamphlet the same year, but no copies are extant, and since Mahon's
interest in parliamentary reform did not begin until considerably later, his author-
ship of a pamphlet at that time seems highly unlikely. See Ghita Stanhope and
G. P. Gooch, *Life of Charles, third Earl of Stanhope*, 1914, p. 38, and Cartwright,
Life of Cartwright, i. 82 n.

[3] Price, *Nature of Civil Liberty*, pp. 52–73.   [4] *Political Disquisitions*, i. 38.

total number of English male inhabitants over eighteen years by 515, to determine the number of electors—roughly 2,900—to each M.P. Cities with the requisite number of voters would return one M.P. or more; smaller towns would contribute their votes to the counties.[1] Cartwright eulogized the independent institutions of Anglo-Saxon times and traced the development of tyranny in succeeding periods.[2]

Take Your Choice was particularly designed to appeal to Richmond for two reasons. Like Price, Cartwright protested against the injustice of the Regulating Act of 1774 disfranchising £500 freeholders in the East India Company, and against the government's invading the company's General Court in 1774 with supporters for the government-directors' instructions for company servants in India.[3] In addition, Cartwright appealed 'to the Whig nobles . . . those patriots who have seen their country carried to the edge of ruin. . . . The author's hopes are with the Whigs, for their creed, would they be true to it, is the creed of free men.'[4] For Richmond, the idealist who once thought the Rockingham party the sole political descendants of Locke and favoured religious toleration because 'their principles [of the dissenters] are the same in religion as ours in Politics',[5] Cartwright had a direct appeal.

He had actually intended the pamphlet for Shelburne and had sent manuscript copies to him in 1776 with the naïve request that Shelburne lead a reform party in Parliament. Shelburne, through Price, demurred.[6] Cartwright then sent printed copies of the pamphlet to all leading Whigs; Richmond responded, called on Cartwright to discuss the tract, and soon became his close friend.[7] Richmond submitted the outline of his Reform Bill to Cartwright before it was

---

[1] Cartwright, *Take Your Choice*, p. 62. [2] Ibid., pp. 15–22.
[3] Ibid., p. 32.
[4] Ibid., p. vi.
[5] Richmond to Rockingham, 26 Apr. 1772, Fitzwilliam MS. R1–789. See Selected Letters.
[6] Price to Cartwright, 2 Apr. 1776, Cartwright, *Life of Cartwright*, i. 95. Cartwright wrote Shelburne directly, 27 Feb. 1777, ibid., pp. 107–12.
[7] Ibid., p. 99. See also Cartwright to Portland, 22 Feb., 31 Mar., and 4 Aug. 1777, Nottingham MSS. Cartwright's testimony at trial of Horne Tooke, *The Trial of John Horne Tooke for High Treason, November 17–22, 1794*, taken by Joseph Guerney, 1795, i. 454.

presented to Parliament;[1] unquestionably Cartwright was the major influence on Richmond's thinking during the entire period in which Richmond was interested in political reform.

Richmond's bill was at the far left of the spectrum of reform plans under discussion in 1780. It is customary to make a division between political and economic reformers; but there is an even greater division within the ranks of political reformers, because the political reformers included both radicals and moderates, and the moderates accepted the tenets of the economic reformers rather than of the radicals; they appealed either to Parliament or to gentry-dominated associations, through 'practical' schemes aiming at a smoother operation of the existing constitution.

There were three types of moderate reformers. The first type consisted of Burke and most of the Rockingham party, supporting purely economic reforms, such as reduction of the civil list. The second type included the younger Pitt, the directors of the second Yorkshire Association, and possibly Shelburne (who claimed to support more radical reform but never committed himself on particulars), suggesting miscellaneous parliamentary reforms usually embodying additional county representation. Among the third type were Wyvill, Sir George Savile, and possibly Fox, who advocated annual parliaments without universal suffrage.

There were two groups of radicals: reformers like Wilkes, William Jones, and Richard Price, advocating universal suffrage, with annual parliaments as a less essential reform to be considered later, and those like Richmond, Cartwright, and John Jebb, supporting the immediate institution of both annual parliaments and manhood suffrage. Both groups held government to be derived from and measured by the needs of individual man. Therefore no just reform could stop short of the restoration of every man's natural right to a share in the legislature. With the dubious exceptions of Wilkes and Richmond, the speculative thinkers were primarily pamphleteers appealing to unrepresented groups and unburdened with responsibility for preparing workable legislation.

Richmond's bill was certainly not intended as workable

[1] Richmond to Cartwright, 5 Nov. 1779, Cartwright, *Life of Cartwright*, i. 128–9.

legislation. A letter to the *Public Advertiser* signed 'Cassandra' had accused Richmond of trying to intimidate the legislature;[1] Wyvill said the objects of the bill could never be attained by constitutional means.[2] Richmond intended only to get the bill on record, then publish it. He himself had written Cartwright,

I almost despair that any House of Commons constituted like the present could be induced to pass such a self-denying law. I am convinced that nothing but an irresistable cry from without doors, could induce them to vote it.[3]

In April 1780 he mentioned to Shelburne 'submitting to the public a plan'.[4] He told Horne Tooke 'not to blame him for failing to get reform legislation through Parliament. Reform was up to the people themselves.'[5]

Contemporaries feared, with good reason, that the only alternative to constitutional channels was force. James Burgh once threatened that the Army might be used to force Parliament to reform itself; Jebb and Cartwright proposed a grand national association to usurp the functions of Parliament by popular acclamation.[6] Richmond seems to have agreed with Jebb in 1780, though he later lost faith in the Yorkshire Association. As pressure he half-heartedly suggested a refusal to pay taxes.

Two factors demonstrated that Richmond intended the bill to instruct, rather than to incite. First was the compromise nature of the bill itself, which aimed at reassuring the propertied classes as well as attracting the disfranchised: Richmond showed no interest, for example, in payment of M.P.s or in the secret ballot. Second was Richmond's own inordinate fear of revolution in England. From the age of seventeen, when Richmond had written Newcastle that he prized liberty 'beyond anything', but that the British 'headstrong tradition was liberty become license, which when one

---

[1] *Public Advertiser*, 28 Jan. 1780.

[2] Wyvill to Brass Crosby, 7 Dec. 1782, *Sound Reason*, p. 118.

[3] Richmond to Cartwright, 5 Nov. 1777, Cartwright, *Life of Cartwright*, i. 128–9.

[4] Richmond to Shelburne, [20 Apr. 1780], Lansdowne MSS. See Selected Letters.

[5] *Trial of Horne Tooke*, ii. 161.

[6] Veitch, *Genesis of Parliamentary Reform*, p. 49.

considers is madness',[1] he had consistently extolled the spirit of liberty but desperately feared the spirit of the mob. The Gordon Riots, for example, had frightened Richmond as much as anyone: 'If the nation can so tamely bear all it has borne, and the evident loss of their own liberty without stirring, and will submit to be led by Scotch fanatics, and to the tune of the bagpipe—set Newgate loose, and burn London, turning against the best friends of liberty, and confounding them with its worst enemies—such a nation *cannot* be saved.'[2] He was hated for his French peerage, his profits from the coal tax,[3] and his ancestry, and stood to lose so much by a general uprising that he considered his estate in Aubigny as a potential place of refuge.

Like all Rockingham Whigs Richmond had always been wary of the voluntary expression of public opinion. He had supported reduction of the land tax to please the gentry in 1767, but had opposed messages of thanks from the Grand Juries on it.[4] He had excused his reluctance to set the county of Sussex petitioning against Wilkes's expulsion, because:

in so doing I should have appear'd factious . . . but when the general sense of the Nation does come unanimously, and their resentment rather kept down and properly directed by opposition they will gain real credit and do real good.[5]

In 1771 when the aldermen of the city of London considered protesting against the government's passivity in handling the Falkland Islands' crisis, Richmond assured Rockingham that he would be extremely cautious in handling Wilkes.[6]

Richmond's one momentary appeal to the public for protection of the East India Company's chartered rights was so disappointing that he disparaged all attempts to elicit

[1] Richmond to Newcastle, 18 Feb. 1752, Add. MS. 32,976, f. 145.
[2] Richmond to Rockingham, 12 June 1780, Fitzwilliam MS. R1–1066. Printed in Albemarle, *Rockingham*, ii. 418–20.
[3] For this, see Butterfield, *George III, Lord North, and the People*, pp. 223, 225, 244–5.
[4] Richmond to Newcastle, 22 Mar. 1767, Add. MS. 32,980, f. 366. See Selected Letters.
[5] Richmond to Burke, 2 Sept. 1769, Fitzwilliam MS. R8–2.
[6] Richmond to Rockingham, 12 Feb. 1771, Fitzwilliam MS. R158–44. See Selected Letters.

a public response against the American War. It was Burke who convinced Richmond 'The people at large [are not] wholly to blame',[1] and urged the party to educate the people. As late as 1781 Richmond hoped that Rockingham himself would educate the people about political reform: he must have intended his own bill as a text, rather than a manifesto.

The bill created very little immediate stir. Richmond probably expected the Society for Constitutional Information to publish the pamphlet, but they voted not to,[2] and the bill was never printed until 1783. Only the city of Westminster sent thanks; in May the Westminster subcommittee had drawn up a nearly identical programme of parliamentary reform.

The King sensibly took the bill with only moderate seriousness; he wrote to North, 'The Duke of Richmond is subverting the whole constitution',[3] but seemed more annoyed at Richmond's absence from court over the previous ten years.[4] North, speaking to Fred Montague of the King's abhorrence for Richmond, left out political reform altogether and mentioned only the failure to appear at court.[5] In March 1782 Richmond expressed concern that his presence in the ministry would offend the King, only because of his prolonged absence from court.[6] He conferred with the King and hostility ceased, though the King was well aware that Richmond had not abandoned parliamentary reform.

The radical reformers, surprisingly enough, were only lukewarm; if anything, Richmond's bill made some of them think twice about the practicability of speculative programmes. Only Thomas Northcote, along with Jebb and Major Cartwright—Richmond's personal friends—defended the bill as entirely feasible because 'Political truth is synonymous with expediency.'[7] Jebb's 'Quintuple Alliance', an organization

---

[1] Burke to Richmond, 26 Sept. 1775, *Burke Correspondence*, ii. 72.
[2] Wyvill to Brass Crosby, 7 Dec. 1782, *Sound Reason*, p. 118.
[3] George III to Lord North, 3 July 1780, *Corr. Geo. III*, v. 96–97.
[4] North Memorandum, July 1780, ibid. 3100–1.
[5] *Walpole Last Journals*, ii. 325. See also Keppel to Rockingham, 9 July 1780, Keppel, *Life of Keppel*, ii. 278.
[6] Richmond to Rockingham, 26 Mar. 1782 (printed incorrectly as 24 March), Albemarle, *Rockingham*, ii. 467–8.
[7] John Jebb to Belfast Committee, 19 Aug. 1783, Dublin, Halliday Pamphlet 455, Royal Irish Academy, pp. 63–73.

of reform delegates from London, Westminster, Southwark, Middlesex, and Surrey, seems to have supported the bill.[1] But Price and Priestley both worried that universal suffrage was not always feasible,[2] and the three peers who had previously supported radical reform, Effingham, Abingdon, and Manchester, all virtually agreed the bill was impractical.[3] The Society for Constitutional Information, begun by Cartwright but dominated by moderates like Wyvill, vacillated. They discussed the bill at least four times, but did not print it until the end of 1783, and then only as an appendix to Richmond's *Letter to Colonel Sharman*. From 1780 to 1783 several pamphlets on reform were published, notably those by William Jones[4] and Cappell Lofft, but none seems to have drawn particularly on Richmond.

Richmond himself, admitting the bill would never receive general support, consistently encouraged more moderate plans of reform. At private meetings—with Pitt and Wilkes in December 1781, and with Pitt and twenty members of the House of Commons in May 1782—he pledged himself to more moderate plans of reform: it was probably at his suggestion that the Sussex representatives at the Yorkshire Association Chamber of Deputies in March 1780 opposed making annual parliaments a *sine qua non* for the association's programme.[5] The same year Richmond had advertised a meeting of the freeholders of Sussex:

My own ideas go to hope that however justly the Public may feel indignation against the authors of our calamities, the business of this meeting may be to look forward, and in conjunction with other counties, to address Parliament for a more frugal expenditure of the public money, for an abolition of many known useless employments, and a reduction of all exorbitant emoluments.

1 Alexander Stephens, *Memoirs of John Horne Tooke*, 1813, ii. 82; Minutes of Quintuple Alliance meeting, 13 May 1783, printed in *Sound Reason*, p. 140.

2 Price to Belfast Committee, 7 Aug. 1783, Halliday Pamphlet 455, pp. 26–30.

3 None of the peers turned up to support the bill, and Effingham wrote the Belfast Committee on 18 Aug. 1783, that demands must be sacrificed to a plan which would achieve unanimity. Ibid., pp. 73–80.

4 William Jones, *Dialogue between a Scholar and a Peasant*, 1783.

5 Resolutions at a meeting of deputies from the several committees in the Yorkshire Association, 20 Mar. 1780, Rev. Christopher Wyvill, *Political Papers*, 1794–1804, i. 127.

Many may think, and with reason, that still greater reforms are necessary; and it may be well worth the attention of the Public, whether, if this nation means to preserve its liberty, it may not be necessary to revert to those principles of a free constitution from which we have been for a long time insensibly but greatly deviating.

Public economy may not directly reach every evil, but goes near the source; and has this advantage that a measure so equitable and necessary must unite all men in its support.[1]

In 1783 Richmond wrote to the Sussex Association expressing his consent to any form of political reform presented.[2] Surrey told the Yorkshire Association 'he wished all radical reformers were as willing to co-operate as the Duke of Richmond',[3] and Wyvill wrote:

when the people had thus decisively given their preference to the more limited plan, their Noble Advocate, far from pressing them with the pertinacity of disputation to reconsider and accept his favoured system, generously labored to accomplish a general coalition on the ground of their [Yorkshire] association. This was the wisdom of judicious statesmen—this was the magnanimity of true patriots.[4]

The Rockingham party had been warned several months in advance of Richmond's intention to present a plan. Close as he was to Shelburne, Richmond would never have told Shelburne in April 1780 of his intention to present a plan[5] without having spoken with Rockingham first. By November 1779 the party must have known Richmond's preliminary outline; by May 1780 they knew most of the details. What they did not suspect was Richmond's intention of attacking party as such. And his attack on 'connexion' was so badly constructed that even after the bill was presented most of the party was not sure what Richmond had intended.

By 'connexion' Richmond meant borough influence, the destruction of which, as Richmond advocated, would have

[1] Richmond to Freeholders of Sussex, 8 Jan. 1780, *London Chronicle*, 13–15 Jan. 1780.

[2] Richmond to William Frankland, 17 Jan. 1783, Wyvill, *Political Papers*, ii. 228–33.

[3] Minutes of York County Meeting, 19 Dec. 1782, ibid. ii. 66–67.

[4] Christopher Wyvill, 'A Second Address from the York Committee of Association to the electors of counties, cities and boroughs within the Kingdom of Great Britain', Oct. 1781, *Sound Reason*, p. 91.

[5] Richmond to Shelburne, [20 Apr. 1780], Lansdowne MSS. See Selected Letters.

lessened the parliamentary influence of the King and also disrupted a party like Rockingham's whose major strength was control of votes in the Commons. But while he asserted that universal suffrage would make patronage unfeasible, Richmond would not 'level the natural Aristocracy' to facilitate the entry of potential 'independents' in the Commons by ballot, payment of M.P.s, or abolition of the property qualification for Parliament, and as long as the old safeguards were retained, the introduction of annual elections, which would be costly even without bribery, would have thrown even more votes to patronage. Richmond envisaged the Commons as a homogeneous annual assembly with little of that session-to-session continuity of membership which is essential to party control. Yet expensive annual elections would necessarily have led to 'arrangements', and hence continuity. Richmond thus approached a complex problem with a superficial solution, but his particular superficiality was the result of weak thinking and his aristocratic background, rather than a fear of endangering the power of the Rockingham party.

Presentation of the bill had no immediate influence on Richmond's party status. When ministerial offers were extended at the end of June 1780, Rockingham insisted on a guarantee that Richmond be made Secretary of State before he would give the offers further consideration.[1] Rockingham himself would not have been averse to considering some plan of political reform, if enough of his followers had supported it: he had almost given way to triennial parliaments in March 1780,[2] and later committed his ministry to political reform in 1782 'if we could amongst us settle some plan that should unite the opinions of the publick'.[3]

Rockingham tended not to take the bill particularly seriously; most of the party thought Richmond an eccentric and were slightly embarrassed to be his associates.

In 1783 the bill was eclipsed by the *Letter to Colonel Sharman*, a far more significant work for subsequent reform

---

[1] *Walpole Last Journals*, ii. 324; Ian Christie, 'The Marquis of Rockingham and Lord North's offer of a Coalition, June–July, 1780', *E.H.R.* July 1954, pp. 388–407.

[2] Rockingham to [unidentified], 23 Mar. 1780, Fitzwilliam MS. R1–1051–1.

[3] Richmond to Shelburne, 20 Mar. 1782, Lansdowne MSS. See Selected Letters.

movements. The letter was originally written in answer to a series of questions on parliamentary reform in Ireland, circulated by the Belfast regiment of the Irish Volunteers in August 1783. Questions were sent to Abingdon, Wyvill, Cartwright, Jebb, Price, and Richmond. All six answers were published together in Ireland,[1] but Richmond's (written at Goodwood within two weeks) was by far the most suitable for a separate pamphlet, and a mutilated copy was circulated in London. In October John Stockdale printed full copies for 1s. 6d. each;[2] in November the Society for Constitutional Information printed and distributed free copies.[3]

Basically the pamphlet showed no development of thought over the bill, unless in the direction of making it more explicit that reforming Parliament was not synonymous with levelling wealth, and of distinguishing between artificial control of politics by wealth and natural leadership by the aristocracy. In other points—the inadequacy of any parliamentary reform (additional county representation) short of universal suffrage, the superficiality of any reform short of full parliamentary reform—the letter repeated the bill.

Altogether the *Letter to Colonel Sharman* went through at least five editions before its last publication in 1859. Two separate editions came out in 1792, by which time Richmond had lost all interest in political reform. The Society for Constitutional Information expressed confidence that Richmond's interest in reform was only dormant;[4] the Sheffield Constitutional Society was 'totally at a loss how to account for the very different opinions now held out by [Richmond] in any other way than the difference of being in and out of office'.[5] The Society for Constitutional Information printed the pamphlet 'to show that all reformers are not levellers', whereas the Sheffield publication aimed at presenting the lower classes with a radical plan safely sanctioned by a peer.

---

[1] Halliday Pamphlet 455.

[2] London, printed for J. Stockdale, 1783 (British Museum Pamphlet). A copy was sent to Stockdale by an Irish Volunteer correspondent.

[3] Notice of the distribution (apparently no copies are extant) is given in the publication of the letter, 1792, by the Sheffield Constitutional Society.

[4] Copies actually sold by J. Johnson at 1d. a copy (British Museum Pamphlet). Reprinted 1795 (Bodleian Pamphlet) and 1797 (copies in British Museum and Bodleian Library).

[5] Sheffield, printed for the Constitutional Society, June 1792.

The Sheffield Constitutional Society was the less radical member in a partnership with Manchester, for whose republican leaders like Thomas Paine Richmond was far too conservative.

Affiliated with the Sheffield Society was the London Corresponding Society, founded by Thomas Hardy, 'captivated by the scheme of representation propagated by the Duke of Richmond'.[1] Though brought to trial for treason in 1794, Hardy was acquitted when he proved conclusively 'that he uniformly acted upon the Duke of Richmond's plan, that he pursued that only which the Duke of Richmond wished to be carried into effect, that he promoted it by the means by which the Duke of Richmond wished to see it accomplished'.[2] The position of the ministry was extremely embarrassing, since both Pitt and Richmond were called upon to testify. Hardy proved that it was 'safe' to go as far as the terms of Richmond's bill. Partly as a result Richmond was dismissed from the Ordnance two months after the trial.

Succeeding publications of the *Letter to Colonel Sharman* in the nineteenth century were either reminders of the safeness of the cause—'I dare you's to the government—or reassurances to the middle classes that annual parliaments and universal suffrage were traditional objects of reform rather than speculative innovations intended to level property. Two editions appeared in 1817, one in *The Pamphleteer*, a non-partisan collected edition of effectively written pamphlets on all subjects,[3] and one printed by William Hone,[4] possibly in connexion with Cartwright's Hampden Club. Cartwright was actively publishing a number of tracts in 1817; there is no evidence that he considered a revival of Richmond's pamphlet at that time.

In 1820 the radical orator William Hunt, stirring up popular demonstrations for political reform, claimed that Richmond had given up reform for lack of popular support.[5]

---

[1] Stephens, *Memoirs of Horne Tooke*, ii. 82.

[2] Summary of the defence, the *Trial of Thomas Hardy for High Treason*, taken down by Joseph Guerney, 1794.

[3] *The Pamphleteer*, xlviii. 351–83; reprinted in 1824 (vol. xxiv).

[4] Ibid., Tract (13).

[5] Hunt to the Radical Reformers of England, Ireland, and Scotland, 22 May 1820, Henry Hunt, *Memoirs of Henry Hunt, Esq.*, 1820, p. vi.

But Hunt was appealing to the lower classes as Richmond had not, and he deliberately did nothing about publishing Richmond's pamphlet itself. Conspicuously, neither did the Chartists: Richmond was referred to in the preface to the printed charter[1] and mentioned again in Duncombe's speech presenting the charter to Parliament.[2] But the Chartists, like Hunt, were intensely desirous of keeping the movement out of the middle classes,[3] and furthermore could never use a plan of reform which omitted their four implementing points—payment of M.P.s and abolition of property requirement for them, secret ballot, and an educational programme for the lower classes. The *Letter to Colonel Sharman*, safeguarding political leadership by the natural aristocracy, was already becoming anachronistic.

Its last publication was in 1859, edited by Henry Brookes, who with less than complete understanding eulogized Richmond as 'one of the very few who preserved through a long and active course a perfect uniformity of conduct; steady in his principles, open and undisguised in their avowal; inflexible in his opinions, unremitting in his opposition to what he thought wrong, and equally unmoved when in defense of what he believed to be right'.[4] Brookes maintained that John Bright's campaign among the middle classes in 1858 to gain support for a programme of reform based on the 1792 bill of Fox and Grey, had stopped too short. He aimed to show that Bright could have reached the same classes with more extreme reforms. But by 1859 the *Letter to Colonel Sharman* could no longer summon enthusiasm: on the one hand annual parliaments and universal suffrage had become the common objectives of all radical reformers; on the other the safeguards Richmond imposed were out of date by mid-nineteenth century.

---

[1] William Lovett, *Life and Struggles of William Lovett*, 1876, p. 167.
[2] 4 May 1842, Mark Hovell, *The Chartist Movement*, 1925, p. 255.
[3] Ibid., pp. 307–8.
[4] London, 1859 (British Museum Pamphlet 8138, C. 74).

V

1780 TO 1784

RICHMOND IN THE ORDNANCE
UNDER ROCKINGHAM, SHELBURNE,
AND PITT

ALTHOUGH Richmond continued to participate in reform committees like the Society for Constitutional
Information and the Quintuple Alliance, still urged
Rockingham, Shelburne, and Pitt to consider reform, and
even mentioned reform as his 'favourite object' until 1784,
his interest in reform was already waning by the time he
wrote the *Letter to Colonel Sharman*. Richmond was accused
by contemporaries of supporting reform only to end the
American War and remove the ministry, an accusation inspired by two factors: the superficiality of Richmond's
approach, and the short duration of his interest in reform
after the break up of the Rockingham ministry of 1782.
But as suggested earlier, the superficiality of his approach
came from elevated social status and limited mental abilities,
rather than any consideration of the effect of reform on the
Rockingham party.

The decline of his support for reform was, furthermore,
not the result of his appointment to the ministry but of
a number of other developments, the most obvious of which
was the rapid decline of the reform movement itself after
1780. On one hand the gentry were frightened by the
Gordon Riots and the propagation of radical plans like
Richmond's; on the other they were satisfied with the ending
of the war and in 1784 with the selection of a prime minister
important not for advocating political reform but for winning
a nominally popular election.

The second factor was Richmond's realization of his own
unsuitability for personal leadership in the reform movement. The radical nature of his Reform Bill should have

directed his greatest appeal to the lower classes, but he was not a popular orator and was so hated by the mob for his coal tax returns that he never dared to appear before a crowd like the freeholders of Middlesex or Westminster. What influence he might have had with moderate reformers was limited by his personal unpopularity and his ineptness at committee work.

A far more important factor was his return to a satisfactory party participation under Pitt, after a period of disillusion-ment and drift. From 1780 until 1783 Richmond's relations with the Rockingham party disintegrated. Richmond failed to get their support on parliamentary issues—for example, the party did not back up his motions for better treatment of American prisoners at Plymouth in July 1781, or for an investigation into the execution of Colonel Isaac Hayne in January 1782.

During this period of political disagreement Richmond's personal alienation from Burke, Fox, and Rockingham became more openly apparent. Richmond held Burke responsible for Rockingham's recalcitrance on political reform and union with Shelburne, and complained to Carmarthen that 'he thought Burke intractable, and [was] convinced that a great deal of mischief arose from thence'.[1] When ministerial offers were extended to Rockingham in June 1780, the Marquis considered taking office without Shelburne. Rich-mond, who was consulted only twice during the negotia-tions, later attributed the omission of Shelburne to Burke. To Barre he expressed fear over 'Burke's wanderings . . . adopted seriously and obstinately by men of far higher description than himself.'[2] With Pembroke he agreed that opposition suffered 'from the too nice distinctions in politicks of learned men, and that in consequence thereof we shall continue to canonade headquarters to no purpose with two and forty pounders loaded with the sublime and Beauti-ful . . .'.[3]

The latent personal hatred between Richmond and Fox

[1] 25 Mar. 1781, *Political Memoranda of Francis Godolphin Osborne, Fifth Duke of Leeds*, ed. Oscar Browning, 1884, p. 42.

[2] Barre to Shelburne, Dec. 1780, Fitzmaurice, *Life of Shelburne*, ii. 68.

[3] Pembroke to Carmarthen, 9 Nov. 1781, *Pembroke Papers*, ed. Lord Herbert, 1950, p. 178.

did not flare up until Rockingham's death on 1 July 1782,
when Shelburne, who in March had refused to take office
without Rockingham at the Treasury, agreed to stay on as
the Marquis's successor. At Fox's instance most of the
party resigned, but Richmond, Conway, and Keppel remained in the Shelburne ministry. Portland's 'heart was
open for their return from their errors',[1] but Fox spoke of
Richmond 'in very harsh terms, and of his ingratitude to
those who have saved him from being an outcast in all
gentlemanlike society'.[2] 'Fox . . . and some of his warm
friends'[3] attacked Richmond violently enough to reduce him
to tears at a meeting of the former ministry.[4]

Until Rockingham's death Richmond remained personally loyal to the Marquis; politically he began drifting from
him at the end of 1780 over parliamentary reform, until in
May 1782 Richmond encouraged Pitt to present his Reform
Bill against Rockingham's wishes and then urged a revival
of the petitioning movement against his own ministry.[5]
In December 1780 he 'worked night and day' with Rockingham over reform.[6] In November 1781 Shelburne proposed
an alliance of opposition factions on the grounds of political
reform. After a violent party altercation Rockingham refused.[7] In January 1781 Richmond had lamented the honest
differences of opinion between Rockingham and Shelburne
—a far cry from his earlier consideration that Rockingham's
party was the sole protector of Whig principles.

The few who are capable of any Exertion are split into miserable
little palliating Politicks, unable to act together,—ununited upon any
System. I blame no Body because I am aware of the Difficulties necessarily arising from what depends so much on the different opinions of
Men. I am sure Individuals will never agree while those they have
just Confidence in differ, and I cannot blame these for following their

[1] Portland to [unidentified], 20 July 1782, Nottingham MSS.
[2] William Eden to Lord Loughborough, 25 July 1782, *The Journal and Correspondence of William, Lord Auckland*, 1861, i. 14–15.
[3] Richmond to Lord George Lennox, 8 July 1782, *H.M.C. Bathurst*, pp. 698–9.
[4] Carlisle to Gower, 8 July 1782, *H.M.C. Carlisle*, p. 632.
[5] The petitioning movement was later continued by Fox against the Shelburne
ministry.
[6] Barre to Shelburne, 7 Dec. 1780, Fitzmaurice, *Life of Shelburne*, ii. 67.
[7] Burke to Portland, 12 Nov. 1781, Nottingham MSS.

own opinions. I can only lament these Differences and their fatal Consequences.[1]

On the whole, Richmond considered the differences between Rockingham and Shelburne as largely personal, and therefore superficial. To Rockingham, Shelburne was self-effacing but ambitious, flattering but unsociable, a treacherous ally who talked in general terms and could never be pinned down to particular promises. To the self-conscious Shelburne, awed by Rockingham's ability to manage a good-sized party, the Marquis seemed recalcitrant, so narrow visioned as to be unable to grasp general problems. Each considered the other vague; to each there was no such thing as knowing how to proceed with the other.[2]

Richmond, consequently, was used as an intermediary on Shelburne's part. With a smaller parliamentary party, less borough influence, and until 1782 no support from the King, Shelburne was understandably the supplicant for Rockingham's support. On at least four occasions—December 1780, March 1781, November 1781, and March 1782 —Richmond was the bearer of some kind of coalition offer.[3] From December 1780, when he considered himself free of Rockingham and seceded from Parliament with Shelburne,[4] until March 1782, when he entered the Rockingham ministry, Richmond was a closer follower of Shelburne than of Rockingham.

In June 1780 Lord North, through Montague, asked Rockingham to draw up terms for a possible coalition, whereupon the Marquis submitted Richmond's name for Secretary of State. Stung by the King's personal rejection of his nomination Richmond tactlessly criticized Rockingham for the entire conduct of the negotiations, and particularly for his failure either to include Shelburne in the demands or

---

[1] Richmond to Rockingham, 18 Jan. 1781, Fitzwilliam MS. R1–1084, printed in part in Albemarle, *Rockingham*, ii. 429–31.

[2] *Leeds Pol. Mem.*, pp. 35 and 41.

[3] See Fitzmaurice, *Life of Shelburne*, ii. 66–70; *Leeds Pol. Mem.*, p. 41; *Pembroke Papers*, p. 178.

[4] *Correspondence of C. J. Fox*, i. 260; Pembroke to Carmarthen, 5 Dec. 1780, *Pembroke Papers*, p. 69. 'The D. of Richmond, I believe, feels himself equally free, though his personal private friendship for Ld. Rockingham is, I make no doubt, as great as ever.'

at least to keep him informed of their development.[1] Rockingham's reply betrayed little preoccupation with policy but
immense pique at Shelburne's almost ostentatious lack of
concern for his personal suffering during the Gordon Riots.
Rockingham's house had been threatened and his life en-
dangered;[2] Shelburne had sent not so much as a message of
congratulations on his escape and had in fact pleaded in
Parliament for sympathy with the rioters.[3]

Immediately after the formation of the second Rockingham ministry Richmond and Shelburne fell out. The one
characteristic which perhaps made Shelburne most difficult
to work with was his tendency to put off unpleasant details.
He preferred a general agreement on vague principles to
thrashing out specific problems.[4] When the Rockingham
ministry was first formed, Shelburne, who unlike Rockingham enjoyed confidential communication with the King,
obtained the royal promise of the governorship of Portsmouth (on the decease of the incumbent) for the Earl of
Pembroke, a former supporter of North who had joined
opposition under Shelburne only two years before. He never
quite found the right opportunity for telling Rockingham or
Richmond, whose brother, commanding officer at Portsmouth and a consistent supporter of Rockingham, also
coveted the position.

Unexpectedly the incumbent died and Shelburne had the
awkward promise to explain. He thought the Duke 'not
irrevocably out of humor'[5]—perhaps not, but Richmond
with typical obstinacy continued to argue about the appointment until the day Pembroke kissed hands, then tried unsuccessfully to exact a promise from the King that when the
governorship of Plymouth fell vacant Pembroke would be

---

[1] Richmond to Rockingham, 9 July 1780. Fitzwilliam MS. R1 66–27–1 and 2.
See Selected Letters. For a complete discussion of the negotiations see Christie,
'Rockingham and Lord North's offer of a Coalition, 1780', *E.H.R.*, pp. 388–407.
Mr. Christie suggests that Rockingham and Shelburne had differed over parliamentary reform in Apr. 1780. It is clear from Richmond's correspondence with
Shelburne that a drift had begun in March but that no formal break had ever
occurred.   [2] *Leeds Pol. Mem.*, p. 35.
[3] Rockingham to Richmond, 11 July 1780, Fitzwilliam MS. R166–216.
[4] For example, he spoke in general terms of the need for shorter parliaments and
a more equal representation but never committed himself to a specific programme.
[5] Shelburne to George III, 29 May 1782, *Corr. Geo. III*, vi. 47.

transferred there, leaving Portsmouth for Lord George, and finally in June was taken in by Fox's half-contrived complaint that Shelburne had betrayed his agent at the Paris treaty negotiations.[1] Two months earlier Richmond could not have thought the story credible. He may also have rightly suspected Shelburne on at least one occasion of betraying his confidence to the King.[2] In any event he soon came to the belief that Shelburne, in spite of obsequious protestations to the contrary, had merely been using him during the previous two years.

After Rockingham's death there was even less harmony between the two ministers. Richmond had with some reason expected to succeed Rockingham at the Treasury, since he was the only member of the cabinet whose appointment would have conciliated the factions of both Fox and Shelburne.[3] He may have anticipated that Shelburne, still recognizing his inability to govern without the Rockingham party, would have yielded the Treasury to him. At a party meeting as early as 7 July he admitted that Shelburne could not be trusted.[4] In the parliamentary debate on the new ministry on 11 July, Richmond disagreed with Shelburne concerning policy;[5] in August Camden wrote Grafton, 'The Duke of Richmond's discontent is marked in his countenance.'[6] Lord George Sackville wrote that Shelburne could not work with Richmond and others 'who professedly do not trust him'.[7]

Certainly Richmond was not in Shelburne's confidence. Shelburne was not particularly anxious to have Richmond in

---

[1] Fox to Grenville, 10 June 1782, *Correspondence of C. J. Fox*, i. 36–70.

[2] Shelburne to George III, 11 May 1782, *Corr. Geo. III*, vi. 15.

[3] Horace Walpole, and from him later historians, assumed that Richmond's great disappointment was Portland's nomination as leader of the Rockingham party after Shelburne had already succeeded to the Treasury and Fox had determined upon opposition. But until Shelburne's appointment Richmond's main reason for expecting the party leadership was that his own appointment to the Treasury might keep the ministry intact; when that reason was removed, Richmond could have had little expectation of leading a party in which he had several hated enemies, in opposition to a minister whose policies he preferred and from whom he was not yet estranged.   [4] 6 July 1782, *Leeds Pol. Mem.*, pp. 72–73.

[5] *Parl. Hist.* xxiii, 11 July 1782.

[6] Camden to Grafton, 1 Aug. 1782, *Grafton Autobiography*, p. 334.

[7] Viscount Sackville to William Knox, 11 Nov. 1782, *H.M.C. Various Collections*, vi. 189.

the ministry and was willing to turn him out if he made
specific patronage demands.[1] Had Fox not played into Shelburne's hands by resigning, Shelburne and the King planned to
ease him out of the cabinet—a manœuvre of which Richmond
was not aware. Richmond stayed in the ministry because
he thought Shelburne shared his interest in parliamentary
reform and reorganization at the Ordnance. But Shelburne
never discussed parliamentary reform with Richmond, and
furthermore, he showed so little interest in Richmond's own
fiscal reforms in the Ordnance Department, that when
Richmond submitted his Ordnance budget in 1783 he later
had to remind Shelburne to read and return it.[2]

Richmond first grew restive at 'consenting to a very
secondary part where he might have claimed the lead',[3] then
suspicious that all along he had been merely led on by Shelburne. It was Shelburne's handling of the treaty with France
which finally turned suspicion to conviction. In September
Shelburne had satisfied Richmond on the American treaty
by examining each article with him; the French treaty, con-
taining far more concessions than most of the ministers had
been led to expect, had been discussed in detail with no one
but Lord Grantham before its presentation to the cabinet
early in December.[4] Unwilling to defend the treaty, Richmond terminated his attendance at cabinet meetings the
following month, though he did not resign the Ordnance.
Shelburne remained his personal friend though never again
a close one: a little later Lady Sarah described her brother as
'a little come off of his friend Lord Shelburne, but still he
approves of him in general though not in detail'.[5]

Curiously, it was not until after Shelburne's retirement in
February 1783 that Richmond finally broke with the rem-
nant of the Rockingham Whigs. A party newly in opposition could never afford to disavow its own members in the

[1] George III to Shelburne, Shelburne to George III, 4 July 1782, *Corr. Geo. III*,
vi. 74–75.
[2] Richmond to Shelburne, 30 Jan. and 3 Feb. 1783, W.O. 46/18, pp. 11, 17.
[3] George III to Shelburne, 5 Dec. 1782, Add. MS. 34,523, f. 367.
[4] For Richmond's leadership of the 'War Party' in Shelburne's ministry and its
effect on the peace negotiations see Vincent Harlow, *The Founding of the Second
British Empire*, 1952, chs. vi–vii.
[5] Lady Sarah to Lady Susan O'Brien, 17 Feb. 1783, *Correspondence of Lady
Sarah Lennox*, ii. 30–31.

government, and Richmond was not entirely ostracized from the party when he remained with Shelburne in July 1782. He himself wanted to bring his former associates into the ministry in December 1782. After Shelburne's resignation Portland asked Richmond to remain at the Ordnance or accept the secretaryship of war.[1] Without further reflection he declined to serve in a cabinet with North, but even after the coalition arrangements were announced, Richmond wavered about keeping the Ordnance as a non-cabinet position.[2] When Portland pressed him for a decision on 4 April, he resigned in anger;[3] a week later his last connexion was severed with a vigorous attack on the Portland ministry in Parliament.[4]

Shelburne himself retired from Parliament after his defeat, leaving a leaderless party including Richmond, Grafton, Camden, Barre, and Ashburton, unable to join Fox and North, and too weak in bidding power ever to form a ministry of their own. Camden considered retiring; Richmond planned an extended trip abroad.[5] By autumn 1783 the aimless group was exactly ready for Pitt, who used them as the experienced nucleus of his ministry, deliberately avoiding Shelburne. Unfortunately Pitt also took in Thurlow and Howe, whom Richmond detested, and began office with an ominous want of confidence in the older generation. But he also provided Richmond a face-saving avowal of support for parliamentary reform, and gave Richmond the extensive patronage which Shelburne had refused: specifically, the Tower and then the governorship of Portsmouth were found for Lord George and the secretaryship of the Ordnance for Charles Lennox. Complaints were circulated about Richmond's inordinate patronage.

A cabinet position with Pitt also brought final reconciliation with the King, first begun 27 March 1782, when the King accepted Richmond as a member of the Rockingham cabinet. Through Rockingham Richmond forwarded a letter

---

[1] Fox to Portland, 4 Apr. 1783, Nottingham MSS.
[2] 24 Feb. 1783, *Walpole Last Journals*, ii. 487.
[3] 24 Feb. to 2 Apr. 1783, ibid., pp. 509–10.
[4] 14 Apr. 1783, ibid., p. 513.
[5] Camden to Richmond and Richmond to Camden, 2 and 3 June 1783, Camden MSS.

ter apologizing for his past failure to appear at court. The following day he had a long audience with the King,[1] and thereafter appeared regularly at court functions.

Inevitably the first stage of reconciliation was a truce and not an alliance. The King did not forget Richmond's Reform Bill and was further infuriated by Richmond's failure to cease demanding the governorship of Portsmouth for his brother after the appointment had already been settled on Pembroke.[2] In December 1782 the King advised Shelburne that 'The Master General of the Ordnance or the first Lord of the Admiralty should not be allowed to make motions in the House without consulting the rest of the cabinet.'[3] When Richmond ceased attending Shelburne's cabinet meetings in January 1783 the *Public Advertiser* gave as the reason his cool reception in the closet.[4]

But Richmond's very continuation with Shelburne, the King's nominee as Rockingham's successor, had been a positive step toward reconciliation with the King. His complaint to George III in December 1782, that he was taking a minor part in a ministry where he might have claimed the lead,[5] displayed a confidence which would have been out of the question a year earlier. Early in January 1783 Richmond announced his intention of retiring from the cabinet; at the request of Shelburne and the King himself he stayed in the cabinet nearly a month more until the treaty of peace with France was signed.[6] In December 1783, when the King 'put full confidence in Richmond, Thurlow, Gower and Pitt'[7] to form a ministry, the reconciliation was complete.

The final reason for Richmond's loss of interest in parliamentary reform was the rechannelling of his obsessive interests into military reform. Although Richmond had at one time intended a full-time military career, it is doubtful whether he would have been a success: he was personally

---

[1] G. Selwyn to Lord Carlisle, 28 Mar. 1782, *H.M.C. Carlisle*, pp. 608–9; *Public Advertiser*, 28 Mar. 1782; Richmond to Rockingham, 26 Mar. 1782, Fitzwilliam MS. R1–1131.

[2] George III to Shelburne, 6 and 8 June 1782, *Corr. Geo. III*, vi. 53–54.

[3] George III to Shelburne, 6 Dec. 1782, Add. MS. 34,523, f. 369.

[4] *Public Advertiser*, 29 Jan. 1783.

[5] George III to Shelburne, 5 Dec. 1782, Add. MS. 34,523, f. 367.

[6] George III to Shelburne, 12 Jan. 1783, Add. MS. 34,523, f. 340.

[7] George III to Pitt, 23 Dec. 1783, P.R.O. 30/8/103.

gallant and reputed a good engineer and artillery expert, but he did not work well with troops and his camp administration was impeded by his attention to trivial detail.

Basically Richmond believed in the separation of civil and military authority. He never, for example, considered military appointments as places: in 1764 he opposed Conway's dismissal from military rank because the General had voted against Grenville in the Commons.[1] In 1760, when Shelburne had been promoted over Lord George, Richmond in protest resigned the Bedchamber, but not his rank. In January 1783, when he disagreed with Shelburne over the French treaty, he left the cabinet but not the Ordnance. In December of the same year he accepted the Ordnance from Pitt, but did not join the cabinet until more than a month later.[2]

In war-time, however, when political capital could so easily be made from military mismanagement, politics and the military became inseparable. Richmond personally detested Sandwich, the First Lord of the Admiralty, and Lord George Germaine, the Secretary at War. Thus when his cousin, Admiral Keppel, was court martialled in 1779, Richmond, who had a preconceived notion that Sandwich would attempt to discredit Keppel, led the Rockingham Whigs in attending the court daily and in turning the trial into an opposition rally.[3] In Parliament Richmond first made a political issue of Sandwich's failure to give Keppel either accurate information about the size of the French fleet or an adequate fleet of his own and then turned his energy to questions of general naval administration.

When Burgoyne complained of bad instructions after his surrender at Saratoga, Richmond turned the complaint into an attack on Germaine and army administration. Occasionally his attacks were on purely military questions—the defenceless state of Devon and Cornwall, the administration of Greenwich naval hospital. Other attacks led into military

[1] Undated short paper in Richmond's handwriting, inserted in the 1766 Journal, Goodwood Small Libr. MS. E.
[2] 13 Jan. 1784, *Leeds Pol. Mem.*, pp. 94–95.
[3] The Duchess made hatbands for Keppel's supporters, and Richmond himself was accused of leading some of the riotous demonstrations after the Admiral's acquittal. See Keppel, *Life of Keppel*, ii. 184.

management from foreign policy: the Dutch declaration of
war, for example, could not be discussed without bringing in
the English Navy.

Richmond, being one of the ablest opposition speakers,
led most of the military attacks in the Lords. In 1780
Rockingham insisted on consulting Richmond about military affairs before he would consider drawing up a plan of
government;[1] Richmond's appointment to the Ordnance in
Rockingham's ministry was apparently by his own choice,
and in Ordnance reform Richmond seems to have found his
forte. Newspaper articles called him the most indefatigable
man in all Europe.[2] Five days after his appointment, for
example, he had reorganized the administration of the
Tower and dismissed superfluous employees.[3]

He had two main projects at the Ordnance, one of which
was budget reform. Townshend, the previous Master-
General, had called the Ordnance budget 'incomprehen-
sible'; on 10 March 1783 Richmond presented a budget
revised for clarification. Salary scales were reorganized, staffs
were cut, and 'extraordinary' demands on the civil list were
reduced by an attempt at accurate anticipation of expenses.

The second project was the concentrated improvement of
dockyard defences at Portsmouth and Plymouth, accompanied by the jettisoning of fortifications at other dockyards
like Chatham and Sheerness. Portsmouth and Plymouth
had been virtually defenceless during the French invasion
scare of 1779; both, incidentally, had been coveted as military commands by Lord George Lennox, who was appointed
to the governorship of Plymouth in 1784.

In May 1782 Richmond visited Portsmouth and Plymouth to investigate defences, and at the time of Rockingham's death Richmond was finishing the first draft of his
fortifications plan. In January 1783 he submitted to Shelburne the revised budget anticipating the expenditure of
£400,000 over an eight-year period for dockyard improve-
ments. The budget was passed with very little debate on
10 March.

---

[1] Christie, 'The Marquis of Rockingham and Lord North's offer of a Coalition',
E.H.R., 1954, pp. 388–407.
[2] *Public Advertiser*, 2 Apr. 1782.   [3] Ibid., 3 Apr. 1782.

At the time of his resignation in April 1783 he was planning an additional survey of dockyards for the summer. The work lapsed under the Portland ministry, but was resumed immediately under Pitt.

It was thus through personal and political association with Pitt that Richmond was able to return to party, become reunited with the King, and enjoy the unfettered pursuit of Ordnance reform. Once separated from the Rockingham Whigs, the Duke went on to new interests and abandoned the projects for parliamentary reform which had consumed for seven short years the larger part of his vast, but erratic energies.

VI

RICHMOND IN THE MINISTRY
OF PITT: FROM DOMINANCE
TO DISMISSAL

THE cabinet Richmond joined in 1784 appeared to be so weak as to leave Richmond a clear field for influence over the inexperienced Prime Minister. Stafford, Sydney, Carmarthen, Camden—perhaps even the Chancellor—were all lights beginning to flicker. The once compelling orators were now slower in retort and less willing to undertake broad policy debates; the once active minds showed less circumspection in seeing many-faceted problems. Whereas the patronage of other members of the Rockingham party had made Richmond's control of two parliamentary seats look inconsequential, few if any of his current cabinet associates had more patronage than he.

Most of the ministers had held office under Shelburne and then floated helplessly looking for a leader during the period of the coalition. Beyond the experience of two years the ministers had few political ties with each other. Stafford was a Bedfordite who had taken office as Lord President of the Council in 1767 and remained there until he resigned in 1779 after a quarrel with North over the prosecution of the American War. Sydney, consistently a follower of Chatham, had taken office as Secretary of War in 1782; Carmarthen had become a follower of Rockingham only after his dismissal from the lord lieutenancy of the East Riding of Yorkshire in 1780. Camden had been a follower of Chatham who stayed on briefly with Grafton after Chatham's resignation in 1768 and then returned to office as President of the Council under Rockingham and Shelburne. Since 1778 Thurlow had served as Lord Chancellor in every administration except the coalition.

Consequently there were no 'caves' in Pitt's administration based on previous political associations. Neither were there at first any family connexions, such as the Grenvilles,

the Bedfords, the Devonshires, nor any geographical ties
such as the Yorkshire ties of Rockingham's closest friends.
Few of the ministers had become close companions. Richmond seems scarcely to have known Stafford at all; with
Sidney he had only a formal acquaintance, which was not
improved by his resentment of Sydney's being given the
lead in the House of Lords.[1] The friendship with Camden
which began in 1783 seems never to have developed further.
On occasion Richmond talked in confidence with Carmarthen and invited the Marquis fox-hunting at Goodwood.
But periods of confidence seem to have come only when the
two were in mutual agreement against Pitt on a particular
question of foreign policy, or when they shared spells of
bitterness over Pitt's lack of civility. Thurlow infrequently
took Richmond into his confidence during the early years of
the ministry, but after the regency crisis of 1788 Richmond
regarded the Chancellor with open hostility.

In the first seven years of Pitt's administration no 'sides'
lined up consistently on issues of foreign policy or domestic
reform. Initially the disputes over foreign affairs centred
around the question of Britain's intervention in continental
affairs, Richmond and Carmarthen, followed irregularly by
Camden, Stafford, and Thurlow, being the most ardent
cabinet opponents of insular isolation. But this ministerial
team worked together only until 1787. Richmond was the
first to break away from support of the general policy, disgusted by the unpredictable impulsiveness of the Prussian
King and the aloofness of the Emperor during the Dutch
crisis. Increasingly thereafter Richmond favoured British
isolation; by 1791, despite ominous news from France, only
Camden stood with Carmarthen in support of continental
intervention. On the Fortifications Bill, the Slave Trade
Regulation Bill, and possibly the question of intervention
against Russia in 1791, disagreements threatened to split
off part of the cabinet, but it was never the same part from
issue to issue, and there was apparently little caballing among
cabinet members. At least once Richmond stayed away from
a cabinet meeting because he saw no reason for discussing a

---

[1] Richmond to Pitt, 24 Nov. 1790, P.R.O. 30/8/171, ff. 157–63. See Selected
Letters.

question on which he would surely be outvoted, only to learn that during the meeting a number of ministers had changed their minds and Richmond's point had been carried.[1]

Probably one reason for the infrequency of caballing was the unimportance of decisions reached in cabinet meetings. With a cabinet of mediocre talents, peers who neither controlled extensive parliamentary support as individuals nor joined forces to form consistent blocs within the cabinet, Pitt frequently made his own decisions on domestic policy, relying on advice which came from men outside the cabinet like Grenville, Dundas, and Wilberforce. On at least two bills, for example—for parliamentary reform and for regulation of the slave trade—Pitt by no means carried his cabinet with him. On foreign policy, where he had little first-hand experience, Pitt was more interested in soliciting cabinet opinions. But the first real threat of war he faced—over the Dutch crisis in 1787—demonstrated that most of the ministers were hopelessly disinterested in foreign affairs. The Dutch Patriot party, with *sub rosa* assistance from France, threatened to overthrow the pro-British Stadtholder William V, brother-in-law of the King of Prussia and grandson of George II. As Prussian and French troops were gathered (or threatened) on the Dutch borders an open conflict seemed unavoidable. But besides Pitt and the Foreign Secretary only Richmond kept himself fully informed of events during the crisis and vigorously offered specific advice. During much of the summer Pitt had to send off instructions to British envoys abroad after random consultations with any cabinet members who happened to be in town; finally, after the Prussian invasion in September, he called a full cabinet meeting. Stafford and Thurlow did not bother to come. Those cabinet members who did attend weighed the alternatives of making France a party to a joint settlement or forcing her to back down alone. On his own initiative Pitt appointed William Grenville to investigate the possibilities of an alli-

[1] On 16 Nov. 1785, at a meeting Richmond had refused to attend because he feared defeat of a memorial to the Dutch Estates General urging opposition to the ratification of a Franco-Dutch treaty of alliance. The cabinet voted to send the memorial. Richmond to Carmarthen, 15 Nov. 1785. Quoted in A. Cobban, *Ambassadors and Secret Agents*, 1954, p. 67.

ance, relaying both sides of the cabinet discussion to him without binding him to either view.[1]

Since Pitt did not consider cabinet decisions binding, the influence of particular ministers often depended upon their personal friendship with Pitt. From 1784 to 1791 Richmond appeared to be one of the cabinet members closest to him and hence one of the strongest. The Duke invited Pitt to Goodwood for fox hunting at least once a year. A scolding he administered to Pitt for being absent from town during the regency crisis in 1789—'I am sorry to disturb you but indeed in time of action our general must not have a furlough'[2]—was written in a metaphoric style indicative of familiarity and affection. In periods of crisis—like the regency negotiations in 1788 or the threatened capture of the Dutch Estates by the Patriots in the summer of the previous year—Richmond saw Pitt for confidential talks almost every day. Moreover, Richmond was the only member of Pitt's cabinet to be interested in three of Pitt's most important proposals for reform—Parliament, the slave trade, and Irish commercial restrictions. Pitt's defence of Richmond's Fortifications Bill was so strong that no one considered the possibility of Richmond's resigning over the issue, even after the bill had nearly split the cabinet and had three times brought defeat to the government. In 1792 Leeds, who must have been referring only to the situation existing previous to his own resignation the year before, remarked that if anyone should know Pitt's opinion on negotiations with the Portland Whigs, Richmond should.[3]

Unquestionably several of Richmond's known opinions coincided with those of Pitt; unquestionably in his early years the young Prime Minister did look both to Richmond's ingenuity and to his almost paternal encouragement in times of crisis. But it was easy to overrate Richmond's political influence on Pitt. The Duke was known for tactless obstinacy, the young minister for a cool hauteur. Assuming that no natural friendship could have developed between two such self-absorbed personalities, outsiders reasoned that

[1] Pitt to Grenville, 23 Sept. 1787, *H.M.C. Fortescue*, iii. 428; Grenville to Pitt, 23 Sept. 1787, P.R.O. 30/8/140.
[2] (5 Apr. 1786), P.R.O. 30/8/140, ff. 143–5. See Selected Letters.
[3] *Leeds Pol. Mem.*, p. 177.

Richmond must secretly tap immense political power which gave him leverage over Pitt. All too often this attitude led contemporaries to a gross misinterpretation of appearances.

When Richmond first joined the cabinet, for instance, there were bitter protests about his inordinate power over the disposal of patronage plums. Charles Lennox was appointed secretary to the Master-General, but the appointment of his own secretary was traditionally the prerogative of the Master-General. Thomas Steele, M.P. for Chichester and a close friend of Richmond, was made Joint Paymaster of the Forces. But Steele was rapidly becoming a closer friend to Pitt himself than to Richmond. Lord George Lennox received an appointment to the Tower and then to Portsmouth. But contemporaries failed to note that at the time it was offered, Lord George was forced in a political shuffle to take Portsmouth against his wishes. The Fitzgeralds, Robert and Henry, were possibly offered diplomatic assignments in the first months of Pitt's administration, but their actual appointments were many years in forthcoming.

Though contemporaries rated his influence high, Richmond seems to have suffered as much as any minister from a chronic want of communication with Pitt. Dispatches circulated late and sometimes not at all; specific suggestions of Richmond's were apparently neither used nor acknowledged. In 1786 Richmond recommended changes in the wording of the Address from the Throne: the address was presented exactly as Pitt had originally sent it to Richmond.[1] In the same year the Duke urged that convicts should not be among the early shiploads of colonists to Botany Bay: Botany Bay was initially settled by convicts.[2] He pleaded in vain that the Commander-in-Chief be included on the Governor's Council in India.[3] There is evidence that in 1788 Richmond recommended setting up a joint council of regents and that Pitt later regretted the ridicule he had first given the suggestion.[4] In 1789 Richmond asked for money to provide

---

[1] Richmond to Pitt, 15 Jan. 1786, P.R.O. 30/8/171, ff. 79–87; *Annual Register*, 1786 (State Papers), p. 254.

[2] 3 Dec. 1786, P.R.O. 30/8/171, ff. 97–98.

[3] 30 Mar. 1786, P.R.O. 30/8/171, ff. 89–91.

[4] Duchess of Devonshire's Diary, 9 Dec. 1788, Sichel, *Sheridan*, 1909, ii. 413; Malone to Charlemont, 4 Feb. 1789, *H.M.C. Charlemont*, ii. 88.

Ordnance employment for dismissed Anglesea coal workers: the money was not forthcoming.[1] In 1790 he recommended that the beer tax be presented to Parliament as a permanent measure: the beer tax was presented as a temporary expedient, to last only one year.[2]

Occasionally Pitt would indicate assent to a proposal and then change his mind. At times he took Richmond's advice, with unfortunate consequences, as when Richmond recommended that the Fortifications Bill be trimmed only slightly for its second presentation in May 1786:[3] the bill was thrown out without a vote, as indicating contempt of Parliament.

Within two years after Richmond joined the cabinet Pitt began to recognize the Duke's increasing unpopularity with the House of Commons, to realize that he was no longer the asset he once had been in the House of Lords, and to consider that he was growing lazy in his cabinet work.

The full extent of Richmond's unpopularity was demonstrated in 1785 and 1786 by the defeat of his extensive plans for fortifications of the dockyards at Portsmouth and Plymouth. The idea of remodelling and extending the defences of two major dockyards as protection against new developments in naval artillery occurred to Richmond during a visit to Portsmouth and Plymouth in May 1782, when the Duke was first Master-General under Rockingham, and the initial plan for financing these fortifications was tacitly approved by Shelburne in January 1783. Subsequently Richmond prepared a total estimate of £400,000 of which £50,000 was to be voted annually for eight years. When the second £50,000 appropriation was presented to Parliament as part of the regular Ordnance budget, Colonel Barre demanded that the total building plan be examined by a board of professional army and navy officers before Parliament was called upon to vote appropriations.[4]

---

[1] 29 Aug. and 13 Sept. 1789, P.R.O. 30/8/171, ff. 139–42 and 145–7.

[2] 7 Dec. 1790, P.R.O. 30/8/171, ff. 163–4. See Selected Letters.

[3] Richmond to Pitt (18 Feb. 1789), P.R.O. 30/8/171, ff. 95–96. See Selected Letters.

[4] Apparently Barre desired revenge on Richmond whom he considered responsible for Shelburne's omission from Pitt's cabinet (Pulteney to Duke of Rutland, 6 July 1785, H.M.C. Rutland, iii. 222). In 1787 Richmond and Shelburne quarrelled

The board, consisting of fifteen army officers and ten navy officers and including Richmond as chairman, was appointed on 13 April 1785, and met beginning on 3 May for a month of tedious work largely answering questions put by Richmond about hypothetical types of enemy attack on the southern coast of England. The board's report was finished in June, well before Parliament adjourned; but against the King's wishes Pitt and Richmond did not present the bill again until 27 February of the following year.[1]

In mid-January 1786 Richmond circulated the report among the cabinet. It is clear from a letter he wrote to Pitt on 15 January that he anticipated only military arguments against the bill. With the preparation of Pitt's speech in mind, Richmond enumerated the kinds of attack against which the fortifications would be useful and the times during a war when such attacks could be expected.[2]

But when the bill was actually presented, its opponents attacked not the military arguments but, first, the supposed unconstitutionality of a measure tending to concentrate large groups of soldiers outside and separate from towns, and, second, the partiality of the Master-General himself in preparing the report: Richmond was charged by members of the board themselves with packing the committee, hamstringing it procedurally by presenting faulty information, wasting time in discussion of irrelevant questions, and garbling the final report presented to Parliament. Sheridan summarized the opposition points by labelling the whole report a fortress of sophistry.

Each of the charges against Richmond had, in fact, some foundation. The report when presented had certainly been

---

over the extent of Shelburne's approbation of the Fortifications Bill in 1783 (Wm. Ogilvie to Duchess of Leinster, 14 Mar. 1787, Fitzgerald Corr. Ogilvie III; Pulteney to Duke of Rutland, 19 Mar. 1787, *H.M.C. Rutland*, iii. 379).

[1] The best summary of the history of Richmond's fortifications estimates is given in the *Annual Register*, 1784–6. See particularly the *Annual Register*, 1786 (Hist. Eur.), pp. 95–103; *New Annual Register*, 1786 (British and Foreign History), pp. 68–84. See also Daniel Pulteney's reports to the Duke of Rutland, 15 Mar., 6 July 1785, 23 and 28 Feb., 1 Mar. 1786, *H.M.C. Rutland*, iii. 190, 222, 283, 285, 286; Cornwallis's reports to Colonel Ross; *Cornwallis Corr*. i. 188–91. The King wanted the Fortifications Bill presented at the end of the session in 1785 (George III to Pitt, 28 Feb. 1786, P.R.O. 30/8/103).

[2] 15 Jan. 1786, P.R.O. 30/8/171, ff. 79–87.

trimmed to omit the arguments of known dissenters like Burgoyne[1] and Captain Macbride.[2] Richmond claimed that the only material suppressed was secret military information, such as estimates of the size of attacking forces. Opponents of the bill, among them members of the board, claimed, apparently with justice, that many of the deletions were not necessary for reasons of military security, and served only to cover up the extent of opposition to Richmond's plan within the board itself.

If Richmond's objectivity in censoring the report was questioned by his opponents, even the Duke's loyal supporters like Cornwallis criticized his handling of the committee. Military procedure was reversed, senior officers speaking first although it was customary in such investigations for junior members to open the discussions, and the Master-General himself asking hundreds of detailed questions, many of them rhetorical. MacBride complained that opponents of the fortifications plan had been cajoled into accepting the report by the ridiculous way in which the Master-General had put irrelevant questions to the committee.[3] Cornwallis, who was probably thinking of MacBride himself as one of the cavilling members, reported,

The King's instructions, drawn up of course by the Duke, contain about a thousand questions, nineteen in twenty of which are nearly self evident propositions, but few of them so clearly drawn as not to admit of some cavilling, to which many of us are much inclined. The Duke himself puzzles the cause very much.[4]

But the most acrimonious debate of all centred on Sheridan's charges that Richmond had packed the committee with officers who were either known supporters of the plan or responsible to the ministry for their positions. Certainly several appointments looked suspicious. Richmond's brother, for example, was on the board for Portsmouth, Sir Guy Carleton was promised a pension of £1,000 in return for

---

[1] General John Burgoyne (1722–92), poet, dandy, and military commander of British forces during the American Revolution, Commander-in-Chief in Ireland during the Fox–North Coalition.

[2] Captain John MacBride (d. 1800) entered the Navy, 1754, as seaman, promoted to Lieutenant on examination 1758, given first command 1761; Rear-Admiral 1793, Vice-Admiral 1794, Admiral 1799.

[3] *New Annual Register*, 1786 (British and Foreign History), pp. 68–84.

[4] Cornwallis to Lt.-Colonel Ross, 8 May 1786, *Cornwallis Corr.* i. 190.

services on the board,[1] and Sir Charles Grey, to whom
Richmond had written, 'My trust in Plymouth is on you',[2]
was known to have favoured a plan of fortification even more
extensive than that which Richmond proposed. On the other
hand, a number of members like Burgoyne, MacBride, and
Barrington were political associates of Fox.

As nearly as can be determined, when the committee first
met in May, Richmond counted on fourteen supporters,[3]
some of whom, like the governors of Plymouth and Portsmouth, and the head of the Royal Engineers Corps, were
virtually *ex officio* members coincidentally owing their positions to the ministry and some of whom, like Sir Guy Carleton, Sir Andrew Hammond who owed his baronetcy to Pitt,
and Major-General William Green who was promised one,
seem to have been packed. Six members of the committee
were apparently undecided before the meetings began.[4]
Four were known to be opponents of the government and
the plan.[5] Thus at most there would have been only ten
opponents of the bill as against thirteen supposed supporters.
When the final report was drawn up, three of the anticipated
supporters opposed it,[6] but all six of the undecideds seem to
have been favourable.

While it does appear, then, that the board was packed,
the connexion between military administration and eighteenth-century politics was so close that Richmond would
have had difficulty in obtaining any qualified board many of

---

[1] George III to Pitt, 28 Mar. 1785, P.R.O. 30/8/103. Sir Guy's pension, in his
wife's name, was voted by Parliament in June.

[2] 6 Apr. 1782, Ordnance Board Outletters, W.O. 46/14, p. 9.

[3] Lt.-Generals Lord George Lennox, Sir Guy Carleton, Wm. Howe, Cornwallis,
Charles Grey, and Sir David Lindsay, on whose behalf as Governor of Plymouth
Richmond had attached Lord Amherst in 1779; Major-Generals Roy and Green;
Vice-Admiral Mark Milbank, Port Admiral at Plymouth; Rear-Admirals Lord
Hood, government candidate for Westminster in 1784, Lord Graves, made Com-
mander-in-Chief at Plymouth in 1787 and Vice-Admiral the same year; Captains
Sir Andrew Hammond, James Luttrell, Surveyor-General of the Ordnance, and
John Jervis (later Earl of St. Vincent), M.P. for Yarmouth, who opposed Fox's
India Bill, later supported Pitt during the regency crisis.

[4] Major-Generals Bramham, Cleveland, Pattison, and Garth; Captains Bowyer
and Hotham.

[5] Lt.-Generals Hugh Percy (later Earl of Northumberland, Richmond's replacement at the Ordnance had Fox taken office during the regency crisis), and Burgoyne;
Vice-Admiral Samuel Barrington, Captain Macbride.

[6] Vice-Admiral Milbank, Rear-Admiral Graves, Captain Jervis.

whose members were not obligated either to the existing government or to one of the opposition factions. Richmond could argue with justice that had he not supplemented these appointees with other supporters of the bill, a majority of opposition officers might have defeated any fortifications plan for political reasons.

Pitt presented the Fortifications Bill early on the evening of 27 February. The personal criticisms of the Master-General which characterized the debate continued throughout the night. At seven in the morning a tie vote was taken, the casting vote of the Speaker defeating the bill.

At Richmond's request Pitt presented a revised bill in May. In the meantime he had worked on government friends who had opposed the bill in February, and had accepted Richmond's plea that only a token sum be removed from the revised estimate.[1] But the second bill was withdrawn without a vote after angry accusations that the presentation of a measure nearly identical to one previously defeated was a violation of the rights of the House. After the defeat of his Fortifications Bill, Richmond gave up all idea of a major system of fortifications on the southern coast of England though he was able to save enough from future Ordnance budgets to purchase limited amounts of land around Plymouth and Portsmouth and to erect small fortifications costing less than £15,000 a year.[2]

The political implications of the bill's defeat were far more serious to Richmond than the military. Not least was the threat to cabinet harmony. As early as January 1786, Thurlow, Dundas, and Howe, First Lord of the Admiralty, had voiced objections to the bill.[3] Howe even allowed members returned by the Admiralty to speak and vote against the revised bill on 13 May;[4] in retaliation James Luttrell, Surveyor-General of the Ordnance, spoke and voted against

---

[1] Richmond to Pitt, 5 Apr. 1786, P.R.O. 30/8/171, ff. 95–96. See Selected Letters.

[2] Rose, *William Pitt and the National Revival*, 1911, p. 212.

[3] There is no record of the opinions of the other cabinet members. Early in May Thomas Steele told Thomas Orde that the passing of the revised bill was more essential to the quiet of the ministry than he might think. Pulteney to Duke of Rutland, 16 May 1786, *H.M.C. Rutland*, iii. 301.

[4] In general the naval officers were the members of the Fortifications Board most opposed to the plan.

an Admiralty regulation three days later.[1] As late as 1788
Richmond seems to have allowed Ordnance Board members
to oppose Howe on a question of navy administration which
ultimately brought about Howe's retirement from the
cabinet.

Far more serious for Richmond, the defeat of his bill
made clear the extent of his personal unpopularity with the
House of Commons. Even the King, who had favoured the
plan, consoled Pitt,

> I do not in the least look on the event as any want of confidence in
> Mr. Pitt from the Members of the House of Commons but their attach-
> ments to old prejudices and some disinclination to the projectors of the
> fortifications.[2]

As long as the Ordnance remained under Richmond's
leadership it was particularly vulnerable to political attacks;
by 1788 there had already been three attacks made on Ordnance administration which involved Richmond personally.
On 17 December 1787, after the presentation of Ordnance
estimates for the following year, Sheridan protested that the
building of fortifications in the West Indies was an unnecessary expense, the principle of which had been defeated with
the defeat of the Fortifications Bill. On the same day he protested against a plan of Richmond's which would lead to the
forcing of civilian employees of the Ordnance to join the
Army by establishing a corps of artificers. After some discussion Sheridan withdrew his complaint and the Ordnance
estimates were voted.[3]

The most persistent criticism of Richmond concerned
electoral corruption. A week after the fortifications defeat
in February 1786, Charles Marsham, M.P. for Kent, moved
to disfranchise officers of the Ordnance and Navy. Marsham
illustrated his attack with a history of Queenborough where
the Ordnance had returned one member of Parliament for
thirty years (the other member was returned by the Admiralty). According to the charges Richmond himself had
claimed in 1782 that Queenborough was full of abuses but

---

[1] Pulteney to Duke of Rutland, 16 May 1786, *H.M.C. Rutland*, iii. 301.

[2] George III to Pitt, 28 Feb. 1786, P.R.O. 30/8/103.

[3] A brief but bitter debate occurred in the House of Lords three months later
over the Mutiny Bill, incorporating the corps of artificers.

upon resuming his place at the Ordnance in December
1783 he had rescinded the order of his predecessor, Lord
Townshend, for an investigation into electoral abuses in the
borough. Since that time the opportunity for corruption had
actually been increased by the Ordnance taking on more
employees for its own ships and gunpowder factories.

Marsham's motion probably had no connexion with the
Fortifications Bill except for its timing to capitalize on the
Master-General's unpopularity. The Ordnance member
from Queenborough, John Aldrich, Storekeeper of the
Ordnance, had no connexion with the Fortifications Board,
though Captain Bowyer, returned from Queenborough
through Admiralty influence and considered by Richmond
to be unfriendly to the Ordnance, actually supported the
bill more strongly than did any of the other naval officers
on the board. Marsham's motion was defeated, but on 12
December 1787 Alderman Sawbridge presented a petition
from four freemen of Queenborough charging that public
money was wasted by the maintenance of extra ships in
order to employ voters and return one M.P. for the Ordnance Board. Although the petition presented by Sawbridge
was tabled on 12 December, Richmond gave the four freemen a hurried hearing in April, dismissing their complaint
with the hardly satisfying explanation that it was less expensive and more convenient for the Ordnance to keep its own
ships in Queenborough.[1]

At Seaford and Shoreham as well as Queenborough, there
is some indication that Richmond was trying to extend
Ordnance influence. In 1788 he wrote asking to see Pitt,

concerning the next general election upon which I have had offers, but
I cannot engage in any of them without feeling that I have the means
of undertaking them with a reasonable prospect of success, and that
depends so much upon my own situation that I must have some
determination upon that subject before I can persuade myself to embark in a business of much trouble and not a little expense.[2]

Six months after the election he mentioned with similar
vagueness 'having been of late so particularly called upon to
take a very active part in a Business of some consequence

---

[1] Richmond to Pitt, 7 Apr. 1788, P.R.O. 30/8/171, ff. 123–6.
[2] 29 Aug. 1788, P.R.O. 30/8/171, ff. 129–30. See Selected Letters.

where it was thought I could be useful'.[1] The reference may
or may not concern Ordnance intervention in elections, but
one point is certain: slightly less than six months before the
general elections of 1790, forty-nine ministerial supporters—
including, indeed, Richmond, Lord George Lennox, and
Pitt—were made non-resident freemen of Seaford, and after
a highly irregular postponement of the election in order to
fulfil the six months' requirement before the freemen were
eligible to vote, the two government candidates were returned. Meanwhile Richmond, wanting to return another
ministerial supporter, Gibbs Crawford, from the controversial Queenborough, returned John Aldrich for Shoreham
instead. As the result of a petition from householders of
Seaford the election was investigated in 1792 when the votes
of all the new non-resident freemen were thrown out. Since
one of the opposition candidates also had several of his
supporters disqualified, one government member and one
opposition member were declared elected and the right of
election was transferred from the government controlled
corporation to the Scot and Lot householders.

Meanwhile in Sussex politics Richmond had lost ground.
Lord George Lennox, who had tired of Parliament, was
replaced by Charles Lennox for the county. But Thomas
Steele was forced by the independent voters of Chichester
to disavow Richmond's support and to run as an independent candidate. After Steele's election Richmond had permanently to yield the nomination of one M.P. from Chichester
to the independents of the city.

Because he was personally unpopular and involved in a
number of patronage disputes with uneven success, Richmond was a liability with the House of Commons. He was
scarcely an unqualified asset with the Lords or even the
cabinet. Six months after the defeat of the Fortifications Bill,
Pitt began to complain that Richmond's participation in
cabinet meetings was slackening. There had been nothing
new in Richmond's declining to come to London before the
opening of Parliament in January 1786, or perhaps even in
his refusal of Pitt's personal request to come to town to

[1] 24 Nov. 1790, P.R.O. 30/8/171, ff. 157–63. See Selected Letters.

support the India Bill in March of the same year.[1] But in September Richmond had to apologize to Carmarthen for his ignorance concerning Dutch affairs. 'I am so much out of the train of reading the correspondence that I am not well able to understand the grounds of the present troubles.'[2] By December Pitt was complaining openly of Richmond's laziness, and particularly of his refusal to attend cabinet meetings. In April 1791 Richmond admitted to Leeds that he had been absent frequently and for long periods.[3]

This diminution of Richmond's industry is difficult to explain, since the Duke had entered office with a reputation for immense energy. Probably his industry had been inspired by an obsession with Ordnance reform, and particularly with the development of improved fortifications. When the Fortifications Bill was defeated, Richmond's interest in Ordnance reform was destroyed. It was replaced by an interest in broader questions of government policy, particularly in foreign affairs. But Richmond did not regularly keep up on issues when he was away from London—'My attendance in town upon the affairs of the North could in my present uninformed state be of little use'[4]—and he was no longer able to arrive in town shortly before an issue was to be discussed and use his remarkable powers of concentration and imagination to capture the high points of a question after a briefing. Furthermore he no longer had a Burke to brief him before meetings and debates. Rogers, his secretary, occasionally summarized reports for him, but Rogers was no Burke, and Richmond generally had to cull material from dispatches himself.

Hence the Duke became erratic in both cabinet participation and House of Lords debates. In cabinet meetings he frequently could say nothing for lack of adequate information. In Parliament Richmond spoke rarely and those unimaginative speeches he did make concerned minor points or personal issues: debating the commercial treaty with France he branched off into a discussion of Anglo-French

---

[1] Richmond to Pitt, 30 Mar. 1786, P.R.O. 30/8/171, ff. 89–91.
[2] Richmond to Carmarthen, 10 Sept. 1786, Add. MS. 28,061, f. 300.
[3] *Leeds Pol. Mem.*, pp. 155–6.
[4] Richmond to Pitt, 1 Sept. 1788, P.R.O. 30/8/171, ff. 131–3.

coastal fortifications. Even in the dispute involving the powers of the Prince Regent during the King's illness in 1788, a subject on which he would presumably have been well informed since he had conferred daily with Pitt and had drawn up a paper setting forth the cabinet's views on the limitations of the powers of a temporary regent,[1] he spoke only twice, once refuting the Prince's right to the King's property and care of the King and once explaining a technicality about putting the Great Seal in commission.[2]

Chatham had once called Richmond the most formidable debater in the House of Lords. But Chatham had nearly always heard Richmond speaking in opposition to the government. As an opposition debater he had been able to criticize particular ministerial shortcomings without being held responsible for the comprehension of total policies. He could, for example, attack the government's failure to support Sir David Lindsay at Portsmouth without being responsible for a total understanding of the system of fortifications there. He could villify Sandwich for sending Keppel to the channel with an insufficient number of ships to meet the French fleet, without having to see channel manœuvres in the global context of naval operations. As a minister, however, he had necessarily to synthesize information from a variety of sources and see problems whole, a talent in which he was lacking. After 1783 Ordnance Board minutes show that he was often in London for months without attending Parliament, even during periods when crucial issues were being debated in the Lords. He was never employed to introduce government motions, and was second in command respectively to Sydney, Carmarthen, and Grenville, none of them outstanding debaters. In 1790 when Grenville was given a peerage specifically to enable him to take the lead in the Lords, Richmond complained,

I trust I have not shown myself a difficult man, when after having had for many years a considerable share in the debates in the House of Lords, I first wished to support your government as an individual and

---

[1] *Leeds Pol. Mem.*, p. 132.

[2] *An History of the Late Important Period; from the Beginning of His Majesty's Illness to the Settlement of the Executive Government in the Appointment of a Regent*, London, 1789.

afterwards defended your measures as a minister under Lord Sydney and the Duke of Leeds. But to continue to act a second part under every change and particularly under one which is avowedly made for the sole purpose of giving the House of Lords another leader, would be depriving myself of every sort of consideration which I may hope to have in that House and rendering myself to tally useless there.[1]

Gradually declining before 1790, Richmond's position deteriorated rapidly after that year when the whole nature of Pitt's cabinet began to change. From a collection of single spent forces the cabinet was becoming a combination of factions built around two rising leaders, Henry Dundas and William Grenville. Grenville, who had served as joint Pay-master of the Forces and special envoy to The Hague and Paris, was made Home Secretary in 1789 in place of Sydney, promoted to the Lords as Baron Grenville in 1790, and finally appointed Secretary of State in 1791; Dundas, who had been in charge of the India Office, took Grenville's place as Home Secretary in 1791. Meanwhile Lord Howe was replaced by Pitt's brother at the Admiralty in 1788, Thurlow was dismissed in 1792, and Camden died and Stafford retired in 1794. Richmond's dismissal in January 1796 meant that Pitt's entire first cabinet had been replaced within six years.

Whereas none of the members of the original cabinet controlled extensive patronage, the new cabinet had two strong centres of patronage—the Grenville–Pitt family and Dundas's Scottish connexions. Whereas Pitt himself had taken decisions out of the hands of former cabinet members, especially Carmarthen, he now appeared to go to the opposite extreme in delegating extensive authority to his leading ministers. He left to Grenville, for example, complete control of negotiations with Russia in 1791, and when Dundas decided on his own initiative in 1793 that Great Britain might contribute forces to the allies for a joint attack on Dunkirk, Pitt announced that Dundas's decision would stand as his own. Whereas all the members of the original cabinet had complained passively of Pitt's inattention the two new ministers were soon in active rivalry for personal

---

[1] 24 Nov. 1790, P.R.O. 30/8/171, ff. 157–63. See Selected Letters.

ascendancy over the young minister. The competition was not materially altered by the entry of the Portland Whigs into the ministry in July 1794, for Portland's supporters ultimately became absorbed into the existing factions.

For Richmond the new cabinet changes meant that whatever influence he had once enjoyed in matters concerning the army or foreign affairs was now blocked off. Dundas, appointed Secretary of State for War, disliked Richmond and at least twice complained behind Richmond's back— once in 1792 about dilatoriness in the building of barracks in Scotland under the provisions of the new Barracks Act,[1] and again the same year about the extent of West Indies fortifications proposed by Richmond.[2] At least twice (concerning the attack on Dunkirk in 1793) Dundas seems to have made decisions involving the Ordnance without consulting Richmond.

Dundas and Richmond were in agreement over a general war policy against France: both preferred the concentration of British troops in colonial areas rather than on the Continent. But for reasons dating back to the Prussian invasion of Holland without concerting plans with England in 1787 and to the Prussian–Austrian attack on Russia despite England's pleas not to go to war in 1791, Richmond was far more sceptical than Dundas of the good faith of continental allies. Rather than join with allies in any combined attack on French borders, as Dundas advocated, Richmond would have preferred to use British troops in support of French counter-revolutionary efforts. Above all, however, he criticized Dundas's dissipation of strength over several theatres of war. Since Richmond's relations with Chatham, First Lord of the Admiralty, were only slightly less strained than they had been with Howe, Richmond was perpetually in conflict with other ministers over military policy after Dundas's appointment as Home Secretary.

With Grenville the clash was not so much on particular issues of foreign policy, where the two ministers were not in disagreement,[3] but on Richmond's position in the House of

---

1 Dundas to Pitt, 15 Oct. 1792, P.R.O. 30/8/157.
2 Dundas to Pitt, 12 Nov. 1792, P.R.O. 30/8/157.
3 See Selected Letters for Richmond to Pitt, 27 Mar. 1791 (P.R.O. 30/8/171.

Lords and in a cabinet where foreign affairs, once thoroughly discussed in meetings, were now left increasingly to the discretion of the Foreign Minister. In December 1790 Grenville was created Baron Grenville, expressly for the purpose of replacing the inadequate Leeds as ministerial lead in the House of Lords. Promoted over Richmond's head, Grenville was thus in a position to watch Thurlow in debate: after the irascible Chancellor had quarrelled with Dundas and George Rose over Scottish patronage his support of ministerial bills in the House of Lords, erratic at best, threatened to become totally unreliable. Pitt and the King agreed that none of the ministerial lords were debaters of sufficient prescience or facility in debate to cover Thurloe; Grenville was therefore given a peerage and the management of Government supporters in the House of Lords. Richmond was shocked and embittered. After a few months of attempting to accept Grenville's appointment with good grace, he began attending Parliament only half as often as before.

Any chance of Richmond's rebuilding his cabinet standing ended with the declaration of war on France in January 1793. In the first place, Richmond was held indirectly responsible for the government's defeat in prosecuting for treason the leaders of radical reform societies claiming allegiance to the principles of the French Revolution.[2] When Thomas Hardy and Horne Tooke of the London Corresponding Society were tried for treason in 1794, they defended themselves by producing the society's constitution, which declared that the Corresponding Society had been constituted solely to carry out the reforms proposed in Richmond's Reform Bill of 1780. Pitt and Richmond were both called upon to testify at the trials—Richmond to identify his Reform Bill and Pitt to acknowledge his own presence at a meeting of reformers in 1784. Horne Tooke

---

ff. 167–8), agreeing with Grenville, not Leeds, on the occasion when Leeds resigned. *Leeds Pol. Mem.*, p. 155. For two years Richmond had been complaining about Leeds's cool behaviour towards his nephew, Lord Robert Fitzgerald.

[1] Pitt to George III (Nov. 1790), P.R.O. 30/8/101; Gore-Brown, *Thurlow*. p. 284; George III to Pitt (21 Nov. 1790), P.R.O. 30/8/103.

[2] Sheridan claimed that Richmond had stationed himself at the Tower one night in May 1794, pretending that he had uncovered a conspiracy (Sichel, quotes Sheridan's speech given 5 Jan. 1795, *Sheridan*, ii. 378–90).

and Hardy were acquitted; Richmond and Pitt were humi-
liated by the renewed publicity given to the reversal of their
own positions on parliamentary reform since 1784. While
the trials were probably not the major reason for Richmond's
dismissal two months later, they unquestionably aggravated
the hostility between Richmond and Pitt.

Far more destructive to Richmond was his involvement in
an anachronistic military organization inadequate to cope
with the conduct of the war. The difficulties in Richmond's
relations with Dundas became only one clog in a war
organization so generally clogged with overlapping authori-
ties that in July 1794, after the secretaryship of State had
been divided between the colonies and the Home Department, Richmond had to ask Portland exactly which letters
should be addressed to him as Home Secretary and which to
Dundas as Secretary of State for War. As Master-General
of the Ordnance, Richmond was responsible for permanent fortifications, artillery, and engineers. As Secretaries
at War Sir George Yonge[1] and later William Windham[2]
were cabinet ministers responsible for military operations.
As Commander-in-Chief, Amherst and subsequently the
Duke of York were at the head of the Army but not in
the cabinet, and first as Home Secretary and later as Secretary of State for War, Dundas was in charge of general
policy decisions on such questions as theatres of concentration. Besides sharing and overlapping his authority with at
least four other officials, the Master-General was even in an
undefined position in the Ordnance Department. Theoreti-
cally his sole functions were to distribute patronage and to
transmit cabinet policy decisions to his Surveyor-General
and Lt.-General, who were in charge respectively of muni-
tions and armaments.[3] In practice the Master-General was

[1] Sir George Yonge, Bart. (1731–1812), M.P. for Honiton, 1754–94; nom.
K.B., 1788; a Lord of the Admiralty, 1766–70; Vice-Treasurer for Ireland, Apr. to
July 1782; Secretary at War, July 1782 to Apr. 1783 and again from Dec. 1783 to
July 1794; Governor of the Cape of Good Hope, 1799–1801.

[2] The Hon. William Windham (1750–1810), M.P. for Norwich, 1784–1802, St.
Mawes, 1802–6, and Higham Ferrers, 1807–10. Secretary to the Lord Lieutenant of
Ireland, 1783, during the coalition; Secretary at War, July 1794, until he resigned
with Pitt in 1801, and again under Grenville, 1806 until his death.

[3] See A. Forbes, *A History of the Army Ordnance Services*, 1929, p. 174.

held responsible for the efficient operation of the entire
Ordnance Department.

The difficulties of the Master-General's position were
clearly shown in the first campaign of the war, and particularly in the battle of Dunkirk. Immediately after war was
declared Lord Auckland, British Ambassador at The Hague,
requested that the Duke of York be sent to Holland in command of a British regiment. When the appointment came
before the cabinet, Richmond staked his remaining influence
on blocking it, because of a quarrel with the Duke dating
back to the regency crisis in 1788–9. During the crisis the
Duke of York had supported his brother's claim to full
rights as regent, a claim which Richmond had vigorously
opposed. After the King's recovery Richmond's nephew
Charles Lennox was promoted prematurely, through the
influence of Richmond and the Queen, to be Captain of a
company in the Duke of York's regiment, the Coldstream
Guards.[1] The Duke, who had opposed Lennox's promotion,
was reported to have insulted him in disguise at a masked
ball and then teased him before the regiment for failing to
answer an anonymous insult. Lennox was visiting Richmond
at Richmond House at the time and must have consulted
him before circulating a letter at Brookes Club asking if
any members had heard the alleged insult; when no answers
were received he challenged York to a duel.[2] On a morning
early in June both parties appeared: Lennox fired once and
missed; the Duke refused to fire. A month later Lennox
transferred out of his regiment, the quarrel still unhealed.

On 18 February 1793, after York had been appointed to
the command of British continental forces, the Duchess of
Richmond, always reflecting her husband's opinions, com-
miserated with him:

The Nation must be ruined that Master Frederick may have a
plaything that I doubt he does not know how to manage, and that will

[1] A rumour reported by the Duchess of Devonshire that the Duke of York's
regiment had been given to Richmond must refer to Charles Lennox's promotion
(27 Nov. 1788, Sichel, *Sheridan*, ii. 408). Grenville defended Lennox against Lord
Buckinghamshire's criticisms, calling Lennox 'a most steady, warm, and deserving
friend' (17 Apr. 1789, the Duke of Buckingham and Chandos, *Memoirs of the
Courts and Cabinets of George III*, 1853–5, ii. 37).

[2] *Gentleman's Magazine*, 1789, ii. 403.

give him a rap on the knuckles; I cannot bear those that are so mean as to give way to this to pay their Court & am delighted you have so clearly given your sentiment on this head and resisted all you could. I look upon this Continental War as a most dangerous unpopular measure & I do not think these times for Princes to play tricks in, but advise them to look at Home.[1]

Immediately after York's arrival on the Continent Richmond's prestige suffered further diminution. York was to attend a conference of the allies at Antwerp, to determine upon a plan of attack against France. Combining his dislike of York with his distrust of continental allies, Richmond wrote two vigorous letters to Pitt urging that British troops be withdrawn from the Continent immediately: '. . . confining our operations to a naval war and to such expeditions on the coast of France or on her possessions abroad as we could manage, we should be sure of support at home and essentially assist the allies'.[2]

Neither letter was answered; indeed, although Dundas refused to commit Britain definitely to the maintenance of troops on the Continent, he encouraged the allies to attack Dunkirk, a fortress of historic interest to England, and convinced Pitt that Dunkirk could easily be taken.[3] At the end of April the Duchess of Richmond ominously advised her husband, 'you should not fatigue yourself for the whims of a silly boy'.[4]

Planning for the Dunkirk campaign began in mid-July. After Richmond left for summer camp with his militia on 19 July the direction of the Ordnance was apparently taken over by the Lt.-General, Howe, and by Dundas himself, though Richmond was daily in touch with his secretary at the Ordnance Board.

There is evidence that before he left for camp Richmond was attempting to obtain more artillery men for Dunkirk than had been requested by the British staff in Flanders. Certainly by the second week in August, two ships had been sent to Ostend, and on 20 August, easily in time for the

[1] 18 Feb. 1793, Goodwood, Box 25, 3d.

[2] Both letters are quoted at length in J. H. Rose, 'The Duke of Richmond on the Conduct of the War in 1793', *E.H.R.* 1910, xxv. 554.

[3] Fortescue, *British Army*, iv, part i, p. 85.

[4] 22 Apr. 1793, Goodwood, Box 25, 3d.

campaign, Richmond ordered two additional ships with supplies to be sent directly from Woolwich to Dunkirk. But at Woolwich the gunners were loaded on a separate ship from their guns without Richmond's knowledge.[1] On 27 August the ship with gunners sailed; the guns, apparently loaded on an Admiralty ship, never left Woolwich.

Partly because of the failure of the artillery to arrive, the Duke of York's siege of Dunkirk had to be given up on 8 September. After the defeat the Duke of York 'insinuated that it had arisen from the neglect or the malicious delay of the Ordnance'.[2] 'He [the Duke] is highly incensed against the Duke of Richmond for not sending the Ordnance.'[3] Sir Gilbert Elliot, visiting in Flanders, found the royal Duke 'violent against the Duke of Richmond'.[4] York wrote at once to the King, blaming his failure primarily on the weakness of the allies, but indicating that his own strength had been seriously impaired by the failure of the artillery to arrive.[5] York himself made no public charge against Richmond, but allowed one of his staff officers to write to the *Morning Chronicle* that 'ministers have sacrificed their duty to the holiday mumery of camps or to the amusements of Partridge shooting'.[6]

Possibly by 31 August Richmond was already aware of the slip-up in dispatching artillery to Flanders. On that date his secretary compiled a report on all orders from the Master-General concerning artillery shipments to Dunkirk.[7] Four days after the attack in the *Morning Post* Richmond 'justified his own share in unanswerable manner by producing the minutest and exactest detail of all the orders received and executed in his department. The consequence of the implication is Lord Chatham's condemnation, and between them

[1] This information is implied in a letter from the Duchess of 10 Sept. 1793 (Goodwood, Box 25, 3d). Richmond's orders to send two ships from Woolwich with Flanders supplies, 20, 23, and 27 Aug., are preserved in W.O. 46/24, pp. 40, 41, 44.

[2] *The Journal of Elizabeth, Lady Holland*, ed. the Earl of Ilchester, 2 vols. 1908, i. 68.

[3] Ibid., p. 94.

[4] *The Life and Letters of Gilbert Elliot, first Earl of Minto*, ed. the Countess of Minto, 1874, ii. 160.

[5] A. Burne, *The Noble Duke of York*, 1949, pp. 73–78.

[6] Ibid., p. 80.

[7] See Rogers to Richmond, 31 Aug. 1793, W.O. 46/24, p. 45.

they have been the means of crowning a rash plan with inefficient execution.'[1]

Ironically, Richmond's defence did almost as much as the defeat at Dunkirk itself to jeopardize his position in the cabinet. The Duchess herself had warned Richmond that he might carry his defence too far: 'Let me entreat you to be guarded on this occasion.'[2] Dundas and Chatham, on whom the blame was indirectly shifted, were certainly not ingratiated by their own implication. Far worse, cabinet members like Grenville who had virtually nothing to do with the defeat still thought the circulation of Richmond's personal defence to be in bad taste. And so, although his defence seemed conclusively to assign the major blame to Chatham, Richmond was nevertheless made a scapegoat for Dunkirk by any one—and there were many—who had other grudges against him.

Grenville, commenting that 'The Duke of Richmond's campaign seems completely to have annihilated the little popularity he ever had',[3] predicted that Richmond would have to resign within a year. He was almost right. But the truth of his prediction could not have been taken for granted at the time he made it. A few months after Dunkirk Richmond retired to Goodwood with a bad case of gout and a liver ailment. Throughout the spring of 1794 he remained in the country, delegating his Ordnance work to Pitt and Howe, the Lt.-General of the Ordnance.[4] And yet in July 1794, when the Portland Whigs joined the government Richmond's place was neither requested nor offered even though Portland asked very high terms.

Possibly he was allowed to remain in office because his relations with the Portland Whigs had been repaired in the years just before they took office. With many of the party, Portland included, he had been out of political touch the four years following his accession to office in 1784. But he

[1] Spencer to Windham, 18 Sept. 1793, *The Life and Correspondence of the Rt. Hon. William Windham, 1750–1810*, ed. the Earl of Rosebery, 2 vols. 1913, i. 153.

[2] 10 Sept. 1793.

[3] Grenville to Lord Buckinghamshire, 1 Oct. 1793, *Courts and Cabinets of George III*, ii. 243.

[4] Lady Louisa Conolly to Duchess of Leinster, 12 Apr. 1794, Fitzgerald Corr. Duchess of Leinster MSS.

had maintained his social connexions with Conway, the Cavendishes, and the Duke of Devonshire; and during the regency crisis of 1788, though he was loyal to Pitt and expected to be dismissed if the Prince of Wales had a chance to reconstitute the government, Richmond had been daily with the opposition at Devonshire House giving information on the King's condition.[1]

Since 1787, when Fox had supported a bill for paying off the Prince's debts and raising his annual civil list allotment, Portland's party had been split. As long as Fox remained in the party, supporting the Prince of Wales and subsequently defending the principles of the French Revolution, Richmond could not encourage any coalition with Pitt. But in 1792, after much wavering, Portland broke with Fox and the way was open for Richmond to press for union.[2] In July he was telling Thomas Pelham at the Sussex races that the ministry was in desperate need of additional strength.[3]

Thus in the rearrangements of July 1794, which removed Stafford, demoted Chatham, and divided Dundas's duties in half, Richmond was not dislodged, and in September, when Windham suggested that the Duke of York might be gracefully relieved of his unsuccessful continental command by appointing him both Commander-in-Chief and Master-General of the Ordnance, Pitt refused.[4] In November the Duke of York was called home on leave while the cabinet decided what to do with him. It was finally determined to make him Commander-in-Chief in place of the ageing and ineffective Amherst.

But Richmond's position at the Ordnance would be untenable if the Commander-in-Chief were an officer, and particularly a member of the royal family, with whom his

[1] See the Duchess of Devonshire's Diary, printed in Sichel, *Sheridan*, i. 403–21.

[2] As late as 1791 Portland, recollecting Richmond's specific opposition to coalition two years before, considered him hostile to a union with the Whigs (*Diaries and Correspondence of James Harris, first Earl of Malmesbury*, ed. the Third Earl, 1844, ii. 430).

[3] *Leeds Pol. Mem.*, p. 177; *Malmesbury Diaries*, ii. 436; Lady Sarah Lennox referred to 'new changes in politics . . . that soften him to the other party'. (Lady Sarah to Lady Susan O'Brien, 30 July 1792, *Sarah Lennox Corr.* ii. 84.)

[4] Windham to Pitt, 16 Sept. 1794, Pitt to Windham, 23 Sept. 1794, *Windham Papers*, p. 240.

relations were at least not cordial. York himself may well have refused to accept the appointment if Richmond remained in office. Cornwallis, who was only slightly more acceptable to York than Richmond, was nominated to succeed him as Master-General.

On 15 December Richmond gave Pitt an opening for the dismissal by writing to ask that his participation in all cabinet meetings, broken off since spring, now be resumed. Pitt stalled, waiting three weeks for Cornwallis's acceptance.[1] On 26 January he wrote to Richmond stating that the breaking off of relations had proceeded solely from the Duke and that the head of the Ordnance must be in the confidence of the Prime Minister. Richmond did not allow the reasons; he protested of his devotion to Pitt, his illness in the spring and travel away from London on Ordnance work in the summer, and his willingness not to speak up in further opposition to military intervention on the Continent, should that be the minister's wish.[2] Both reasons he presented for his absence from the cabinet were honest—he had suffered severely from gout in the spring and had spent several months in summer on a tour of dockyards—and his offer not to oppose continental intervention had been rejected previously. Pitt was hedging.

In a subsequent audience with Richmond the King was more truthful than Pitt: 'I thought it but justice to say that Mr. Pitt yielded to the arrangement to prevent a want of concert in the cabinet which the Duke himself must allow would be highly detrimental to the conduct of affairs at so critical a time as the present.'[3] Cornwallis assumed his predecessor to be the victim of the Portland Whigs. Richmond himself, in letters written to the Duchess at the time and to Charles Lennox nearly ten years later, assumed more logically that Pitt, his one-time friend, had given in easily to Dundas and York:

---

[1] See Cornwallis to Lt.-Colonel Ross, 30 Dec. 1794, *Cornwallis Corr.* ii. 279.

[2] Copies of the letters concerning Richmond's dismissal (Richmond to Pitt, 15, 21 Dec., 12, 23, 26 Jan.; Pitt to Richmond, 20 Dec., 24, 26 Jan.) are printed in *H.M.C. Bathurst*, pp. 708–11. Manuscript copies are among the Bathurst MSS., the Fitzgerald MSS., and the Chatham MSS., P.R.O. 30/9/171.

[3] George III to Pitt, 29 Jan. 1795, P.R.O. 30/8/103.

After owing me a great deal at a time he stood in much need of my assistance, and being served by me with all the fidelity of the warmest Friendship, he turned me out of office and in the most shuffling manner, without aledging any cause but evidently to sacrifice me to the Duke of York and Mr. Dundas' jealousy.[1]

[1] Richmond to Charles Lennox, 6 June 1804, Richmond Papers, Dublin, no. 1274. See Selected Letters.

VII

YEARS OF RETIREMENT:
THE WISHFUL OBSERVER

RICHMOND was mortified by his unexpected dismissal. He remained in town pleading laryngitis as a reason for not attending Parliament during February[1] and for the rest of the year attended the Lords less than half a dozen times, twice for readings of a private bill concerning the will of his father-in-law, General Conway. Charles Lennox was employed as a go-between with Pitt to arrange for his remaining on the staff:[2] in April Richmond was appointed Colonel of the Horse Guards Blue and a year later, Field Marshal.

Three months after his dismissal Richmond retired to Goodwood where the Duchess was confined by illness. There he contented himself with caring for her until her death in 1796, with entertaining occasional guests on the estate,[3] and with supervising the planning and construction of a race track. From 1796 to 1800 Richmond appeared in Parliament on only two occasions—once in 1799 and again in 1800 during readings for a bill authorizing the sale of his coal duties to the government for an annuity of £19,000. The *Public Characters of 1799* remarked that 'The Duke of Richmond now lives a retired life, principally at Goodwood'.[4]

Only a family crisis brought Richmond temporarily out of his retirement. In May 1798 Lord Edward Fitzgerald, hot-headed son of the first Duke of Leinster, and member of the United Irishmen plotting to seek French military assistance for Irish independence, was shot resisting arrest in Dublin. His wounds became infected and in June Lord Edward died in prison, leaving a French wife who was widely

---

[1] Duchess of Richmond to Richmond, 28 Jan., 3 and 13 Feb. 1795, Goodwood, Box 25, 3d.

[2] Lennox to Richmond, 27 Jan. 1795, *H.M.C. Bathurst*, p. 712.

[3] In Sept. 1795, for example, the Duke and Duchess of Devonshire visited Goodwood. (*Georgiana, Duchess of Devonshire*, ed. the Earl of Bessborough, 1955, pp. 214–15.)

[4] *Public Characters*, p. 171.

believed to have encouraged him in the conspiracy. Lady
Edward's immense unpopularity in Ireland made her seek
refuge at Goodwood even before her husband's death, and
she was joined there shortly by the Duke of Leinster and
two of Lord Edward's sisters.[1]

Richmond knew Lord Edward to be unsteady, possessed
of a weak mind and weaker character, easily led. In 1790
Richmond had obtained the command of a military expedition to Cadiz for him, only to learn the next day that
he could not accept because he had also accepted a seat
from his brother in the Irish Commons binding him to
oppose the government. Two years later the impetuous
young lord was in Paris with Thomas Paine, publicly dis-
carding his title. Four years after that he had become a
leader of the United Irishmen, working in secret for Irish
independence.

The crusader's obsession reinforced by personal ambition
had impelled Lord Edward to join the United Irishmen.
During the regency crisis of 1788 Earl Fitzwilliam, a Portland Whig associated with the Prince of Wales, had
befriended a number of Irish leaders including Thomas
Conolly and the Duke of Leinster, who had supported a
petition to the Prince offering full powers of regency in
Ireland. Upon his nomination as Lord Lieutenant of Ireland
after Portland's coalition with Pitt in 1794 Fitzwilliam
hinted incautiously of his intention to allow a greater
measure of Irish self-government, with particular concessions guaranteed to enhance the prestige of his old friends.
For this indiscretion Fitzwilliam was recalled several months
after he was appointed; when it became clear that the
Leinster and Conolly families would never be in favour with
Fitzwilliam's successor Lord Camden, Lord Edward joined
the agitators for complete Irish independence.

For their cause Richmond had little respect. Commercial
oppression of Ireland he had opposed consistently; but political connexion he considered indispensable to mutual safety.
Any connexion was better than none; in fact, he feared Irish

---

[1] *Lady Holland's Journal*, i. 235–6; Richmond to Wm. Ogilvie, 9 June 1798,
printed in Thomas More, *The Life and Death of Lord Edward Fitzgerald*, 1831, ii.
108–14.

independence so much that in 1780 he had urged Thomas Conolly to oppose unconditionally any demonstrations for independence by the Irish volunteers.[1]

Fifteen years later he was even more urgent in admonishing Conolly to oppose all political concessions to Catholics until the Irish and English Parliaments could be united, since a Catholic-dominated Parliament at Dublin might sever Ireland's connexion with England. In a legislative union, 'The whole argument and justice of the case . . . becomes against them [the Catholics], and the Protestant king, religion, and government may be maintained in Ireland'.[2]

Nevertheless, as head of the family Richmond warmly and unquestioningly accepted an obligation to salvage his sister's fortune, reputation, and morale. To Lady Emily, still in Ireland, and to the other Irish members of the family assembled for protection at Goodwood he eulogized on Lord Edward: 'A more generous, good hearted soul I believe never existed than poor Edward possessed. His faults were errors of imagination but I am sure no man acted more from principle (mistaken as it was) than he did.' Momentarily ardour even overcame pride: in June he called upon Pitt to solicit a delay in Lord Edward's trial, and some time later he wrote him directly to ask that the minister's powers be used to prevent a bill of attainder. By drafting letters for Lady Emily to the King and the Prince of Wales, writing directly to Camden and Lord Clare, the Chief Justice of Ireland, and by signing a petition to the King, Richmond tried, though without success, to prevent the passing of a retroactive bill of attainder depriving Lord Edward's heirs of his estate.[3]

Such efforts attested two changes in the ageing Duke— a mellowing sense of family responsibility, unknown in his treatment of Lady Sarah thirty years before, and, more

---

[1] Richmond to Conolly, 23 Nov. 1780, MS. of Prof. G. H. Guttridge. See Selected Letters.

[2] Richmond to Lady Louisa Conolly, 27 June 1795. Quoted in W. E. H. Lecky, *History of England*, 1892, vii. 134–6.

[3] More, *Edward Fitzgerald*, ii, *passim*. Richmond's letters on the occasion are primarily in the Bunbury MSS. (E18/750/2) and Add. MS. 30,990. Pitt's letter to Grenville, mentioning that Richmond had written, is printed in *H.M.C. Fortescue*, iv. 273.

important, an interest in entering the circle of the Prince of Wales. It was the Devonshire House circle whom Richmond's niece called upon when she came to London on behalf of Lord Edward, and it was the Prince of Wales (and through him the Duke of York) who supported Lady Edward's unsuccessful attempt to inherit her husband's estate. Significantly, when Richmond made a brief return to politics in 1802, it was as a friend of the Prince and his circle in opposition to Pitt.[1]

After the King's refusal to support a bill in 1801 allowing Catholics to hold political office, Pitt had resigned office, giving his promise never to oppose Addington, his successor at the Treasury. Grenville and Dundas had resigned at the same time; but Grenville, leading a party of his own, had gone into open opposition to Addington, while Dundas represented Addington in coalition negotiations with Pitt. In June 1803 Pitt declined to give Addington his promised support any longer. But six months later he also refused a proffered alliance with Grenville, who thereupon negotiated a working alliance with Fox. Consequently when Pitt accepted office again in April he was faced with the combined opposition of Grenville and Fox, since Grenville, advocating the formation of a broad-bottomed ministry, declined to come in without Fox and the King would not see his habitual foe in any cabinet position. Thus Pitt was forced to form a ministry from the only individuals left— the former ministers whom Richmond held most responsible for his own removal in 1795. The Duke of York continued as Commander-in-Chief. Melville was First Lord of the Admiralty. (Richmond, not expecting him to take the Admiralty, had previously said he would not support Pitt if Melville came in as War Minister.[2]) Of the other cabinet members six were hold-overs from Addington's ministry and five were new supporters of Pitt. Richmond scarcely knew any of them. But they were new-comers without influence; to Richmond this was reason enough for expecting Melville's

[1] In Aug. 1801 Richmond referred with great pleasure to meeting the Prince at the Duke of Norfolk's home (Richmond to T. Pelham, 2 Aug. 1801, Add. MS. 33,107, f. 216).

[2] Charles Lennox to Richmond (draft), 6–12 June 1804, Richmond Papers, Dublin, no. 12749.

faction to predominate without Grenville's to offset it, and above all for 'that inordinate ambition of his [Pitt's] (to) make him expect to be sole and only minister to the Exclusion of that just share of influence and power which others have to the full as much and in some cases more claim to than he has'.[1]

The mutual jealousy between Grenville and Melville beginning when Dundas entered the cabinet in 1791, had been intensified in the following decade. At first it was Grenville who complained most heartily of Dundas's pre-eminence. In 1798 Dundas considered that Grenville definitely had the ascendancy in Pitt's mind,[2] while in ministerial negotiations of 1803 Grenville warned, 'If they [the ministers] take in Lord Melville as their sole dependency, it is easy enough to see that ten days will not elapse before he becomes their master'.[3] Moreover, it was no secret that Melville was highly unpopular with Fox's coterie.

Grenville, despite all of Richmond's ill humour over his promotion to the Lords in 1790, had never been one of the Duke's strong enemies in the cabinet. Furthermore his following now included a majority of the former Portland Whigs (though not their leader) with whom Richmond had been on good terms for several years before his dismissal. Finally, through his co-operation with Fox, Grenville had won the patronage of the Prince of Wales. Ordinarily the Prince consorted with Richmond's old antagonist the Duke of York; now, for a brief period the brothers had quarrelled. In September 1803 the Prince of Wales had asked his brother's intervention to obtain a regiment the King had refused him. The Duke refused to jeopardize his own position with the King, angry letters were exchanged, and by May 1804 the brothers' confidential association still had not been resumed. When the King was again reported insane, the Prince claimed to have received extensive information on the King's health from every member of the royal family except the Duke of York.[4]

[1] Richmond to C. Lennox, 12 June 1804, Richmond Papers, Dublin, no. 1273. See Selected Letters.   [2] Furber, Dundas, pp. 103, 122–3.
[3] Grenville to Buckingham, 22 Mar. 1803, Courts and Cabinets of George III, iii. 267.   [4] Buckingham to Grenville, 30 May 1804, H.M.C. Fortescue, vii. 224–5.

The Prince apparently had a high regard for Richmond as a political strategist, although he did not think him a strong enough person to be included in the cabinet. It was enough for Richmond that the Prince of Wales represented at this time the most effective opposition to the Duke of York within the royal family.

Thus, almost by coincidence, in the spring of 1804 Richmond found all of his personal friends under one colour and all of his enemies under another. Equally important, he was able to attack the government on the issue which he knew best—military policy. He had first broken his long parliamentary silence in June 1802, with a speech describing the humiliating peace of Amiens as necessitated solely by incompetence in prosecution of the war, especially in the hiring of mercenary troops for continental fighting. A year later he spoke again, this time opposing the resumption of hostilities.

But personally, Richmond was most concerned about the government's methods of recruiting the armed forces and the directives issued to 'drive' the southern counties in case of invasion. On the latter issue his chance to express opposition came only at the level of the county meeting. Major acts for levelling the countryside, burning crops, and destroying livestock in case of invasion were passed in 1801 and after the resumption of war in 1803. On both occasions Richmond had a Sussex county meeting called to draw up resolutions of protest; on both occasions he wrote in outrage to the Secretary of State. The first of the two meetings was attended by Thomas Pelham who promised to intercede with the Commander-in-Chief and Secretary of State. Possibly as a result Richmond was invited to serve on a committee on the defence of the country, but his participation seems to have terminated in ill feeling after less than a week.[1] At the second meeting a protest was drawn up against the new levy of troops for the county, the £20 penalties imposed for failure to meet the quotas, and the plan for levelling the county in case of invasion.[2] The protest

[1] Richmond to Pelham, 5 Aug., 1 and 7 Sept. 1801, Add. MS. 33,107, ff. 226, 393, and 442; Richmond to Lord Hobart, 14 Aug. 1801, P.R.O. 30/8/171.
[2] Richmond to Pelham, 17 July 1803, Add. MS. 33,111, f. 277.

was shown to the Secretary of State but never presented in Parliament and Richmond never had occasion to debate the directives in the House of Lords.

In Richmond's opinion the nearsightedness demonstrated by the government's civilian directives in case of invasion was equalled by the stupidity manifested in the programmes for raising manpower to meet an invasion emergency. As Lord Lieutenant Richmond was at least in part responsible for the recruitment of the Sussex militia. After the resumption of hostilities with France in May 1803, the total number of militia was ordered to be increased, the regular army was allowed to recruit from it, and the Lord Lieutenants were burdened with the administrative intricacies of drawing up lists of all civilian men eligible for week-end training.[1] In December the Addington ministry brought in a bill attempting to harmonize the existing mass of mutually contradictory military legislation. While debates on the new bill were dragging on with increasing confusion through the spring of 1804, Richmond was preparing a pamphlet setting forth a system of recruiting for militia eleven months each year and allowing the regular army the twelfth month. Combined with this he proposed a programme of exempting civilian volunteers from training at such periods as harvest time.[2] When Pitt replaced Addington in May, he requested a copy of the paper, then turned it over to Dundas who criticized it page by page, implying by his comments that the paper was useless. Without consulting Richmond again or even returning his manuscript, Pitt scrapped the pending legislation and brought in an Additional Force Bill, at odds with every one of Richmond's proposals. Richmond opposed the bill in the House of Lords, refused either to carry out the act in Sussex or to pay the £20 fine demanded for every man short of the quota, and subsequently refused to take orders from inspecting field officers of lower rank than himself, sent to supervise recruitment and drilling of Volunteers. When it was clear that the act had failed to raise the troops

---

[1] For a full discussion of the subject see J. Fortescue, *The County Lieutenancies and the Army, 1803–1814*, 1909, chs. i and ii.

[2] Richmond to Charles Lennox, 12 June 1804, Richmond Papers, Dublin, no. 1273 See Selected Letters.

anticipated, because of the general opposition of Lord Lieutenants to it, Richmond supported Lord King's unsuccessful motion for a committee on the state of defence.

Richmond's speech concerning the Committee of Defence established in 1805 was his last appearance in Parliament. He had re-entered politics with some hopes of returning to a cabinet position if Grenville should replace Pitt or join him. A dinner of leaders of opposition at which 'the Prince of Wales seemed engrossed with the Duke of Richmond' seemed to lend substance to the hopeful anticipation. He confided to his nephew that he might be a minister again.[1] But poor health, declining powers of debate, and the absence of any political influence, even with his nephew, Charles Lennox, who now supported Pitt, or with friends like Thomas Steele who had remained with Pitt after 1795, meant that Richmond was never seriously considered for a cabinet position. In keeping with the principles of his Reform Bill, he declared himself to be above party; what he really meant was that he was outside it and would very much like to be in. With polite gestures he was passed by, and when he died two years later, no party mourned the loss of an elder statesman.

In his last illness the Duke was cared for by Lady Sarah Napier, whose loving attendance made Richmond a gentle patient. There was no sign of the tactless obstinacy which had lost him the companionship of party, the friendship of the King, and the respect of the House of Commons, no sign of the obsessive energy which ebbed at the edge of greatness and made its possessor an eccentric rather than a reformer. But there was just enough obstinacy and just enough narrowness of vision for the might-have-been statesman not to regret, nor indeed, even to realize, what he was.

[1] Buckingham to Lord Grenville, 30 May 1804, *H.M.C. Fortescue*, vii. 224–5.

SELECTED LETTERS

Not including his official correspondence at the Paris embassy, the Southern Department, and the Ordnance, over 1,000 of Richmond's letters survive, nearly all of which are letters from the Duke preserved in the collections of people to whom he wrote. The only explanation for the absence of letters to Richmond seems to be the unexciting one that he threw most of his personal papers away. In 1792 a fire destroyed Richmond House in London, but a contemporary newspaper report of the event, clipped and underlined by the Duke himself, stated explicitly that all his papers were salvaged. Generous collections of papers belonging to the second and fourth Dukes remain at Goodwood along with a diary of the third Duke, scattered financial accounts and a few bits of personal correspondence—particularly with Wolfe in 1757, with Conway over Richmond's marriage to Lady Mary Ailesbury in 1757, and with the Duchess in 1793–5. Had Richmond left any of his political correspondence at Goodwood there is no reason why it should not have survived.

Both in style and in numbers Richmond's existing letters are an index of his political friendships. Stylistically, Richmond's ease can often be detected by his use of metaphor, as when in 1768 he described the political calm to Newcastle as a leap year, or when he wrote to Shelburne in 1780 comparing the ministry to a tooth which must be extracted. Clusters of letters to Newcastle in 1768, Rockingham in 1770–6, and Pitt, 1786 to 1790, augment the stylistic indications of warm political association in those periods. Thus it is largely from the Newcastle, Fitzwilliam, Lansdowne, and Pitt manuscripts that the letters now included have been chosen. But I have also included several singletons —to Dowdeswell or Lord Mahon, for example—which are the tantalizing survivors of correspondence which may also have been extensive.

It is possible to include only a suggestive sample of Richmond's letters, not a comprehensive collection. With great reluctance I have arbitrarily eliminated all letters not bearing directly on Richmond's political career, all family notes, and his 'official' correspondence as Ambassador to France, Secretary of State, and Master-General of the Ordnance, letters to Richmond, letters which have been printed elsewhere, either whole or in large part, and those to be published in the forthcoming *Burke Correspondence*. Beyond these rules I have followed the criteria of instinct, choosing letters for indications of variety in Richmond's associations and in the circumstances of composition, and, equally important, for barometric readings of the moods and interests of their mercurial author.

It remains only to say that I have intentionally kept the Duke of Richmond's own spelling and punctuation wherever possible, adding occasional corrections for clarity.

Richmond to Albemarle

Albemarle MS. L1/1/13 (9)   4 July 1765

In the ministry formed on 30 June, Rockingham was at the Treasury, but Cumberland, who had negotiated the arrangements from 'remnants' of opposition, was virtual head of the government. Albemarle, Richmond's cousin and former guardian, had been Cumberland's close supporter since 1762 and though he held no cabinet position was now his go-between with the rest of the ministry. Richmond had twice offered himself to Cumberland—directly in May and indirectly through Lord Frederick Cavendish at the end of June. This letter, clearly intended to be shown to Cumberland himself, represents a third attempt; four days after writing it Richmond came up to London to talk with Albemarle in person.

Though offering to be a 'silent supporter', Richmond realized that he would be considered for a minor office and was bluffing for a major one. The letter, requesting advice while stating his position firmly, gives early evidence of Richmond's ability to compose masterful letters.

Goodwood, Thursday
July 4th, 1765

My Dear Lord,

I am indeed very happy that my conduct meets with the approbation of H.R.H. I think the King's situation truly to be pitied, and that every good subject is called upon to support His Majesty on this occasion.

The Duke's behaviour throughout the whole raises if possible my admiration for him, tis worthy of him, and I sincerely hope he will pursue this plan of undertaking with his friends the King's business, and after having once saved the nation from destruction, now save the crown from disgrace.

As to myself I thought that writing my thoughts on this occasion would appear busy, but I desired Lord Frederick who was going to London to make them known if he had an opportunity. But since H.R.H. has done me the honor to say he was pleased with them, it now becomes my duty to beg of your Lordship to assure H.R.H. that the utmost of my ambition is to show my attachment to the King on this occasion, and particularly to support an administration formed under H.R.H.'s auspices, and composed of the Whig families, with whom my father was connected, and from whom if I have differ'd in opinion, I have never ceased to esteem.

I cannot express the high sense I have of H.R.H.'s goodness in offering in the arrangement to facilitate any wish of mine relative to myself, but I must beg of your Lordship to do it for me in your own words, which will be far better than any I can offer. I can safely say, you cannot express it stronger than I feel it.

The only wish I have as to myself is to be in that situation where I can be most useful. I flatter myself that your Lordship and my friends will not suspect me of seeking any thing advantageous to myself. Indeed nothing that takes me much from this place, can be at all what I should wish if I consulted my pleasure or my abilities. And if tis thought that my silent support can be of most use to the King's measures I am sure I shall be satisfied. But if in the present crisis when so violent an opposition is to be expected that even some of your friends go off, and most of them are shy and doubtful, my taking a more active part can be of use, I am ready to do it, and can only say for myself that I will not be wanting in zeal and steadiness, and perhaps I might have more influence over some friends. I shall therefore leave this entirely with H.R.H. and your Lordship whose advise upon all occasions I shall be happy to receive, but must beg it now. And it will be a

particular satisfaction to me to be as closely connected with
you in politicks as I am in blood: for it is with the utmost
esteem and regard that I am my dear Lord
Ever your most obedient and sincere humble servant,

RICHMOND.

Richmond to Newcastle

Add. MS. 32,975, f.246   23 May 1766

Newcastle had strongly criticized Richmond's appointment as Secretary of State at a cabinet meeting on 14 May, in letters to Albemarle,
Rockingham, and the Bishop of Oxford, and particularly at a private
audience with the King on 22 May.[1] On the following day, having
characteristically broadcast the details of the audience, he wrote Richmond a letter of congratulation assuming that the young minister was
fully informed of his hostile efforts.[2] ('As I could not concur in the
advice that was given . . . I thought, as an honest man, I would write
him a word so.')[3]

Richmond was aware that Newcastle, who had scarcely been consulted at all, imagined himself an instrumental opponent of the appointment. His astutely diplomatic answer, written immediately upon
receiving Newcastle's message and feigning the sincere supplication of
a novice for the indulgence of a venerable statesman, delighted the old
Duke, who displayed the answer to the King and all of Rockingham's
friends.[4]

Whitehall. May 23rd, 1766

My Dear Lord,
I am honor'd with your Grace's letter of this Morning
and should be very much concerned indeed if the Honor
His Majesty has done me in giving me the seals met with
your Grace's disapprobation from any personal dislike, as
without flattery I can assure Your Grace that no man has a
higher Regard and sincerer Esteem for You than I have,
and of course the not having your good opinion must have
given me great concern; but I am perfectly satisfied that the
meaning of Your Grace's objection was as You say the
troublesome business in the House of Lords which I entirely

[1] Add. MS. 35,975, ff. 225, 203, 187, 254-7.
[2] Add. MS. 32,975, f. 244.
[3] Newcastle to Albemarle, 25 May 1766, Add. MS. 32,975, f. 270.
[4] Ibid., f. 271.

agree with you in thinking myself by no means equal to: I might add the business of office, which I fear I shall not do as I could wish. These Circumstances would undoubtedly have made me decline this employment, had I not hoped that all these disadvantages might be made up by diligence in office, Duty to the King, and the having no view that can draw me from acting with the utmost cordiality with His Majesty's Servants, who are men I have the highest Esteem for and Confidence in And I have been the more determined to undertake this arduous business as I have not I hope stood in the way of, or interfered with any other person whatever. I therefore thought I owed it to my friends to assist them in any post they think me worthy of.

Your Grace's goodness in offering me your assistance is what I most readily accept of, your experience will be of infinite Service and I beg leave to assure Your Grace that I shall always pay to it, that deference which is due to you in every shape. I am with the utmost Esteem and Regard My Lord

Your Grace's most faithfull and obedient humble servant,

RICHMOND.

Richmond to Newcastle

Add. MS. 32,976, f. 25   6 July 1766

Richmond to Newcastle

Add. MS. 32,976, f. 31   (7 July 1766)

Two letters indicating the lack of either preparation or unanimity in the Rockingham ministry before its dissolution. Richmond's first letter was written immediately before a meeting with Rockingham, Dowdeswell, Winchilsea, and Conway, at Richmond House on the evening of the Chancellor's resignation. Rockingham had arrived early and was writing to Newcastle at the same time: unlike Richmond he attributed Northington's resignation to passion rather than design and predicted that the crisis might force the King to obtain an accession of strength for the existing ministry.[1]

[1] Add. MS. 32,976, ff. 19–21. See also *Walpole Memoirs*, ii. 238–9. (Walpole's chronology is correct, but his dating for the period 6–10 July is mistaken.)

Richmond apprehensively wished to prepare constructive proposals for the strengthening of the ministry, should the King press for a plan when he saw the cabinet on the morning of 9 July. But no proposals were agreed upon at the meeting of 6 July,[1] and Richmond's two attempts to obtain a subsequent cabinet discussion before seeing the King were unsuccessful.[2]

Whitehall Sunday 5 o'clock
July 6th, 1766

My Dear Lord,
The Chancellor has been today with the King in a very ill humour saying he cannot attend Councils, and that to keep the seals and not attend would be indecent, he therefore will resign. He did not confine his reasons to the want of communication he complains of, but said he thought the system weak:[3] that it was intended to gain Strength by the disposal of vacant offices, but that nothing was done, and he could not go on so. His Majesty did not seem much disconcerted, but told us, this was so great a diminution of assistance, that altho' he wished us well, he must consider what was to be done. In short My Lord it looks very like a break, and not of our bringing on. Your Grace will I am sure think this material enough to excuse my sending a Messenger with this. I hope you will come to town tomorrow at latest, that we may see together what is to be done. I am My Dear Lord ever with the Sincerest and most perfect Regard
Your Grace's most obedient Humble Servant,
RICHMOND.

(Richmond to Newcastle)   Whitehall. Monday night

My Dear Lord,
I was very much disappointed indeed in arriving at Lord Rockingham's a few minutes after Your Grace was gone as was Mr. Conway. I immediately went to Mr. Onslow's[4] but

---

[1] 'All agreed in not lamenting the approaching crisis' (Rockingham to Newcastle, 6 July 1766, 10 p.m., Add. MS. 32,976, f. 23).

[2] Add. MS. 32,976, ff. 29 et seq.

[3] Northington had known since 5 June (Northington to George III, 5 June Corr. Geo. III, i. 356) of the King's determination not to continue the ministry unchanged.

[4] George Onslow (1731–92), M.P. for Guildford, a Rockingham supporter until 1767, when he went over to Grafton. He later opposed reporting of parliamentary debates, conciliatory overtures to America (1777), and economical reform (1781).

was again too late. Had I had the least idea of Your Grace's intentions of returning to night to Claremont, I would have neglected some people I had appointed to be with me, and have called on You before dinner; but—on so important a crisis, I thought it was necessary we should meet all together, and imagined it could not be till the evening as Mr. Conway as well as I was engaged,[1] and no meeting had been appointed. I am the more vexed at this, as indeed we ought to settle what is to be done, and have time to talk it over, which I fear we shall be pressed for on Wensday Morning, especially if there should be any diversity of opinions. In order however to have as much time as possible Lord Rockingham and Mr. Conway have promised to be here at my house at Eleven in the Morning;[2] I hope Your Grace will not be later. The only news I can inform Your Grace of as certain is that the Duke of York was last night two Hours with Mr. Stone, whom I believe H.R.H. consults a good deal with upon Political affairs.[3]

> I am My Dear Lord with the utmost Esteem and Regard
> Your Grace's Most obedient Humble Servant,
> RICHMOND.

On the morning of 8 July Newcastle answered Richmond's second letter, explaining that he had come to town the day before, expecting a party meeting, only to return to Claremont when he found there was to be no discussion before the ministers saw the King.[4]

[1] Both men visited Horace Walpole in the afternoon. Walpole convinced Conway, but not Richmond, of the advisability of resigning and recommending Pitt for the Treasury (*Walpole Memoirs*, ii. 238).

[2] Newcastle did not come, and no further meeting was held until Wednesday afternoon, 9 July, when Newcastle, Conway, Rockingham, and Richmond met immediately after seeing the King and decided to ask the King his intentions the following day (Richmond's Journal, 9 July; Albemarle, *Rockingham*, i. 362; Rockingham to Portland, 9 July 1766, Nottingham MSS.).

[3] The Duke of York was the King's brother most averse to the Rockingham ministry for their failure to provide for the support of the royal Dukes and was erroneously believed to be negotiating with Pitt. Less than a year later the Duke vehemently supported Rockingham's attack on the Pitt ministry's neglect of Canadian affairs. Andrew Stone (1703–73), formerly M.P. for Hastings and sub-governor to George III as Prince of Wales, was one of Newcastle's private secretaries.

[4] Add. MS. 32,976, f. 35.

Richmond to Rockingham

Fitzwilliam MS. R1–386   8 July 1766

Since rumours were fairly common that Pitt had been summoned, it is difficult to tell how seriously Rockingham took Richmond's information. Richmond's injunction of secrecy originally kept Rockingham from discussing the letter with other members of the ministry, and he was later prevented by the need to feign complete surprise at the King's announcement on 10 July that 'Mr. Pitt had been sent for'. Richmond must have written immediately after receiving the information, since he had seen the Marquis late in the morning. There was probably no written answer to Richmond's letter, since Richmond was to see Rockingham the following day.

My Dear Lord,

I have intelligence that Pitt has been sent to. It comes to me in a very extraordinary way and from one I should give no credit to, if he had not told all that the Chancellor had said to the King and almost in the same words His Majesty used to me. And this on Sunday evening. As he is so right in one instance, tis possible he may be so in the other, and he speaks to it with equal certainty.[1]

If this is so is it not possible that the Duke of York in his late journey to Bath and Bristol, and Lord Egmont in his into Somersetshire may have had some interview with Mr. Pitt.[2]

I confess I suspect my information to be true. But think you had better not communicate it to anyone but Mr. Conway for if it is known and that Mr. Conway's sentiments[3] gett among our friends it will be a race among them who shall go first to Mr. Pitt. Past experience I fear justifies my supposition but too well.

Adieu My Dear Lord. I am ever Most Sincerely Yours,
                                                    RICHMOND.

Tuesday. ½ past two.

[1] There is no evidence as to the person to whom Richmond refers.

[2] There is no evidence of either interview; on the evening of Northington's resignation the King sent for Pitt via Northington, whom Richmond did not suspect.

[3] To resign (see Richmond to Newcastle, 7 July, p. 116, n. 1). Richmond did not tell Conway of the information concerning Pitt's summons. The information led even Richmond to consider resigning. See Brooke, *Chatham Administration*, pp. 22–23.

Richmond to Newcastle

Add. MS. 32,976, f.103   11 July 1766

On 10 July the King had told Newcastle, Rockingham, and the two
Secretaries of State that he had sent for Pitt.[1] Immediately after the
audience Newcastle left for Claremont; the following morning he
wrote almost identical letters to Richmond and Rockingham asking
particularly whether negotiations were being conducted by Camden
and whether Pitt had yet seen the King himself or discussed the intended ministerial changes with General Conway.[2]

Richmond must have replied late in the afternoon: he mentions the
report that Pitt saw the King in the morning, a rumour which was
circulated at the King's levee early in the afternoon. By evening
Richmond had learned definitely that Pitt had not seen the King until
1:00 and was seeing Northington in the evening.

Rockingham still considered the summons to Pitt as merely the
successor to four abortive attempts since January to form an alternative
ministry. Richmond, who had not been in office during the previous
attempts, was clearly chafing in the role of 'quiet . . . spectator'.

Whitehall. Friday 5 o'clock
July 11th, 1766

My Dear Lord,
    I do not indeed wonder at Your Grace's wishing to know
what is going on, for to unconcerned people it must be a
matter of great Curiosity, and as such I believe we may now
look upon ourselves.

But I can give your Grace no manner of information that
can be at all satisfactory, for His Majesty has neither yesterday or today utter'd one word to us about the Change. The
Report today at St. James's was that Mr. Pitt was this morning an hour with the King before the Leve, but one of the
pages assured me it was not so. So that if the meeting has
been, it must have been at Richmond. I am pretty sure
Mr. Conway has not seen Mr. Pitt.[3] The Duke of Grafton

---

[1] Newcastle to Ashburnham, 18 July 1766 (Add. MS. 32,976, f. 52). The King
yielded the information only when pressed by the ministers.

[2] Add. MS. 32,976, ff. 65, 67.

[3] Conway did not see Pitt until 12 July (cf. Richmond's Journal, in Appendix
B, 13 July, and *Walpole Memoirs*, ii. 241–2). The speculation about Conway stemmed
from the King's remark that he wished always to see Conway in his government—
implying that Conway was a participant in the ministerial negotiations (ibid.,
p. 240).

I believe knew nothing of it.[1] Your Grace's information that Lord Camden and the Chancellor negotiated this affair is I believe very true, and very extraordinary unless Lord Camden is to be Chancellor and Lord Northington retire with a pension.[2] The only thing for us all to do in this moment in my opinion, if Your Grace will give me leave to give it is to be perfectly quiet and only spectators, and neither declare a wish for, or against. By this means we shall not be accused of interfering or preventing this great plan from succeeding. And when we see what is intended, we shall be at Liberty to take what part we please.

I believe I have often been accused of being hot, Your Grace will now I hope do me the Justice to say I am cool enough, but tho' I am for being calm and taking time to decide, I hope we shall never take a cool part when we do take one.

I am My Dear Lord, With the sincerest Esteem and true Regard Ever Your Grace's most obedient Humble Servant:

RICHMOND.

Richmond to Newcastle

Add. MS. 32,976, f.277   [26 July 1766]

Both Richmond and Newcastle agreed that members of the Rockingham ministry who were not dismissed by Pitt should keep a party patronage foothold in office. Both, however, resented being singled out particularly for dismissal, and both openly blamed Rockingham's lethargy for the fall of the old ministry. Of the two men, Richmond was more angered: Chatham had supplanted him by Shelburne—the rival he most detested, and had offered instead an embassy, the post he least wanted. Unlike Newcastle, Richmond, still connected with Lord Holland, was not disturbed by the prospect that Pitt might turn to the King's Men in the absence of support from Rockingham.

Richmond had seen Newcastle at court on 25 July[3] but had seen

[1] Grafton expected to see Pitt on 17 July, but Pitt was taken ill and did not see Grafton for nearly a week (Richmond's Journal, 17 July, Goodwood, Small Libr. MS. E).

[2] Northington became President of the Council and Camden Lord Chancellor. Both appointments were so generally anticipated that it is difficult to understand Richmond's ignorance of them.

[3] 'The Duke of Richmond went in first, to whom H.M. did not say one single word relating to Adm[n].' (Newcastle Memorandum, Add. MS. 32,976, f. 235).

the King first and left before Newcastle's audience. Newcastle had gone at once to Claremont and from there written Richmond the same evening asking to be kept informed about ministerial changes and to continue having reports on cabinet business sent him until the Rockingham ministry was formally dismissed.[1]

My Dear Lord,

Whitehall. Saturday morning

As I am as much a Country Gentleman as Your Grace, tho' living at this moment in London, I know as little news as any body. Nothing new has come out since Your Grace was here. The Reports about Chas Townshend vary every hour. I think the last are that he remains Paymaster.[2] James Grenville is talked of for vice treasurer,[3] but nothing appears to be settled more than what was at first declared. I suspect the Great man is waiting for resignations, that he may have it to say he was forced to take the Butes.[4] He was Yesterday with the King a great while at the Queen's House before the Levy. The Duke of Grafton is gone out of town and Mr. Conway talked of going to Park Place till Monday. Your Grace shall have the papers sent to you as usual as long as we remain in place which I hear is to cease on Wensday next.[5] I hope it is needless to add with how much esteem and Real Regard I am My Dear Lord

Your Grace's Most Sincere Humble Servant,

RICHMOND.

Richmond to Newcastle

Add. MS. 32,977, f. 421   [18 November 1766]

On 17 November Conway told Rockingham of the dismissal of Lord Edgecumbe from the treasurership of the Household, with an offer to be Lord of the Bedchamber instead, a junior position for which he was too old. The dismissal, which Newcastle had feared since August, was to make room for Newcastle's cousin Jack Shelley, a new Chatham adherent, member for Newcastle's borough of East Retford, and

---

[1] Add. MS. 32,976, f. 245.
[2] After considerable hesitation about giving up the paymastership (at £7,000) Charles Townshend became Chancellor of the Exchequer (at £2,500).
[3] James Grenville was not included in the new ministry.
[4] Conway had suggested the idea to Richmond at their meeting on 13 July (paper inserted in Richmond's Journal, Goodwood, Small Libr. MS. E).
[5] The ministers were dismissed on Wednesday, 30 July.

automatically up for re-election, subject to Newcastle's approval.[1] Portland[2] and Keppel[3] had already notified Newcastle before Richmond wrote.

The following day Newcastle and Richmond attended a meeting of the party which decided, over Newcastle's opposition, that the four Lords—Portland, Monson, Bessborough, and Scarborough—who had remained in office under Pitt should resign. After an ineffectual attempt by Conway to have Pitt retract the dismissal, the four Lords resigned on 27 November.[4]

Whitehall. Tuesday morning

My Dear Lord,

Altho' Your Grace will certainly hear from other hands and perhaps before the receipt of this, I could not resist writing by Lady Albemarle to inform Your Grace that Lord Edgecumbe received last night his dismission.[5] He was offer'd to be made a 13th Lord of the Bedchamber immediately, which he refused, and persisted in, notwithstanding the Great man sent for him and pressed him to accept, telling him his place had been long ago destined and that it was a determined measure that Mr. John Shelley was to have His Lordship's stick.

I have not yett seen Conway, but Lord Rockingham has, and says he was not apprized of the transaction till yesterday evening, and but a few hours before the letter was wrote to Lord Edgecumbe, and I think that the dismission must have been sent before the answer to Conway's letter could arrive.[6]

[1] Had another of Newcastle's cousins, Thomas Pelham been displaced for Shelley, as Newcastle initially feared, the Duke would not have re-elected Shelley. Since Newcastle had no personal ties with Edgecumbe, he reluctantly planned to agree to Shelley's re-election (Newcastle to Rockingham, 1 Oct. 1766, Add. MS. 32,977, f. 201). For a full discussion of the incident see Brooke, *Chatham Administration*, pp. 52–56.

[2] Add. MS. 32,977, f. 394.   [3] Fitzwilliam MS. R2–86.

[4] For a fuller discussion in printed sources see Williams, *William Pitt*, ii. 246; Albemarle, *Rockingham*, ii. 19–30; *Grenville Papers*, iii. 344–8; *Chatham Correspondence*, iii. 126–30. In manuscripts, see Add. MSS. 32,977, ff. 394–400, 32,977, ff. 1–84; Fitzwilliam MSS. R9–1, 2, R2–86, R1–450, 1; Grafton MS. 777.

[5] George Edgecumbe (1720–95), Baron of Mount Edgecumbe, a faithful Rockingham adherent, former Clerk of the Council of Duchy of Lancaster, and Lord Lieutenant of Cornwall, was appointed Treasurer of Household, P.C., and Commander-in-Chief of Plymouth, 1765; he was later joint Vice-Treasurer (1771), and Admiral of the White (1787), and was created Earl of Mt. Edgecumbe, 1789.

[6] It is difficult to excuse Conway from blame; Conway claimed that he though,

Lord Rockingham says that Conway feels very sensibly
on this occasion, and indeed so he must. He has wrote a long
letter to Lord Chatham but we do not yett know the Contents, or what will be the determination upon it.[1] I think our
friends seem to warm upon this measure, which to be Sure
must open the eyes of those who were not before convinced
of Lord Chatham's insincerity. I was not of that number but
hope Your Grace will always permit me to be among Your
most sincere friends as it is with the truest Regard that I am,
My Dear Lord, Your Grace's Most Obedient and most
Humble Servant,

RICHMOND.

Do's Your Grace intend to rechuse Mr. Shelley?

Richmond to Newcastle

Add. MS. 32,980, f. 366   [22 March 1767]

On 26 February the Bedfords, Grenvilles, Rockinghams, and some
followers of Chatham under pressure from constituents combined to
defeat the government on Dowdeswell's motion to lower the land tax
from 4s. to 3s.[2] The motion was irresponsible, but popular, and a few
Grand Juries moved thanks to their M.P.'s for supporting it.[3]

On 19 March, the day before Richmond left London for the Easter
vacation at Goodwood, he left with Newcastle a proposition that the
Grand Jury in Sussex thank their representatives. The idea was not his;
he forwarded it only as a formality. Newcastle answered on 20 March,
opposing the proposition because 'everyman may start a disagreeable
thing in a Grand Jury, who can do no Hurt in the County. It may put
it in the Head of some Lively Genius to give instructions; Or, at any
Time, to observe upon the Votes, and Behaviour of their Members,
which would not be pleasant'. Newcastle sent his letter first to Richmond House, mistakenly assuming that Richmond had remained in
London.[4]

at an earlier time he had talked Pitt out of dismissing Edgecumbe (Rockingham to
Scarborough, 20 Nov. 1766, Albemarle, *Rockingham*, ii. 19), but his opposition had
characteristically been too weak to be effective. He must have realized then that the
subject had not been dropped.

[1] On 17 Nov. The date is erroneously assumed to be 22 Nov. in the *Chatham
Correspondence*, iii. 126.

[2] See Albemarle, *Rockingham*, ii. 34–43; *Chatham Correspondence*, iii. 222–5;
Grenville Papers, iv. 211–12.

[3] *Public Advertiser*, 7 May 1767.

[4] Add. MS. 32,980, f. 354.

Goodwood. Sunday night

My Dear Lord,

I have just received Your Grace's letter and am much obliged to you for it. What I had heard was only the single opinion of one Gentleman, and he did not mention it as a thing he had determined upon, but as what he thought would be right if any other person proposed it, as he is no orator I am persuaded he will not propose it himself. But at all events the methods Your Grace has taken will put a stop to it, which I entirely agree with Your Grace in thinking very proper to do. I am not more explicit as I write by the post but Your Grace will understand me. I have not sent to the person who spoke to me, as if he means to be present, my letter to him would certainly be too late. He must be sett out before this. I am much concerned to hear of Mr. Pelham's indisposition but hope it will not be anything of Consequence.

My journey here was a little sudden but as I am always in the Country on Lady-Day for a very good purpose, to receive Rent and dine with my Tenants, I was glad to gett a few days before, to hunt and have got the Duke of Devonshire,[1] Lord Fred; and Lord John Cavendish, Lord Carlisle,[2] My Sister Sarah and the Dutchess with me. All but the Duke of Devonshire and the Dutchess of Richmond return to London to morrow. The Lords Cavendish left town on Friday after the House of Commons and return so as to be there on Monday, this Your Grace will allow is alert to gett two Hunting days and yett not miss one day in Parliament.

I propose returning to London on Thursday if I hear of any thing worth attending to, if not I shall stay till Sunday.[3]

Your Queen as you are pleased to call her is much obliged to Your Grace for remembering her. She desires me to

1 William Cavendish (1748–1811), Duke of Devonshire, was later Lord High Treasurer of Ireland, Governor of County Cork, 1776, Colonel in Army during service, 1779, K.G., 1782. After Rockingham's death Devonshire was one of Fox's best known supporters.

2 Frederick Howard (1748–1825), Earl of Carlisle, K.T., 1767, later Treasurer of Household, and P.C., 1777, Commissioner to treat with America, 1778, President of Board of Trade, 1779, Lord Lieutenant of Ireland, 1780–2, Privy Seal, 1783, K.G., 1793. Though Carlisle and Richmond differed widely over the American War, they remained close friends until 1783.

3 Richmond returned to Parliament on 30 Mar.

assure you of her best Compliments and that you will make them acceptable to the Dutchess of Newcastle, to whom I also beg of Your Grace to present my Respects. I am Ever

My Dear Lord, Your Grace's most obedient Humble Servant,

RICHMOND.

P.S. I have just recollected that my best way is to send this letter by Lord Frederick Cavendish, so that I need not have been so prudent. The Subject of the first part of my Letter Your Grace will easily have seen is Mr. Bettesworth's[1] idea of the Grand Jury's thanking the Members for the County for voting for the 3rd land tax.

Richmond to Newcastle

Add. MS. 32,984, ff. 208–9   7 August 1767

Burke, visiting Goodwood early in August, found Richmond unwavering in personal respect for Rockingham, but uncertain about his own activity in the next parliamentary session.[2] Richmond's letter to Newcastle significantly illustrates his dissociation from the party, encouraged by his realization that the party held him partially responsible for the failure of the Bedford negotiations.

Richmond may have intended to sound Newcastle on the opinion of Rockingham's friends who had met at Claremont on 1 August;[3] his own opinions expressed in his letter had been thoroughly discussed with Newcastle on 26 July when Richmond visited Claremont on his way to Goodwood.[4] The two men had 'parted friends' and Newcastle was delighted with the renewed confidence.

The major part of the letter concerns the county meeting at Lewes on 19 August, to nominate the M.P. for Sussex.

Goodwood. August 7th, 1767

My Dear Lord,

I am much obliged to Your Grace for Your letter, and can inform you that almost every man I have spoke to has promised to be at Lewes; but not knowing how far it might

---

[1] Possibly William Bettesworth, of Rogate, a supporter of Richmond in Chichester.

[2] Burke to Rockingham, 18 Aug. 1767, *Burke Correspondence*, i. 138.

[3] *Public Advertiser*, 1 Aug. 1767.

[4] Newcastle to Keppel, 26 July 1767, Add. MS. 32,984, f. 58.

be agreable to Your Grace to have *every body* at Halland,[1]
I desired them to be at Lewes only for the 19th. However I
am still in time to acquaint several of Your Grace's kind
invitation, and shall certainly bring those who go with me.

The Duke of Dorset and Mr. Sackville will be at Lewes if
His Grace's Health will permit.[2] Lord Halifax I doubt will
be absent, he seem'd to have a mind to come too, but some
reason or other (which I believe may be guess'd at) keeps
him away.

I found in a news paper an advertisement about Lewes
which I inclose lest Your Grace should have overlook'd it.
I suppose it is something as idle as that for the County was
in the Winter.

I know of no Political News but that Lord Townshend goes
to Ireland and that the Townshends expect a green Riband
for the Duke of Bucleugh and a Peerage for Lady Dalkeith.[3]

This I have from good authority tho' not from Conway.
I have not heard from him since I left London, but am not at
all angry with him for it, and I hope he is not so with me
for differing a little in opinion with him.[4] I also hope my
other friends are not displeased with me for not agreeing
with them. My situation is indeed odd enough, differing a
little from all of you[5] and yett having the highest and truest

1 Newcastle had asked Richmond and his 'western gentlemen' to dine with him
at Halland before the meeting.

2 Charles Sackville (1710–69), Duke of Dorset, had been M.P. for East Grinstead,
1734–42, Sussex, 1742–7, Old Sarum, 1747–54, East Grinstead, 1761–5, a Lord of
the Treasury, 1743–7, Master of the Horse to the Prince of Wales, 1747–51, P.C.,
Feb. 1766, and was Lord Lieutenant of Kent, 1766–9.

John Frederick Sackville (1745–99), nephew and heir of the Duke, was M.P. for
Kent, 1768–9, Lord Lieutenant of Kent, 1769–97, later Ambassador to Paris,
1773–89, nom. K.G., 1788, Lord Steward of the Household, 1789–99.

3 Lord Townshend, elder brother of Charles Townshend, was appointed Lord
Lieutenant of Ireland to replace the incumbent Lord Bristol, who declined going to
Ireland itself. Charles Townshend's wife, daughter of the Duke of Argyll and
Greenwich, had married first the Earl of Dalkeith, son and heir of the Duke of
Buccleugh. After the death of Dalkeith in 1750, and of Buccleugh in 1751, her son
became Duke of Buccleugh. On 28 Aug. 1767, four days before Townshend's
death, the Countess of Dalkeith was created Baroness Greenwich in her own right,
and on 23 December the Duke of Buccleugh was nominated Knight of the Thistle.

4 Richmond had criticized Conway's refusal to serve in any ministry with George
Grenville, whose connexion with Bedford both men overestimated. Both Rockingham and Conway opposed Richmond's repeated suggestions of alliance with the Butes.

5 On 18 Aug. Burke wrote of Richmond: 'He cannot be pursuaded of the propriety of not accepting the late offers, or at least of not having gone further than you

Regard for you. And tis particular enough that I who am reckon'd warm and hot, think you all in extremes, and could have wished that we had all gone a little father to meet. I mean the Marquis and the Duke of Grafton etc., who I believe did seriously mean to agree. And if it could have been brought about I do think great advantages would have arose to the Country and to the Party.

As to the Bedfords I must say I saw, and was sorry to see that they were then entirely governed by Mr. Grenville's politicks,[1] and I think the surest way to have got them would have been for the Marquis to have agreed with the Duke of Grafton.

We have now I think no prospect but confusion for some years at least! God grant some good may come of it.

Your Grace sees I write very freely, I am sure you will approve of it, altho' you may not agree with me in every point; but as my opinion influences no body and does not make me the less attached to my friends I trust Your Grace will not be displeased with me for it, for I must assure you that I am ever With the Sincerest Regard My Dear Lord Your

Grace's most obedient Humble Servant,

RICHMOND.

Though Newcastle was clearly pleased with Richmond's confidence, he urged in reply that without the Bedford alliance Rockingham would have entered office merely as a tool of the King. The rest of his letter described the friendly letters he had received from Halifax and Dorset explaining their extended absence from the Lewes election.[2]

Richmond to Rockingham

Fitzwilliam MS. R1–565   13 December 1767

By attempting to retain his friendships in the Rockingham party and his place in the ministry of Pitt, Conway had split Rockingham's party

did to put all ministers in the wrong by driving them to avow more of a closet system than they admit publicly' (Burke to Rockingham, 18 Aug. 1767, *Burke Correspondence*, i. 138).

[1] Grenville actually had only a tenuous connexion with Bedford through the unreliable Rigby.

[2] 10 Aug. 1767, Add. MS. 32,984, ff. 239–40.

so widely that periferal members (Newcastle, Hardwicke at one extreme, Richmond and the Cavendishes at the other) were virtually in
open disavowal of Rockingham himself. Yet Rockingham continued
to give the appearance of good relations with the General. Scarcely
understanding Rockingham's feelings, and unaware of rumours circulating in London of a Grafton–Bedford coalition to which Conway
was to be the voluntary sacrifice, Richmond wrote this ill-timed reprimand. In a letter of 14 December the Marquis sarcastically reassured
Richmond: yes, he had done his duty and paid Conway his call; he
could now enjoy a gentlemanly wish that rumours of Conway's
predicament might prove true.[1]

Goodwood. December 13th, 1767

My Dear Lord,

I have but a moments time to save the post and yett must
write to scold you heartily for not returning Conway his
visit, when you had told me you would go to see him even
before you expected he would call upon you. Surely whatever
either of you may feel, tis wisest to keep up forms at least,
that your coming together may not be render'd impractic-
able. That you may is my only wish, as I think it the only
sensible plan, exclusive of my real friendship for you both,
and who knows but the time may be near at hand. I may be
mistaken, but I think I see a glimmering of light. Pray
therefore be friendly at least in appearance to the world.

I must have done or I shall be too late.

Adieu My Dear Lord. I am ever most heartily and
sincerely yours

RICHMOND.

Richmond to Newcastle

Add. MS. 32,989, f. 294   3 April 1768

On 28 March John Wilkes had been elected to Parliament from
Middlesex, and five days later he left for Bath to await consideration of
an outlawry sentence by the King's Bench.[2] Richmond had left London on 10 March and thereby missed all of Wilkes's tumultuous
electoral campaign.

---

[1] Fitzwilliam MS. R9–8. In Lady Rockingham's hand—to the Duke of Portland
or the Duke of Richmond.
[2] For Wilkes's campaign see Bleackley, *Wilkes*, pp. 180–202.

During Rockingham's administration Richmond had known of a ministerial bribe to keep Wilkes out of the country, though he had not subscribed to it; he now supported Wilkes only as a new issue on which to embarrass the government. He took very little interest in Wilkes's petitioning movement and no interest at all in the accompanying movement for parliamentary reform.

The argument over Wilkes was the beginning of Richmond's split from Lord Holland, who supported Luttrell.[1] With Newcastle, however, Richmond's friendship steadily grew, as attested by fifteen affectionate letters, mostly concerning local patronage, exchanged between the two between April and November, when the old Duke died.

Goodwood. April 3rd, 1768

My Dear Lord,

I beg leave to enquire after Your Grace's Health and that of the Dutchess of Newcastle, and hope that the compleat unanimous success we have met with in the West of Sussex will in some measure make up for the disappointment at Lewes;[2] I can safely assure Your Grace You have in this part of the County to the full as many friends as ever, and as hearty. Mr. Wilkes' success is an event which I think must produce somethink. I should be glad to know Your Grace's sentiments upon it. For my part I confess that though I hate a mob that rises against law and acts by force, I am not sorry the ministry should see that there is in the people a spirit of liberty that will shew itself on proper occasions, as in the choice of their members. For whatever men may think of Mr. Wilkes' private character he has carried his election by being supposed a friend to liberty, and I think it will shew the administration that though they may buy Lords and Commons and carry on their measures smoothly in Parliament yett they are not so much approved of in the nation.

But Your Grace will judge of these Events much better than I can, and I shall be happy to learn Your Sentiments. I hope Mr. Pelham got safe to London, he made us all

---

[1] See Riker, *Henry Fox*, ii. 299.

[2] Newcastle's candidate, Combe Miller, was defeated by Colonel Hay and Mr. Hambden. Newcastle admitted the defeat 'might easily have been prevented if the Duke of Newcastle's friends had had proper attention and had taken due care of his interest' (Newcastle to Rockingham, 17 Mar. 1768, Add. MS. 32,989, f. 198).

very happy here, and I will venture to say that the more he is known the better he will be liked.[1]

I am My Dear Lord Ever Your Grace's most obedient and faithfull humble servant,

RICHMOND.

Newcastle expressed his entire agreement with Richmond the following day in a letter virtually echoing his words and urging a visit at Newcastle House whenever Richmond was on his way to London.[2]

Richmond to Rockingham

Fitzwilliam MS. R1–650   10 March 1769

For the entire spring Richmond did not attend Parliament, although he was frequently in London. He was not especially occupied with Goodwood, Chichester, or his militia; his 'nameless disposition' seems to have been a psychological depression following an illness in January. He contented himself with entertaining relatives at Goodwood and semi-seriously planning a continental trip which did not materialize until August.[3] Rockingham's letter may have hinted at the desirability of Richmond's return to Parliament. Richmond's answer culminates the first development of his personal devotion for Rockingham, while indicating the formal relations the two men still observed.

Richmond had been in London from 20 January until 6 March and must have talked to Rockingham near 1 March about the vote on payment of the King's debt, on which he returned the proxy. He returned to London for the last two weeks of March and again for the end of April. He wrote to Rockingham at least twice more in the spring, giving his proxy on one Militia Bill and extending an invitation to visit Goodwood.[4]

Goodwood. March 10, 1769

My Dearest Lord,

I am much obliged to you for recollecting the Proxy and

---

[1] Richmond had seen Pelham at the East Grinstead Assizes on 21 Mar. (Richmond to Newcastle, 20 Mar. 1768, Add. MS. 32,989, f. 230) and had returned immediately for the county elections in Chichester. Pelham probably stayed at Goodwood house during the election.   [2] Add. MS. 32,989, f. 299.

[3] Originally Richmond planned to leave in the middle of March to visit the Bentincks and spend the summer in Geneva (Caroline Fox to Emily, Duchess of Leinster, 27 Feb. 1769, Corr. of E. Duchess of Leinster, p. 565. Thomas Conolly to Duchess of Leinster, 7 Mar. 1769, Fitzgerald Corr. Misc. Addenda, Irish Nat. Library, Dublin). The trip was put off by a visit to Goodwood by Lady Louisa Conolly, Lord Holland's hesitation to take Lady Cecilia, who was dying of consumption, to Paris to meet Richmond, and the elopement of Lady Sarah Bunbury with Lord William Gordon (Corr. of Lady Louisa Lennox, Bunbury MS. E. 750, Bury St. Edmunds).   [4] 27 Apr. and 7 May, Fitzwilliam MS. R1–651 and R1–654.

sending it me; I have sign'd it and return it enclosed, begging you will have it enter'd for yourself. My reason for begging this so particularly is that I have always been very much against proxies and have never given one before; but am glad to deviate from my general principles in this particular to shew the world, (or rather yourself who alone are acquainted with my opinion on this head) the implicit confidence I have in you. And indeed I do hope the World will see it, as a mark of the sincere esteem, good opinion and friendship which you have on every occasion made me conceive for you. I am very sorry I have it not in my power in more essential points to be of some real use to your Lordship, for I should be happy to make some Return for the many kind acts of Friendship I have receiv'd from you. I have, unhappily, hitherto thrown away my esteem on those who have been unworthy of it and should now be glad to make some amends by doing justice to the few Honest men I know; but in the present situation of my mind I doubt I can do little more than wish you well and profess the Esteem I have for you.[1] The good opinion of your friends is what you are so much used to, that it may appear of little consequence but I know that you set more value on it than on things of more apparent advantage. Mine is God knows sincere and disinterested, but is no compliment from a man whose discernment proves to be so bad.

It gave me great pleasure to hear you had exerted Yourself to speak in the House,[2] and I am particularly pleased that you returned to the charge the second day and replied,[3] for it gives me hopes that you will get rid of that ill placed timidity which has hitherto chequed you. Indeed my Dear Lord you owe it to yourself, to your friends and to the cause

[1] A flattery unusual for Richmond, and indicative of a still formal relationship with Rockingham. He may refer to Holland, who opposed Wilkes, as the friend on whom he had thrown away affection.

[2] On 2 Mar., opposing a ministerial address which stated the willingness of the Lords to pay the King's debts (£513,000) 'even Lord Rockingham attempted, though under great perturbation, to open his mouth; and, being very civil and very gentle, he was well heard' (*Walpole Memoirs*, iii. 228).

[3] On the following day the Opposition demanded papers concerning civil list expenses under Bute and succeeding administrations (presumably to indicate that Bute had used the civil list to 'bribe highest' and Rockingham had used it least). Rockingham spoke with 'spirit unusual to him' (ibid., p. 230).

which you stand at the head of, to deliver those sentiments in public which have made you so many private friends. I will not say all I think because I dread the idea of flattery which it might have the appearance of, tho' I trust you would not accuse me of it. But be assured you cannot speak too often, practice will make it easy to you, you will do yourself credit, the cause good, and take away the only objection your enemies can raise against you as a minister.

The division of 26 on so very courtly a point as paying his Majesty's debts and enabling him to bribe higher is I think a very strong one, and although I am sorry to observe that the national importance of a question seldom makes so much difference in votes in the House of Lords as it does in the House of Commons, yet one must hope that it will not always be so and any point can detach a courtier one should think the Nullum Tempus would.[1]

I entirely agree with you in thinking the times require every exertion of publick spirit, and even I feel a desire of attending this bill if it is opposed, but as I know that I could not be of the least service, and should only suffer most exceedingly I trust I shall be forgiven staying away. You will do me the justice to say that I have not hitherto spared myself and you have seen to how little purpose! If this was the case when my spirits were good, how little reason have I to hope that I could not do any good. Indeed My Dear Lord I must for some time at least indulge myself in my present disposition which I will give no name to. I will hope that time will wear it out, (crossing out, erasure illegible).

Adieu My Dear Lord, I trust you know me to be most sincerely yours,

RICHMOND.

Richmond to Rockingham

Fitzwilliam MS. R158–44   12 February 1771

Lady Rockingham had been taken ill in December and was moved to Bath, where she remained too ill for Rockingham to leave her until March. In the interim (and during the illness of Portland, who would

---

[1] Sir George Savile's bill to secure ownership of land after sixty years' possession (see Richmond's letter to Portland, 21 Feb. 1771, Portland MSS.).

have been Rockingham's first choice) Richmond, eager for experience but afraid to be considered usurping Rockingham's position, took over leadership of the party. At the time the Rockingham and Chatham factions, convinced that ministerial offers were unlikely and a union of opposition groups therefore not essential, were engaged in an irresponsible quarrel over Dowdeswell's bill for restoring the rights of juries in determining cases of libel;[1] in vain Richmond attempted to divert their energies instead to an attack on the cabinet's inadequate demands on the Spanish government after an attack on Falkland Islands by the Governor of Buenos Aires the previous June.[2] Richmond's discussions with Chatham on 1 February in the Lords, on 2 February at Chatham's home, with Manchester, Savile, Montague, Germaine, Lords John and George Cavendish and Brook at Manchester's home on 3 February, and with Camden, Chatham, Lord John, and Dowdeswell on 4 February, all reached a deadlock over Dowdeswell's bill.

This letter concerns private talks between Richmond and Chatham on 5 February. Rockingham, clearly less interested in the general discussions about a union of opposition factions than in the fate of Dowdeswell's Enacting Bill and uncertain from one of Dowdeswell's letters whether Richmond would defend or sacrifice the bill,[3] had intended to come to London to support its immediate presentation and was prevented from doing so only by Lady Rockingham's relapse.[4] He did not receive Richmond's letter until 14 February and immediately wrote Dowdeswell with obvious relief, 'The Duke of Richmond's letter gave me the satisfaction of seeing he thinks we should proceed in our own Mode.'[5]

Whitehall, Tuesday morning
feb: the 12th 1771

My Dear Lord,
I thought the Bath Stages went and came in one day, and

---

[1] During the trial of Woodfall, publisher of the *Public Advertiser*, for libel in June 1770, Lord Mansfield had instructed the jury to determine only upon the fact of publication and not upon the criminality of the libel. Dowdeswell's bill would have made such a limitation upon the jury illegal for the future; Chatham would have declared that Mansfield had already acted illegally. (For background see Williams, *William Pitt*, pp. 275-7, and W. S. Holdsworth, *A History of English Law*, 1903, vii. 342-5.)

[2] See Julius Goebel, *The Struggle for the Falkland Islands*, 1927, pp. 275-7, and J. F. Ramsay, *Anglo-French Relations*, 1763-70. University of California Publications in History, XXVII, no. 3, 1939, chs. iv, v, vii-x.

[3] 8 Feb. 1771. Fitzwilliam MS. R1-126-14. Rockingham had not heard from Richmond since 1 Feb. (Fitzwilliam MS. R158-43).

[4] Rockingham to Dowdeswell, 11 and 14 Feb. 1770, Fitzwilliam MSS. R1-770 and 771.　　　　　　　　　　　　　　　　[5] Fitzwilliam MS. R1-771-1.

therefore proposed sending you a Proxy (which Lord Fitz-william told me you desired) by Monday's Coach. The Letter you sent him desiring the Proxy might go by Saturday night's post was not sent here till ½ past Eleven that night, so that it was impossible then to get a Proxy and send it you by the Post.

But I think it of so much Consequence, that your sentiments should be known and Your Vote given upon this occasion, that I send my Servant with this Letter inclosing a Proxy as you desired.[1]

Pray dont keep him too long, for in this snow He will not be able to travel fast, and I must have the Proxy by 12 o'clock on Thursday to get it enter'd before prayers.

I am not sorry that this opportunity offers of writing to you in a safe manner, that I may give you an account of many Things here.

I shall first thank Your Lordship for Your Letter of the 6th instant which contains exceeding good observations on the Declaration, in one point only You are mistaken where you say the Spaniards have no Spanish name for these Islands, tis true the Spanish Ambassador has not in the Declaration but by the Papers it appears that the Governor calls them the *Magellan Islands*.[2] Your observation upon the Restitution of *Fort and Port Egmont* not of the *Falkland's Islands* is a very just one,[3] and your remark that the Spaniards may now settle in another part of the Island without breaking this Declaration is very true. This Point we thought once of putting into one of our Resolutions, but upon considering it, we thought it might have the appearance of encouraging the Spaniards to break the Peace, and therefore not fit to stand as a Resolution, but very proper for Discourse. There is another curious Thing worth observing, but which for the same Reason must not be in a Resolution, viz: that Lord Rochford's acceptance is in other words than

[1] Rockingham wanted to send the proxy for Thursday, 14 Feb., when the papers relative to the Falkland Islands were to be considered.

[2] The Governor of Buenos Aires may have referred to the islands as the Magellan Islands by mistake, since they were 350 miles from the Straits of Magellan, but the Spanish generally called them the Malouines.

[3] In the Declaration Spain agreed to the restitution of Port Egmont but did not admit British claims to the rest of the islands by right of prior discovery.

the Declaration,[1] and therefore the King of Spain may refuse to ratify, upon that Ground, and it is not impossible he may for the secret is thought to be, that France absolutely refused to join in the war and pressed Spain so much to accomodate that at last the King of Spain said, well I leave it to be settled by my Brother *the King of France, I trust my Honor in his Hands* and accordingly Mons: Francois obliged (Masserano) to sign the Declaration[2] which He did with Tears in His eyes. So it is not impossible the K. of Spain may be glad of an excuse to break this off.

Your Lordship will see by our Resolutions which I inclose, the other Parts which we mean to attack upon and I wish you would send me a short Letter with Reasons, or at least a directory Letter without reasons for using your Proxy in Support of these Resolutions, and in opposition to any address of Compliment upon this occasion. I could wish Your leave to read such Letter in the House, or at least to say that I had Your Directions how to use Your Proxy, which I would use on this great occasion only, For I have in general great objections to giving, and receiving them. They are a most usefull engine to all Administrations,[3] but a very bad and dangerous one; that which may be clearly right in the Judgement of those present by a great Majority, may be over-ruled by the Proxies of foreign Ambassadors and Governors at Petersburg and at Virginia, and I think some day of making an attempt to abolish them, at least in Part, that is that they shall not be given if out of the Kingdom, nor without Reasons sign'd by the Giver of the Proxy and for one particular Business.

I should therefore wish to use Your Proxy only on *this* occasion, and by particular Directions. And in this manner I think it right to use it, that as Your opinion has great weight with a great many People both within and without Doors, it may be known.

[1] For a comparison of the Spanish Declaration and Rochford's acceptance, see Goebel, *Falkland Islands*, pp. 358–9. The Spanish King accepted the Declaration on 8 Feb.

[2] There is some basis for Richmond's report. On 20 Dec. Louis XV wrote Charles III strongly urging peace. Prince Masserano, the Spanish Ambassador to Great Britain, had been taking orders indirectly from Choiseul, involving a reduction in the Spanish demands. See Ramsay, *Anglo-French Relations*, pp. 225–6.

[3] Cf. Richmond to Rockingham, 10 Mar. 1769; proxies usually ran in the ratio of 5–1 in the government's favour.

I cannot say how much I regret on every occasion the illness of Lady Rockingham and its tedious Continuation. The miserable feelings and continual anxiety which must be on Your Mind, are by far the most grievous part; but permit me also to lament it on account of Politicks which Your Absence is a great check to. Your Presence is greatly wanted both for Your opinion how to proceed as Business arises, and to speak to People and keep them together.

Dowdeswell, Lord John, and Burke have pressed me very much to stay in town and in some degree to supply Your Place. I confess I am much averse to it, from the idea that (not you or our very particular Friends will have but that) others may entertain, that in Your absence I am setting up for myself and endeavouring to draw the lead into my own Hands. I talked with Keppel upon this Subject and He agreed with me that it was much to be wished upon my own account that no such Business or employment should fall to my Lot, as could give the smallest Suspicion of such a design, and yet when we came to talk the matter over with Lord John, Dowdeswell, and Burke, they thought it absolutely necessary that I should call the Meeting to consult upon Business at my House that I should speak to people to attend, and now and then give dinners, in short put myself in a Situation liable to the Construction I fear, for that otherwise in your Absence no Business could be done and opposition must break. I felt the Truth of this and have therefore risked the imputation knowing it will not come from those whose Esteem is worth having, and knowing that my future Conduct will convince the world, that I have no Ambition to supersede You; the little I see of it, makes me think it no tempting situation, and I beg leave to say I have too sincere a Friendship for You not to act in the most punctilious Manner. I thought it necessary to say this much to you lest you should think my being so meddling was of my own accord, and as your Friendship to me has ever been (exclusive and inclusive of Politicks) of the highest Sort, I cannot bear the most distant Idea of being thought a Betrayer. But I have done upon this Subject.

The Spanish papers were read in both Houses Yesterday sevnight, that is Monday. On the next Day, Tuesday, I called a meeting of both Lords and Commons to consider of them. About 23 out of 30 came: (Barry)[1] was here as was Serjeant Glynn.[2] Dunning[3] sent an Excuse on acct. of Business. Pulteney[4] sent an excuse that having conceiv'd differently of the Peace than our Friends did, He could not attend. He added that he had the highest opinion of us, and had no thoughts of acting with the present Ministers, but on such great occasions thought it right to follow the best opinion he could form. I did not ask Sir Wm. Meredith.[5] The Persons present I send a List of. All agreed in damning the Peace and finding great faults with the whole Negotiation, but in not starting any thing that would tend to break it. The whole of the Business was fully discussed: no differences of opinion, but all good humour and zeal. It was then agreed that Dowdeswell should draw up the Resolutions upon a plan He had proposed, and that we should meet again here on the *Sunday* following,[6] which we did. The same people attended as before, except Barry, who did not send an excuse, and who had rather found fault with the rough draft that Dowdeswell had shewn him as being not strong enough. At the meeting, several amendments and alterations were made, and I send you the Result.

There are however still a few alterations to be made, and the Copier has I believe by Mistake taken the wrong one of two Resolutions proposed to wind up the whole. There was a short and a long one. He has taken the short, whereas we agreed upon the long one which has a recapitulation of the Facts.

[1] It is clear from the lists attached that Richmond was referring to Colonel Isaac Barre.

[2] Sergeant John Glynn (1722–79), Sergeant-at-Law, was counsel for Wilkes in 1763 and 1768, for Almon in 1765, and Alderman Townshend in 1772, M.P. for Middlesex since 1768, and member of the Society of the Bill of Rights. In 1772 Glynn was elected Recorder of London.

[3] John Dunning (1731–83), M.P. for Calne, had been Solicitor-General under Chatham and Grafton. He was created Baron Ashburton and Chancellor of the Duchy of Lancaster in the second Rockingham ministry.

[4] William Pulteney (1721–1805), M.P. for Cromarty, was the nephew of Governor Johnstone.

[5] Sir William Meredith (1725–90), M.P. for Liverpool, had been a Lord of the Admiralty in the first Rockingham ministry. He went over to the government as Comptroller of the Household, 1774–7, and afterwards retired from politics.

[6] 10 Feb.

We expect the Ministers will start first and move an address of thanks. We shall endeavour to get the Lead, but in the Lords they may do as they please, as the House determines who shall speak first, but in the Commons it is the Speaker[1] (who is at present out of humour) and may call to Dowdeswell first. The Debate and Division may perhaps be as strong against a fulsome Address as upon the Resolutions, but we must have the Resolutions stand on the Journals. Our Protest will be founded upon the Resolutions and I have great Hopes the City will address the King and make use of our Words.[2] Wilkes sent to me for this purpose saying he intended proposing an Address and asking my advice, declaring he meant to follow it. I sent him for answer, that, I thought nothing could give more weight to opposition and to the City, than the appearance of union and acting together. That therefore I thought His meeting which was to have been on Friday last, should be postponed till our Effort had been made in Parliament, that we should take the Lead and the City follow and that after our Resolutions had been attempted and our Protest enter'd, They should address the King and nearly copy our words. This would shew Concert, and add weight to both. He sent me for answer that he would implicitly follow my advice and accordingly did put off the Business til ours is over. I shall be very cautious how I proceed with him.

Your Lordship will not be sorry to hear of the proceedings of Yesterday. Sr. Wm. Meredith in the H. of C. moved his amendment to the Nullum Tempus Bill.[3] it turned out luckily that Lord Carlisle and the D. of Marlbro' thought

---

[1] Sir Fletcher Norton had been Speaker since Jan. 1770.

[2] The city did not address the King on this occasion.

[3] In Dec. 1767 the Treasury granted Sir James Lowther a crown interest in the forest of Inglewood and the socage manor of Carlisle, properties the Portland family had claimed for over sixty years as part of the unspecified 'appurtenances of Penrith' granted to the Earl of Portland by William III. In 1769 a bill presented by Sir George Savile was passed abrogating the maxim of 'Nullum Tempus occurit Regi' on which the crown interest had been granted to Sir James, but leaving a loophole allowing Sir James to prosecute for the properties within a year. Sir William Meredith's bill repealing the loophole clause was thrown out of the Commons on the third reading, 25 Feb. 1771, but when the trial finally came on in November Sir James was non-suited on a technicality. In two letters to Portland, 21 and 22 Feb. 1771 (Nottingham MSS.), Richmond urged the need of obtaining Lord Camden's support should Sir William's bill reach the House of Lords.

their Interest still more concerned in this Business than the D. of Portland's,[1] and therefore took a warm part. Lord Charles Spencer[2] seconded the Motion, and the Bedfords were with us (Rigby alone excepted who has not attended Parliament for some time) Charles Fox and Lord Carlisle's Macaroni Friends[3] also were with us. And Lord North, Dyson, Jenkinson, Sir Gilbert Elliot, and all the Junto and real Ministers against us. Lord North had, luckily, sent His Cards out before He knew the stirr the D. of Marlbro' and Ld. Carlisle made. He was therefore obliged to support it, but did it as I hear, in ill Humour, and to my great Satisfaction was beat by a majority of 19. The Division was as I hear 152 for Sr. Wm. Meredith 133 against Him. I think this must make ill blood and some mischief among them. Sr. James Lowther spoke.

Sr. Geo. Saville's Bill[4] upon the right of Electors had not so good a fate, we were sadly beat. People will not attend so old a subject.

Lord Chatham made a great deal of His Questions which He wanted to put to the Judges.[5] We divided 22 or 23.

Yesterday I made a motion for recalling the Press Warrants. We took great care to steer it clear, of giving any opinion upon the legality of them, and of having any intention to advise to disarm, all we contended for was, that if the

1 The first Duchess of Marlborough had received a lease for 'fifty years at first' (but never renewed) of ground in St. James's Park, on which Marlborough House was built in 1709. Carlisle was Lowther's rival over the parliamentary representation for the borough of Carlisle and the county of Cumberland, in which the disputed territory would have increased Sir James's political influence (Sir William Musgrave to Carlisle, 22 Sept. and 1 Oct. 1767, *H.M.C. Carlisle*, pp. 213 and 215).

2 Lord Charles Spencer (1739–1820), second son of the second Duke of Marlborough, M.P. for Oxfordshire, was a Lord of the Admiralty. In 1779 he was appointed Treasurer of H.M. Chamber, in 1782, one of the Vice-Treasurers of Ireland, and in 1801, Joint Postmaster-General.

3 The Macaronis were a group of young 'dandys' including Carlisle, Fox, and the Earl of March, within Almacks, a gambling club which later became Brooke's Club. See *The History of Whites*, 1892, p. 126.

4 That expulsion does not create incapacitation. See *Cavendish Debates*, ii. 245–56.

5 On Tuesday, 5 Feb. 1771, Chatham moved to put two questions concerning Falkland Islands to the judges: could the crown hold any territory except in sovereignty, and, if it could not, could the Spanish declaration restoring Port Egmont be accepted without derogating from the maxims of Sovereignty (see Richmond to Chatham, 5 Feb. 1771, P.R.O. Chatham Papers 1/54/53).

Peace could last only a twelvemonth, it was cruel and need-less to go on pressing. The Ministers (as we expected) flew out very injudiciously and said it was disarming or at least relaxing the Preparations that it was madness to think of so doing. That nothing was *settled as yet*. The Ratification not come, Spain and France still arming and in an Hostile Manner. in short they viz. Lord Rochford, Lord Halifax, and Lord Hillsbro',[1] blunder'd out in opposition to our Motion the best reasons in the world for believing the Peace insecure and against an address till the Ratification was arrived. It was partly with this view that I moved the Ques-tion. Lord Chatham and the D. of Bolton[2] supported me admirably, and at last we said that finding from the Mouths of all the Ministers that tho' they did not deny our fleet to consist of upwards of 30,000 men, they still thought the Peace so insecure, the Ratification so uncertain and the state of other powers such, as to make it necessary to go on with pressing, I would on these new lights withdraw my Motion. Lord Gower[3] finding the scrape they were got into, unsaid all they had argued, but as the Rest did not unsay their own words I persisted to withdraw my Motion. Lord Suffolk[4] then insisted the Motion should be put. I said I had no objection to its being put for if the Ministers voted against it was confessing they thought the Peace so bad as to make pressing necessary. I have not time to relate more particu-lars, but it was a very good Day for us. Lord Chatham ex-ceeding himself as did the D. of Bolton. Lord Craven spoke and their inferiority in Debate was remarked by their best friends.

[1] Rochford and Halifax were Secretaries of State for the South and North respec-tively; Hillsborough was Colonial Secretary.

[2] Harry Powlett (1719–94), Duke of Bolton, was Governor of the Isle of Wight, 1766–70, and again in 1782, Vice-Admiral of Hants and Dorset, 1767, Admiral of the White, 1775, Lord Lieutenant of Hants, 1782. He was a nominal supporter of Chatham.

[3] Granville Leveson-Gower (1721–1803), Earl Gower, had been M.P. for Bishop's Castle, Westminster, and Lichfield before succeeding to the title in 1754. He was Lord Lieutenant of Staffordshire, 1755–1800, President of the Council, 1767–79, and 1783–4, High Steward of Stafford, 1769, K.G., 1771, and was created Marquis of Stafford in 1786.

[4] Henry Howard (1739–79), Earl of Suffolk, was High Steward of Malmesbury, 1763–7, Deputy Earl Marshal, 1763–5, P.C., 1771, Lord Privy Seal, 1771, Secre-tary of State for the North, 1771, K.G., 1778.

I must now tell your Lordship of two long Conversations I have had with Lord Chatham. I should first premise that We had a meeting Lord John, Dowdeswell and I, with His Lordship and Lord Camden upon the Jury Bill.[1] Dowdeswell first gave his Reasons for the Bill. Lord Camden next gave his opinion that it was better to leave things as they are and do nothing. Lord Chatham scouted this thought, said it was betraying the Rights of Jurors and the people, but was for a declaratory act, not an enacting one. proposed the alteration, and to say that Jurors *have been are* and *shall be reputed* competant, etc., Dowdeswell objected. Lord John and I supported him. Lord Chatham then said he was sorry but must *oppose* our bill that is he must bring into the H. of Lords a declaratory Bill, so we broke off. The next day Lord Chatham asked me if Mr. Dowdeswell meant to move it soon. He hoped He would consider of it. I told him we were firm, and thought we could not alter without giving up our characters to the Publick which being our best Foundation, that had never as yet fail'd us, we could not (risk) it now. He said he was sorry; that he should not oppose in ill blood and hoped we should differ like Friends.[2] I told him, that certainly it should make no Difference in our Zeal for the public Cause, but that it would be giving great Advantages to the Court who would profit by them, and that it was impossible but that some of our Friends should be displeased at His opposing our Bill. That if He did not approve it we could not desire him to support, but that it seem'd needless to opose it, which would by some be looked upon as Hostile, and endeavouring to make the publick think we were not sincere in their Cause. He said he meant no such Thing, but as this would appear as a measure held out to the publick which we should all support if in power, He thought it right to shew it was not the Thing He meant. for that if Ministry would give us our Bill He would not take it, He thought it so bad.

He then went out of His way to talk upon Politicks in general, said much upon the various parts of opposition,

[1] The meeting was held on 4 Feb.

[2] Cf. Chatham's reference to the bill as a 'compound of connection, tyranny, and absurdity' (Chatham to Barre, 21 Feb. 1771, *Chatham Correspondence*, iv. 100). 'My arguments not being stamped with the name of Rockingham were disapproved of' (Barre to Chatham, 21 Feb. 1771, ibid., p. 101).

that there were many excentrick men who would not belong
to a Party, that they were the Real Strength of opposition.
And then head and shoulders he lugged in His future ideas
about the Treasury without my giving him the smallest
inducement so to do, and repeatedly returned to the Charge
upon the same matter in a very mark'd manner. He said that
he thought a great defect in our Party was disposing before
hand of the Treasury for Your Lordship, as a *sine qua non*.
That this was making a man the object of the Party and of
opposition. That for His part we could never subscribe to
that: He did not mean to say that He had the smallest
objection to Your being in that office. He thought you fit for
it, you had a very good Judgement, Abilities sufficient, and
the most agreable, affable, and gentlemanlike Manners, and
from the weight of your Party was a Considerable Man in
this Country: If therefore His Majesty thought of putting
you there He should have much pleasure in seeing it. but if
the King put all other things to rights and only wished that
office for another man proper He did not see why all should
break for the single object of Your having that particular
office. I thanked His Lordship for the openness and Confidence with which he had spoke, I told him I thought it
much best always to deal so, and that in return I thought
myself obliged to speak frankly too. I said that it was not the
true light to consider our insisting on the Treasury for you
as making one man the object of opposition. That the
Treasury carried with it the Government of this Kingdom.
That my principles were, that the Court had adopted a system destructive of the Constitution viz: to have the Minister
depending solely on the will of the Crown and not on the
opinion of the Publick for His situation weight and Consequence. that this idea had been started by Lord Boling-
broke to the late P. of Wales, improved by Lord Bath, the
Princess, and Lord Bute. That it arose from the Whigs in
Sr. Rob. Walpole and the Pelham's time having perhaps
carried things with too high a Hand in the Closet. that the
means of effectuating their system was to break all Party in
which they had been too much assisted and had succeeded
too well. That I took this to be the true Source of all the evil
and confusion, that had happen'd, and therefore to remedy

it, the only way was to reunite in Party, to hold steadily together, and by acting upon true whig principles, to recover the weight and Party of the whigs. Upon these grounds I said we were a Party and should stick together. That since we had been glean'd of some rotten Limbs we were sound all over and I believed nothing could now detach a man from us. That reduced as we are, we were still the most numerous corps in either House of Parliament and in the nation, indeed we were the *only* Party now left. And were very respectable by our numbers, Fortune, Rank, and especially by our characters. That for these Reasons we thought our Party ought to be the foundation of any good administration, that you was the Head of our Party and as such the Man to be Minister. That it was not anything personal in Your Favor, but the Minister must be from among our Corps, and no one amongst us stood in Competition with you. That we did not confine our Pretensions here, for we should expect to have the Majority of the Cabinet from our Corps and the Efficient offices the Admiralty, Plantations, etc, that in short we meant to be the Ministers to govern the Country by the Corps of Whigs, and that having secured this we should leave Ribbons, white sticks, and Court places to any assistants we could meet with. That we did not mean to proscribe any man or set of men provided they would join us upon our own principles. That the larger our Party was the better it would answer to our idea of what a party should be, but we look'd upon ourselves as the only Party at present subsisting. That we should be happy to rekon Lord Chatham amongst us, and as many more as would act with us upon our own principles.

To this He answer'd that Burke's Pamphlet had done great harm. That He was the Oldest whig in England and could not now submit to be call'd only an *ally* of the Whigs, He was a *Whig*. That he approved of and could go along with me in almost every title I advanced, in every point, the fatal system of disunion so much practised by the Court, the necessity of a large Union, That the Whigs alone could and ought to make the only Party, and he would never support any Administration of which we were not the Foundation. That He loved you and thought you deserving the elective

situation where you had been put; in all this He agreed, the
only point he differ'd in was, that if the King should be persuaded His present measures were wrong and should set to
rights all the Constitutional Points should alter His whole
Ministry, should take the Whigs, at the Basis of a new one,
would it then be worth while to break all off if H.M. should
destine one place for another man than Ld. Rockingham?
would it not be acting for one Man. He Lord Chatham
should be very happy if the King thought of you. If the
King consulted him and told him He had you in his eye for
the Treasury, he should answer *Sir, you cannot have a more
proper man in every Respect,* he added, *nor indeed so proper a
one.* But on the other hand, if the King should name another
person B instead of A equaly a Whig, of known Principles,
Honor, and abilities, He could not break off for A instead of
B. He mention'd Lord Temple as a man who had no
thoughts of perhaps ever coming again to the House, but as
an Instance. That He could not say to the King that if He
pitched upon Lord Temple, it was improper.

I told Lord Chatham that He might remember the Time
of the first opposition when the King offer'd the D. of
Newcastle, the D. of Cumberland and Mr. Pitt the whole of
the Ministry, Carte blanche, all but one little place (the
Treasury) which He kept for Lord Bute. That this was then
thought a sufficient ground of opposition, and for one man.
That if it was realy meant to take in the Whigs as the Basis
of an Administration it was natural to let them chuse the
Minister, or to chuse their Leader for such. That proscribing
him must make every man think the offer fallacious and
hollow. especially as you was not a man who could ever have
given offence in the Closet by any indecent Behaviour to
cause a proscription of you. and therefore the only Reason
for excluding you must be Your known firmness and steadiness not be made a fool of. That the idea of taking in a Party
and proscribing the Head of it, was in my opinion quite
ridiculous, and such a plan as I was sure the Party would not
trust to. Lord Chatham then said he had held the same
Language to You on many occasions, and that you had taken
it well, and he should hope, if it was ever to happen, that you
would deprecate Your Friends not to make a stand on Your

Account. I said possibly the fear of appearing self interested might make you do so wrong a thing, but I was sure than in perhaps this single point You would have no weight with us. I added that I could not conceive why H. Lordship should suppose that if the K meant to take in the Party He should think of not giving you the Treasury. That there might have been some Difference of opinion among the Members of opposition, while Mr. Grenville was alive. His age, abilities, and having been in that Department might in the eyes of some, make him Your Rival, but that now there was no Body that could stand in competition with You. Lord Temple seem'd to have left the Stage, Lord Chatham had never turned his Mind towards Finance and therefore I supposed He would rather prefer foreign Affairs and that then, there was no man in opposition who had the smallest pretence to stand in Competition with You. This in general he admitted, dwelt a little upon Lord Temple, said he had no thoughts of it for himself, and in a particular manner assured me, and desired me to remember that He would never support, and should not think it safe, if the Treasury was not in the Hands of some man who is now at this moment standing forth in support of the Rights of the People and in the opposition. That He did not mean any man who was come out lately to sweeten himself, but such as were now in declared opposition. That I might guess whom he meant. I did not press him that day but the next day I did, to tell me whom He had in his eye. He then said he only meant Lord Temple, He had no thoughts of any one else, nor that He Lord Chatham would think of it. He only argued Hypotheticaly. And then repeated all He had said the Day before with additional and great compliments to You. He thanked me too for speaking plain. I told him I thought it best He should know the Full of my Opinion and what I believed was the opinion of the Party.[1]

I may have omitted some little circumstances, but I have related the substance of these Conversations as well as I am

---

[1] Richmond's defence of the right of a ministry to choose its own first minister is in contrast to his opposition to 'tying the King's hands' in 1767. By 1782 the same disillusionment with party which led Richmond to advocate parliamentary reform, led him back to his position *vis-à-vis* the King in 1767.

able, after having wrote so much which has not a little
fatigued me. You will see it is wrote in much haste. I have
communicated this Conversation to Lord John Cavendish
and to Admiral Keppel. They have advised me to let it go no
farther. Dowdeswell was develish sulky at Lord Chatham
already,[1] and Burke is all combustible.[2] The Event he talks
of may never happen, but it is right you should know what
passed. Perhaps he may have or expect, some offer. perhaps
He thinks we may have one, and wanted to pin us down
to your having the Treasury. if so, I am glad of what
passed. At all events if He does not give up His opposition to the Jury Bill, it will create uneasiness amongst our
Friends but it is best to make the matter as little bad as
possible.

Adieu my Dear Lord I can realy scarce hold my pen, my
hand is so much tired, cramped, and cold. I am ever with the
most sincere Friendship and Esteem

Your most Faithfull humble Servant,

RICHMOND, etc.

P.S. Lord George Germain is clearly against our adopting
Lord Chatham's Declaratory Bill, but rather wishes the
whole was dropt. He is entirely in this with Lord Mansfield,
but we shall pursue our own plan.
Names of the Gentlemen who were at Richmond House on
Tuesday the 5th of Feby. 1771.[3]

---

[1] Dowdeswell had written, 'The hostility agt us must be of Malice aforethought
to depress or destroy us. . . . The Duke of Richmond himself from nothing but an
anxiety to keep the opposition together wishes for such further concessions as might
either reconcile our opponents or put them most manifestly in the wrong for their
dissention.' Dowdeswell, who was being unusually petulant, wanted Rockingham
to come to London because 'it is material for my weight in the party' (Dowdeswell
to Rockingham, 8 Feb. 1771, Fitzwilliam MS. R126–14).

[2] Burke wrote, 'Indeed the Duke of Richmond is very attentive to any method of
keeping us together, and of connecting us with the high and mighty allies', and
praised Richmond for his conciliatory, firm manner (Burke to Rockingham,
16 Feb. 1771, Burke Corr. Book, ii. 171). He also wrote Dowdeswell, of Chatham,
'The great aim of that party is that you should do nothing that is useful. This will
be a trial of firmness between Mr. Dowdeswell and Ld. Chatham' (Burke to Dowdeswell, n.d., ? 2 Feb. 1771, Burke Corr. Book ii. 183).

[3] Of the twenty-one men on the lists, twelve (Burke, Savile, Townshend, Dowdes-
well, Scarborough, Keppel, Montague, Lords George and John Cavendish,
Dempster, William Burke, and Fitzwilliam) were well-established members of the
Rockingham party, and the erratic Milton usually followed Rockingham. Sir
George Yonge (1731–1812, M.P. for Honiton) and Barre (1726–1802, M.P. for

Richmond to Rockingham

Fitzwilliam MS. R158–45–1   16 February 1771

On the morning of 14 February Rockingham wrote Richmond urging
him to get the lead on Chatham by giving notice of Dowdeswell's bill
before the Easter holidays; later the same day Richmond's letter of
12 February arrived at Wentworth, and Rockingham wrote a second
letter condoning the Duke's firmness with Chatham.[1] Richmond's
answer is significant for giving the most complete account extant of
the previously unreported debates in the House of Lords on 14
February.

On 16 February Dowdeswell and Burke also wrote to Rockingham.[2] Dowdeswell mentioned only the revised preamble to his own
bill and some ideas for a motion on the Falkland Islands. Burke gave
news of the success on 13 February of the first reading of Sir William
Meredith's bill for the repeal of a clause in the Nullum Tempus Act.
All three letters made it clear that the strong force of Rockingham's
personality, so often under-estimated by later writers, was genuinely
missed.

Whitehall. Saturday
Feb. the 16th, 1771

My Dear Lord,
    I am much obliged to you for the two letters which your
Servant and mine brought from Bath. It gives me great
pleasure to find that you approve of what I have done in
Conjunction with the Rest of our Friends upon the various
matters that have arose. It is very certain that we every Day
feel the Want of your Presence; very much in Points where
Consideration is necessary, altho' by Letter we find some
assistance as we hear from you so often; But the Want of you

Chipping Wycombe) were former members of Chatham's government, Glynn
and Manchester were radicals inclined to Chatham, and Tankerville (later Postmaster General under Shelburne and the younger Pitt) was probably on the border
between Rockingham and Chatham, and Germaine, a Rockingham adherent, both
went over to the government in 1774; Governor Pownall (1722–1805, M.P. for
Tregony) and Sir Beaumont Hotham (1737–1814, M.P. for Wigan) both went
over to the government in 1775. The two lists, when studied with the list of names
discussed in Richmond's letter of 1 Feb., indicate the great uncertainty of membership even within the nucleus of the Rockingham party. Between both Houses the
established adherents could not be said to number more than fifteen.

    [1] For Rockingham's comments on the letters see Rockingham to Dowdeswell,
14 Feb., Fitzwilliam MSS. R1–771 and R1–771–1.
    [2] Dowdeswell MSS.; Burke Corr. Book, ii. 171.

to keep people together particularly the H. of Commons
Gentlemen is too apparent. There are many of them who
will upon most occasions vote with us, but want to be spoke
to, and to have the matter explain'd to them beforehand.
This is a part I cannot supply, for I do not know ½ of them,
and the Thing that influences them is the personal Regard
they have for you which will make them do for your speaking
what they will not for another man's. But of this you will
hear more from Dowdeswell as I suppose. He will also have
told you of what passed in the H. of Commons on Wensday
when our Friends divided upward of 250, no despicable
minority.

In the H. of Lords on Thursday the Division was

$$\begin{matrix} \text{Pres: } 35 \\ \text{Prox. } 3 \end{matrix} \right\} 38$$

which as Lords Thanet and

$$\begin{matrix} \text{Pres: } 92 \\ \text{Prox: } 15 \end{matrix} \right\} 107$$

Strafford went away shews we
are 40 in the H. of Lords without a single *Grenville* or
Temple Man. I hear the Ministry are much surprised to find
opposition so numerous in the two Houses, it is what they
did not expect for they thought the late desertions and
absences had reduced us to nothing. Our Debate was long,
we did not divide till Eleven at night.[1] The Speakers were
The D. of Newcastle[2] (who moved the Address), Coventry,
Holderness, Radnor[3] Rochford, Shelburne, Abingdon,
Manchester, Richmond, Rochford again, Paulett[4] Camden,
Mansfield, Chatham, Weymouth, Rochford again, Richmond
again, Weymouth again.

Coventry spoke well and short, His Grace of Newcastle
short and very Complimentary. Lord Holderness very well
as to manner, the Matter, that we were in the wrong, had no

[1] Cf. Horace Walpole's similar but less complete account, mentioning both the
absence of Temple and Lyttleton, and Richmond's call for proxies on Rockingham's
orders (*Memoirs*, iv. 182–4).

[2] Henry Pelham-Clinton (1720–94), Duke of Newcastle, cousin of the first Duke
of Newcastle but never on good terms with him, was Lord Lieutenant of Notting-
hamshire and Steward of Sherwood Forest.

[3] William Bouverie (1724–76), Earl of Radnor, a political eccentric, was normally
a follower of Chatham.

[4] Vere Poulett (1710–88), Baron Poulett, was Lord Lieutenant of Devon but
ordinarily took very little part in politics.

right to and hoped we should not keep Falkland's Islands, our possessions already greater than we can manage. Rochford very manly, not very guarded; Abingdon short; Shelburn exceedingly well and answer'd Lord Holderness that to this Ministry perhaps our possessions were more than they could manage, but another Ministry might be had that could govern them. The D. of Manchester was very short, I much too long. Lord Paulett very dull. Lord Camden very well, Lord Mansfield full of false arguments, one hath he said, that the fleet had been so neglected we were not fit to go to war, to which Sandwich nodded approbation. Lord Chatham spoke an hour and 50 Minutes so dull and heavily that no body could follow him or would attend to him. He meant to be very argumentative in which He always fails. Weymouth spoke better than ever I heard him, justified His own Conduct, but would go no farther, would not say whether the Declaration is tantamount to this First Demand or not and rather made an Excuse for voting for it. It is in vain to think of giving you an account of the Debate the Protest of which I inclose a Copy will do it better than I can.

Dowdeswell, Lord John, Keppel, and Burke are to be here this Evening. You may be assured we shall be steady upon the Jury Bill. all you have said upon it is perfectly true and I hope it will be brought in next week.

We shall also see what other Business there is to bring on. I dont foresee any for our House immediately, I therefore think of running to Goodwood for about a fortnight after having previously settled the Business that is to come on.

You are very good to think of my Health. I complain'd of my fingers being so cramped and cold as they were the immediate impediment to my writing any more, but I have been worse in my Health for this last month than for ten months before. a good deal more pain in my Bowels and stomach which among other Reasons hinders my being so active as I could wish at this moment. However I stirr a good deal and occupation does make me forget my Disorder for a Time. I am worst at waking in a Morning. I must not conclude this Letter without telling you that altho' we want you much here, I am one who think that your own feelings and your attention to Lady Rockingham so necessary at this

Moment, is to be attended to preferably to all Politicks. Pray therefore My Dear Lord do not think of leaving Lady Rockingham, as soon as she is able to travel bring her to London, but do not distress yourself or Her and be persuaded that Your Friends will do in Your absence all they can for the Publick Cause. I am ever with the most Sincere affection and Regard My Dear Lord

Your Most obedient and faithfull Humble Servant,

RICHMOND, etc.

P.S. I did not sign the Protes(t) for you. I had not time to consult the D. of Portland who could not attend and I did not care to do it alone.

Richmond to Dowdeswell

Dowdeswell MSS.   20 May 1771

A friendly letter occasioned by personal business and significant as the only extant letter from Richmond to Dowdeswell. Richmond had remained in London until 13 May and then gone to Goodwood before setting out for Bath; Dowdeswell was evidently at Bagshot.

My Dear Sir,   Bath, May 20th, 1771

I am sorry that my butler by the misdelivery of my message should have occasioned you the trouble of writing to me. I thought you might possibly know who was the dealer in cider in London who might be best trusted and who could furnish the best liquor, and therefore told my servant to enquire of you with my compliments. It is not worth while to give you the trouble of chosing some in the country and sending it to Sussex and therefore I shall take your advice of tasting some from the dealers in London.

You are very good to enquire after my health: my journey here was on a visit to my sister Conolly, but at the same time I am making a short trial of the waters for the complaint I have had in my stomach and bowels for these two years. The Duchess of Richmond is much obliged to you for your enquiry after her, she is perfectly well and sends her compliments.

Your account of Lady Rockingham gives some hopes. It is much to be wished that this tedious disorder which keeps her in such continual and violent pain and him in such cruel anxiety would end in one way or other, for even the worse end must be to both of them better than her present situation.

All politicks but those of the City seem to be at a stand.[1] And I think we shall have now leisure to attend to our farms: perhaps it may be better that we should, and leave our present unnatural and weak leaders to commit as many blunders as they please. They will soon role (sic) like a ball of snow and increase to such a size as to be apparent to all the world, and perhaps as great heaps of snow some times did, fill up the whole valley and choke up the stream. Then the inconvenience will be felt by all, and all hands will be set to remove it. I say it possibly may turn out best to let this fever come to a crisis before a cure is applied, but I confess I shall be for taking it in time, and doing things effectually. I would give James's powder at once and not lose time with worm wood draughts. I mean that a general union of all the discontended parties in the kingdom, upon a full explanation of our principles and a right understanding of our preten- sions, is necessary; and that so many subdivisions of the weakest party the opposition, can never overturn the great majority which the influence of the Crown gives to Court.

I am etc.,

RICHMOND, etc.

Richmond to Rockingham

Fitzwilliam MS. R1–789   26 April 1772

On 14 April a bill relieving Dissenting ministers from the obligation of subscribing to the thirty-nine articles passed the Commons 70–9, with the surface support of the government, who counted on throwing it out in the Lords.[2] It was brought to the Lords on 19 May supported by Chatham and Shelburne,[3] but not by any of the Rockingham party

[1] In May and June Parson John Horne (allied with Alderman Richard Oliver whom Wilkes had defeated for Sheriff of the City of London on 24 Apr., and sup- posedly backed by Shelburne) published in the papers a series of twelve letters attacking Wilkes's private character. Wilkes replied with one serial letter, and was generally acknowledged to have got the better in the altercation. See *The Controver- sial Letters of John Wilkes . . . the Rev. John Horne, and their Principal Adherents,* 1771.

[2] North to George III (3 Apr. 1772), *Corr. Geo. III*, ii. 335–6.

[3] Richmond spoke between an hour and two hours and 'equally pleased and

except Richmond,[1] and was defeated, 102–29. Rockingham himself took no interest and was absent when the bill was brought up. Richmond had been at Goodwood since 3 March; he returned to London on 1 May and attended Parliament sporadically until the end of the session on 2 June.

Goodwood, April the 26th, 1772

My Dear Lord,

You are so often ill without being dangerously so, and are so offen doctoring yourself that when I first heard you was not well I concluded it was only a surfeit of Phisick and I am told that it might possibly be owing to your not letting yourself alone that you have been ill but that your disorder has not been a slight one. However I am sincerely glad you are now better, and hope you will not take so much apothecary stuff in future. No one is realy more anxious for your health than I am, but I did not enquire after you at first as it would be endless to ask how you do after every time you Phisick yourself.

I suppose this letter will find you return'd from Newmarket, Rich or Poor as Mr. Singleton and other Grooms have chose. But the subject of this Letter is to inform Your Lordship that I have had many applications from the Dissenters in Sussex and in London desiring my assistance in the support of their Bill to release their ministers from subscribing to the 39 articles. As I think the Bill a just one, founded on Reason good Policy and the true Principles of Whiggism and tolleration, I have promised to support it. I conclude you have had like applications and am persuaded that your giving it a warm support will greatly recommend you to that weighty Body of men the Dissenters, who all over England are very powerfull and who stick pretty much together. I confess I wish you the more to be well with them as their Religious Principles and our Political ones are so very similar and most probably will make us generaly act together.[2]

---

delighted his auditors' (*Parl. Hist.* xviii, 19 May 1772; *Walpole Last Journals*, i. 88).

1 'Though I must do justice to the Duke of Richmond's present facility of disposition yet I suppose it doubtful how far he and Mr. Burke will approve anything that does not come from the same quarter' (Shelburne to Chatham, 18 May 1771, Fitzmaurice, *Shelburne*, i. 441).

2 Richmond and Rockingham were both very lax members of the Church of England (Richmond later—1780—attended the Unitarian Church). Rockingham

I wish therefore you would see some of their leading men and write to as many Lords as you possibly can to attend for I understand the scheme of the ministry is to throw it out in the H. of Lords by the Bishops. Now the more of Your Friends appear in the list of the Minority the better. I am My Dear Lord ever Your most Sincere and obedient Servant,

RICHMOND, etc.

P.S. I shall be in town on Wensday night on purpose to attend this Business. The Dss of Richmond went to town on Friday last, I was obliged to stay here for our Quarter Sessions which are on Tuesday next. I beg my best Respects to Lady Rockingham. I hope she is well.

Richmond to Rockingham

Fitzwilliam MS. R1–796   2 November 1772

A friendly letter apparently intended to bring himself into touch with Rockingham, whom he had not seen or written since June. Geographical distance kept Richmond out of the neighbourly meetings of the Northern party leaders—Rockingham, Portland, and Sir George Savile—and he was not included in the normal weekly correspondence between Rockingham, Burke, and Dowdeswell. Apart from old news and inquiries, the chief interest of the letter is the evidence of Richmond's view on the proposed secession and of his contacts with others, including Burke, in this connexion. There is no evidence that Rockingham replied.

My Dear Lord,   Whitehall. Nov: 2d. 1772

I have been on a shooting Party with Lord Thanet[1] in Norfolk, and as I was curious to see some matches that were to be run at Newmarket, I thought you would not be displeased with me, if I took the Liberty of begging a lodging at your House there.[2] Your Servants were most exceedingly civil and obliging and I found it a very neat comfortable Habitation.

I was much pleased at the Horses for whom you know I

was particularly unreceptive to Dissenters' requests, since he had recently been lampooned by them for holding social and political meetings on Sundays.

[1] Sackville Tufton (1733–86), Earl of Thanet and brother-in-law of the Duke of Dorset, was hereditary Sheriff of Westmorland.

[2] Rockingham had left Newmarket early to meet Dowdeswell at Harrowden Rockingham to Dowdeswell, 30 Oct. 1772, Fitzwilliam MS. R1–795).

have a great leaning. As to the gambling and match making
it is very entertaining to observe, but as prudent not to be
concern'd in it. I found the *Sampsons* greatly out of Repute
and Your Stable full of them. However you have a Horse
call'd *Galen* for whom (as no Sampson can possibly run) I
should be glad to deal with you as a Hunter, for he is in my
opinion a very fine Horse. Mr. Singleton says that a *Sampson*
he bought of you is far preferable to *Galen*, but I do believe
People are sometimes prejudiced in favor of what is their
own, and will sometimes puff a Horse they want to sell.

But I must leave the Turf to enquire after Your Lordship's Health which is a Subject truely interesting to me. I
have heard with infinite Satisfaction that you was got into
Yorkshire better than you have been for some years. Pray
let me hear that you continue so.

I also hear that you say you do not feel inclined to attend
Parliament at the Meeting.[1] I have talk'd with some Friends
upon this Subject and find many agree with You, but all
think that it should be a measure pursued by all or none, that
we should all determine to attend and give a warm opposition, or all agree to stay away. I greatly incline to the latter,
And have promised to write to you to know what you would
wish, and I told Irwin (the General)[2] that I would let him
know your answer, that he might in the mean time consult
Tommy Townshend and Lord George Germaine,[3] whom he
was to see, about it. Perhaps as I am going to Goodwood it
would be shorter for you to write to them.

There is no news in Town but that Townshend is Lord
Mayor,[4] and that India affairs are in strange Confusion. Sir
Geo. Colebrooke has lost His Majority among the Directors,

[1] Richmond had seen Burke at the end of October. Burke had already written
Rockingham of Richmond's opinions (Rockingham to Dowdeswell, 30 Oct. 1772,
Fitzwilliam MS. R1–795).

[2] Major-General Sir John Irwin (1728–88), M.P. for East Grinstead, Sussex,
along with Lord George Germaine, was appointed Commander-in-Chief of forces
in Ireland, 1775–82.

[3] Richmond had sent a copy of the original plan of secession to Lord George
Germaine. Apparently neither Germaine nor Townshend supported secession (see
Rockingham to Dowdeswell, 17 Nov. 1772, Fitzwilliam MS. R1–797; Burke to
Rockingham, 29 Oct. 1772, *Burke Correspondence*, i. 350–1).

[4] After a lengthy altercation leading to a scrutiny, Wilkes and Townshend were
declared elected aldermen on 29 Oct. On the same day Townshend, who had polled
second to Wilkes in the livery, was elected mayor by an 8–7 vote of the aldermen.

at least they have carried against him the Supervisors He would not wish to send, but I hear He hopes to beat them in a general Court.[1] I have been tollerably well of late but not quite free from my Disorder. Pray present my best Respects to Lady Rockingham and believe me my Dear Lord with the most sincere Friendship ever most truely yours,

RICHMOND, etc.

Richmond to Rockingham

Fitzwilliam MS. R158–53   10 September 1773

In June a government bill regulating the financial administration of the East India Company had been passed. Before its presentation Richmond had opposed the voluntary acceptance of any government proposals by the General Court of the company; after its passage he worked obsessively to obstruct its implementation by company directives.

By the terms of the Regulating Act, the franchise in the General Court, after 1 October 1773, was to be limited to holders of £1,000 of stock.[2] Richmond's letter is a patient attempt to interest Rockingham in qualifying voters in the court to offset those the government was enlisting. Although Rockingham gave Richmond token support, he was never very interested, and his energies were soon diverted to the Irish absentee land tax.[3] Possibly the letter had a negative effect, because Richmond's emphasis on the qualification of voters for the election of directors in April led Rockingham to underestimate the importance of Richmond's campaigns in the court in December and January.[4]

Richmond had not attended any General Court since June and had not seen Rockingham since the end of the parliamentary session.

Goodwood Sept: the 10th 1773

My Dear Lord,

I wish you would consider of such of our Friends as have

---

[1] On 23 Oct. Colebrooke's nominees for the Supervisory Committee were defeated in the Court of Directors. The General Court postponed consideration of the directors' list until 24 Nov., when the list was thrown out and a ballot appointed to elect a new one.

[2] Normally the stock was to be held a year, but within the first year stock had to be purchased by 1 Oct.   [3] See following letter.

[4] See Richmond's letter to Rockingham, 15 Jan. 1774.

money and get as many of them as you can, to lay out
£1 500 (sic) of it, to purchase a Vote in E. India stock.

You well know the very low state of our Affairs in respect
to Politicks, That altho' we have no selfish views to get
places or good Things, and when we were in, shewed we
had no view but the good of the Publick, yet we have not
been able to succeed in destroying that System of Government which has prevail'd almost constantly during this
Reign, the grand Principle of which, is to make the King
govern by his own Power and the weight of His Influence,
instead of the old system of governing by that Party or Set
of men who had most personal Influence in the Country.
The obvious Difference of these two Systems is this, that by
the old, the leading men were obliged to consult the Good
of the People and court them as deriving their power from
them: but by the new, the ministers court only the Crown
from whom alone they derive any Consequence. This evidently tends to despotism, and the more so as those who are
laid aside, the whigs, were united upon principles of Freedom
and Liberty.

Clear as all This is, and felt as it is by the reflecting Part
of mankind, various Circumstances have prevented its being
so generaly understood as to produce the reasonable consequence, a warm support of the Whigs and steady opposition to the present System: It is true, that it is despised and
hated as universaly as we could wish, but there is an indo-
lence and Supineness that will not let the People act with
Vigor till some strong attempt makes them feel the weight
of Power. This is not in our Power to command and we must
wait to improve the Lucky Moment when it comes. There
is however one great obstacle in our way, The immense influence of the Crown which goes on steadily, daily doing its
Business, corrupting first one man, then another, by degrees
debasing almost every Character in the Nation, and unless
disturbed by some violent Commotion will as certainly
bring about in the long run, its end, as the falling water will
perforate the stone. This I fear it is not in our power to
prevent, but the late attempt of getting such an increase to
that Influence by the additional Patronage of the E. Indies
will greatly accelerate the Business, and therefore I think it

the Duty of those, who mean to try to stem this Torrent, to do all we can to prevent it from taking Place. This only view has made me take the Pains I did last year in Leaden Hall Street, and I think I have some merit with the Publick for so doing. From the little Knowledge I have been able to acquire of the Company, I think that the whole of its Independency rests upon the Choice of the next Directors, if the Court who are Making their Friends buy in, carry their Direction at the next Election, all is over.[1] But if we carry ours I shall not despair of baffling every attempt of the Ministers (powerfull as they are) to get the Patronage of the Company. And if our Friends will be a little active in becoming Proprietors and getting their Friends to become so, I believe we shall succeed. I therefore beg leave to recommend this matter most strongly to Your Lordship to be active in, and hope you will recommend it to our Friends as a very essential national Point. I must confess I look upon it as the last Effort, and if I do not meet with the support of our Friends in this Instance, the only one I have sollicited, shall despair of any future good. Your Lordship knows that the stock must be purchased before the 1st of October. As my only object is the next Election in April, They may sell again after that as soon as they please.

I am My Dear Lord ever most sincerely yours,

RICHMOND, etc.,

I inclose a list of a few of the many who might become purchasers.[2]

Richmond to Rockingham

Fitzwilliam MS. R1–818   31 October 1773

On 30 October Rockingham sent out copies of a circular letter calling a meeting in mid-November to concert opposition to a possible absentee land tax in Ireland.[3] He enclosed a memorial to North, copies of a letter written on 16 October to inquire North's position (signed

[1] See Burke to Rockingham, 19 Aug. 1773, *Burke Correspondence*, i. 434; Sutherland, *East India Company*, p. 266.

[2] The list is missing.

[3] *Annual Register*, 1773, pp. 217–20 (Eur. Hist.). Bessborough to Rockingham, 4 and 30 Sept. 1773, and Rockingham to Bessborough, 20 Sept., Fitzwilliam MSS. R1–811, 813, and 814.

by Devonshire, Milton, Upper Ossory, and Rockingham himself), and
North's reply on 21 October that the ministry would not oppose the
tax.[1] To a few friends like Richmond and Dowdeswell he wrote an
additional letter soliciting their presence at the Privy Council when
the tax was to be discussed.

Richmond and Sir George Savile hesitated to oppose the tax, and
Dowdeswell refused to attend the Privy Council,[2] but the great
majority of the party supported Rockingham. Partly because of the
pressure Rockingham was able to bring, North watered down his
support of the tax. On 30 November the bill was defeated in the Irish
Commons.[3]

My Dear Lord,   Goodwood October the 31st 1773
I am much obliged to you for Your Goodness in the two
Letters you have taken the Trouble to write me and the
copies of those between the 5 Lords and Lord North upon
the subject of the Irish absentee Tax bill.

Both your Letter to Lord North and Your circular Letter
seem to me well wrote and full of sound argument,[4] and
upon the whole I think every dispassionate Man must consider the Measure as liable to the objections you urge against
it; and yet I confess I cannot wonder at the Irish, who in
every Instance are so unjustly treated by this Country, endeavouring to catch at any means of recovering some part of
the Money which so regularly goes out of their Country,
and which this Country will not allow them the fair chances
of Commerce to recover. This is in Fact a tax upon England
to assist Ireland, as such I think the Irish would be very
right to attempt it, if it was not at the same Time partial and
unjust upon the individuals on whom it falls. As such I
think we ought not to Consent to it as Englishmen, but the
Irish have much to say in their Defence tho' they should
admit it partial and unjust, by considering it as a just retaliation for the partial and unjust treatment they receive from us,
for as you may truely say *why am I not allow'd the free enjoyment of the full profits of my Estate because I live in England, is
that a Crime?* the Irish Trader and even Landed man may

---

[1] According to Poyning's Law all Irish money bills had to be approved by the
Privy Council before being presented to the Irish House of Commons.
[2] Dowdeswell to Rockingham, 26 Nov. 1773, Dowdeswell MSS.
[3] Rockingham to Dowdeswell, 30 Nov. 1773, Fitzwilliam MS. R1–822.
[4] The letters were composed by Burke.

say also, *why am I not allow'd the free enjoyment of the full Profits of my Trade and the Produce of my Land because I live in Ireland, is that a Crime?* When once a System of Partiality is established, when one Part of our Dominions are excluded from any advantage for the Benefit of another Part, one must expect Retaliation when in their Power.

But notwithstanding that I think the Irish very excusable in wishing this Tax, I think the English would be very inexcusable to suffer it. I am not among Brothers for retaliating injuries. I am for having the original evil redressed, and tho' I fear there is no great Probability of that, and that a counterballancing Injustice may bring things more upon a par, yet I am not for obtaining Justice by multiplying injuries.

Should it therefore ever come before Parliament, I should be against this Measure.[1] But Your Lordship seems to think that as a Privy Councillor I can oppose it. This is a matter of some weight; and should be well consider'd whether in the present Situation I am in, in professed opposition, and unconcerned personally in this Affair, it would be right on this particular occasion to attend the Council which I have not been near on any other. I confess I see such a measure as liable to many objections, among which it would be said that my personal attachment to Your Lordship had influenced me. I trust you will believe that this attachment is most sincere, and I had almost said without Limit, that I make no secret of it, and am ready to publish it, if possible, still more than I do. but I know you would not wish that any personal Consideration of yours should influence my Vote in the Council, and therefore you would not wish any Thing that had the appearance of it. I know very well in my own mind that I should be governed only by what I thought Right and that if I was in a Situation to be called upon to give my opinion on this Measure it would be against it on publick grounds. But that is not the Question, the Question is whether in my present Situation any Thing but my attachment to you personally could make me attend the

[1] Richmond does not seem to have known the opinions of his two brothers-in-law, Thomas Connolly and the Duke of Leinster, Irish privy councillors, both of whom supported the tax.

privy Council. and whether therefore my going there would not do you more harm than good, or be proper? I do not pretend to decide as yet whether it will or not, and wish you to consider of it, and let me know Your opinion.

The next Point is my attending the Meeting,[1] and here again I think I should do more harm than good. Having no kind of Business there of my own, it would with Reason be said, it could be only to encourage every kind of opposition, and would damn the Cause with the name of a Party-Measure. My Most sincere Friendship for you induces me to tell you thus sincerely my Thoughts. They are by no means fixed ones, but such as Strike me in the first instance.

I am my Dear Lord with the most sincere and unalterable attachment

Your most faithfull humble Servant,

RICHMOND, etc.

Richmond to James Adair[2]

Burke MS. 4a   1 December 1773

A letter concerning a meeting with Burke, Wier, Dempster, and Adair some time during the period 7 to 16 November,[3] to discuss a set of administrative instructions drawn up by the East India Company's Court of Directors to implement the Regulating Act in India.

Instead of presenting his alternative instructions when the directors presented their instructions at the General Court on 7 December, Richmond volunteered to head a committee of seven proprietors to prepare a set of alternative instructions within a week. The completed set, presented on 15 December and probably modelled on Richmond's original instructions, contained seventy articles covering first, the powers of the Governor and Council over territorial acquisitions in Bengal and over commerce, and second, the creation of an independent exchequer in India.[4]

Goodwood Dec: the 1st, 1773

My Dear Sir,

I think I collect from the Tenor of Your Letter of this

---

[1] The proposed meeting to organize opposition to the tax was never held.

[2] James Adair (d. 1798), Serjeant-at-Law, known as a Wilkesite, was later Recorder of the city of London, 1779–89. After Rockingham's death Adair supported Fox until the outbreak of the French Revolution.

[3] Burke to Rockingham, 7 and 14 Nov., Burke Corr. Book, ii. 413 and 417.

[4] *Public Advertiser*, 9 and 17 Dec.; *St. James Chronicle* 14–16 Dec.

day's date that you, Burke, Dempster,[1] and Wier[2] approve of my Drafts of Instructions, and prefer them to those of the Directors, and as you do not make any objections to any Part of them, nor have made any notes upon them, I am almost led to flatter myself that you like every Part: indeed they were drawn as nearly as I could comformable to the Ideas we had all agreed upon in Conversation. However I cannot still think but that there must be many inaccuracies at least in Language and form, which I wish you would correct, especialy as I think Your opinions seem to be that they should be offer'd to a General Court and stand a Ballot in Opposition to those of the Directors. I am clearly of this opinion, for I entirely agree with You in opinion that if the Company can be induced to send such Instructions to the Governor and Council as those prepared by the Directors, and make their Board of Trade so dependent upon the Gov: and Council as they do, there is at once an End of the Independence of the Company.[3] I think it amounts to an Absolute Surrender of the little Power that is left to us, and rather than agree to these Instructions, I should prefer sending none, but leaving the Governor and Council to manage the whole Trade and all, and make them the more responsible. Indeed it may be a matter of some Doubt whether if the Company should continue steady and united in resisting the Efforts of Government to gain Influence amongst them, such Resistance will be effectual and whether Parliament will not proceed still further to take away the little Independency they have left us. However I should rather hope that if the Company is steady they will in the end defeat the Ministry, at least it will force them to appear still stronger

[1] George Dempster (1736–1813), M.P. for Perthburghs, and a director defeated for re-election in Apr. 1773, was a well-established supporter of the Rockingham party. See *The Letters of George Dempster to Sir Adam Ferguson*, ed. James Ferguson, 1934, particularly pp. xv–xxi.

[2] Daniel Wier, one of three directors who had not been on the house list in April. (Wier had been on the original house list, but on an amended one issued two days after the first, his name was omitted.) In the previous autumn he had been one of the directors' nominees for the supervisorship to be sent to India.

[3] The first of Richmond's alterations in the directors' proposals was to make the Board of Trade independent of the Governor and Council and to give it the appointment of commercial chiefs. The other two major changes were the establishment of an Exchequer Board to keep the company's money, and the prohibition of hiring sepoys in civil arrests.

in their natural Characters and shew themselves the true despotick men they are. But if the Company cannot be made sensible of this and chuse to rush on to their own Ruin, or if the Ministry have with the Direction, so much undue Influence among them, it is to no purpose to attempt any longer to save those who are resolved themselves to be ruined, or who are bribed to it. We cannot make our Trial of strength in my opinion upon a stronger Question than this, but I wish we were a little better prepared for it, however this does not depend upon us, for if the directors will drive this measure, which indeed now they cannot avoid, we must meet them.

I am exceedingly glad to hear that Gov. Johnstone[1] is for certain to be in town on to morrow. No man is better able to Judge what is right to be done, more hearty in the Cause, or more happy in the method of preparing and conducting Business. I hope he will approve of what has been done and agree with us all in opinion. I should advise the writing some Letters in the Papers to prepare the Proprietors and apprize them of the nature of the Business, as well as to get a good attendance.[2] I think that one might easily state the heads of the Plan of the Directors point out the Defects and bad Consequences and shew the importance of this trial. I wish Burke or you would undertake this business. I would also wish that you would amend and put into good form my Plans, so that we might offer them in the stead of those of the Directors on Tuesday and call upon all our Friends from behind the Bar to stand forth and support us openly.

I feel myself particularly unhappy in not being able to obey Your Summons of attending on You in London Instantly, but have for this four months settled a large Party of Friends who are come here today to fox hunt, and to stay a Month. In this Situation it is next to impossible for me to leave them immediately but I propose on this weighty occasion to leave them on Sunday and to get to town that night.

[1] George Johnstone, an active enemy of Colebrooke, had been the leader with Richmond and Adair of the proprietors' opposition to government's bills. Like Dempster he was an unsuccessful candidate for the directorship.
[2] Several letters, very probably written by Adair, had appeared in the papers during February and March, but there is no evidence that Adair wrote any more in December.

If you will have a meeting of our confidential Friends with
Johnstone at 8 o'clock on Sunday night, and send word to
my House where it is to be, I will attend it, and I should
think we might have a more numerous one on Monday. We
may then I hope prepare ourselves as well as Time will admit
to meet this Business and settle our order of Battle for Tuesday. You give me much too great Importance in thinking
that my Presence can be of much use, but little as I know it
is, I regret not being able to give my full attendance; I hope
however that this Letter which conveys so fully my Thoughts,
and my being in Town for some Days on Sunday next will
prevent any difficulties that you think my absence might
occasion.

I am my Dear Sir ever with the most perfect Esteem and
Regard Your most faithfull and sincere humble Servant,

RICHMOND, etc.,

P.S. Not to delay your Messenger I beg leave to refer Mr.
Wier to this Letter which I beg you would shew to him,
Burke, Johnstone, and Dempster.

Richmond to Rockingham

Fitzwilliam MS. R1–824   15 January 1774

An unsuccessful attempt to bring Rockingham to town for the balloting for instructions on 25 January. Reassured by the failure of several
directors to support the directors' instructions, by the apparent absence
of new government supporters in the General Court, and by victories
in three minor court votes in December and January,[1] Richmond was
optimistic about the outcome of the ballot. But the 'sudden appearance
of many courtiers as proprietors' on 25 January led to the defeat of
Richmond's instructions, 406–308[2]

Rockingham did not reply either to this letter or to one Richmond
had written on 2 January urging his attendance at debates on the
instructions.[3] Because he mistakenly assumed from Richmond's letter
of 10 September 1773 that the only important issue to come before the
company would be the selection of the directors in April,[4] he did not
come up to town at all for the voting in January.

---

[1] On 7, 15 Dec., and 11 Jan.
[2] *Walpole Last Journals*, i. 286.
[3] Fitzwilliam MS. R2–145.
[4] Rockingham to Burke, 30 Jan. 1774, Burke MS. 312.

London Jan: the 15th, 1774

My Dear Lord,

I hear from Adair and from Burke that you talk of being in London, but *not sooner* than the 21st, by which I understand you may be later, which makes me trouble you with this letter to beg you not to be later, as I believe our Ballot will be on that Day. We had two very good days Debate last Tuesday and Wensday[1] in which we went through our Instructions and those of the Directors, both underwent some few alterations, we gave up our Preamble[2] by which we got about 30 votes, and we postponed the consideration of our mint which was the only point upon which any of the Lawyers doubted, so that we have now the opinions of Sayer, Glynn, Dunning, MacDonald, Wallace, Jackson and Skinner[3] that every tittle in our instructions is strictly legal. On Monday we shall have our general Debate on their corporative merits,[4] and I believe the Ballot will be on Friday the 21st. At least I shall endeavour to put it off till then in order to get your vote: for besides the weight that your support gives to the cause and which I realy want because People think that You and the Friends I have leaving me so much by myself in the India House as you do proceeds from your disapproving the Part I am acting there which your presence would remove; I say this Reason and the very near point to which this question is drove make me very desirous of getting every single vote I can.

Indeed I am in great Hopes of success. We beat the Court 3–1 upon a Division in the House on Wensday[5] and I have some notion that the ministers have used the Directors so ill, and abuse them so much that they begin to be sensible

---

[1] 11 and 12 Jan. See *St. James Chronicle*, 11–13 Jan. and *Public Advertiser*, 13 Jan.

[2] A short preamble drafted by J. Smith was substituted for Richmond's preamble, which was objected to as being too condemnatory of the legislature.

[3] All the lawyers except Sayer thought the instructions were compatible with parliamentary law. Sayer was doubtful on the legality of giving the company coinage rights.

[4] The proprietors' instructions were discussed on 11 and 12 Jan., the directors' instructions on 17 Jan.

[5] Moore, clerk of the House of Commons, had moved that the two sets of instructions should be put separately to the ballot (to enable the court to defeat both sets of instructions). The motion was defeated 60–22.

of it, and are not so strenuous for their own plan,[1] but still we cannot be too cautious to get every Vote we can in so important a Matter which will certainly decide the fate of the Company.

I got Lord John Cavendish and Sir Charles Saunders to attend both days.

Our Friends here have agreed to be very silent in Parliament till some matter of great Consequence calls them forth which seems to me to be very wise. Adieu My Dear Lord I am too much hurried to be able to write more. I most sincerely hope that your Health and Lady Rockingham's will continue as well as your friends wish it.

I am ever yours most sincerely,

RICHMOND, etc.,

Richmond to Rockingham

Fitzwilliam MS. R1–828   8 April 1774

In the contest for a new Court of Directors in the East India Company three lists of candidates were put up—the directors' 'house list' recommending all the incumbents, the government's 'house list amended' omitting the names of ten directors who had opposed the government over the selection of a Commander-in-Chief in February, and the 'independent proprietors' list' omitting ten government men and restoring the incumbents removed from the 'house list amended'. Most of the incumbents, who were double-listed, were re-elected; all of the candidates Richmond personally endorsed were defeated.

Rockingham and Burke considered Richmond's efforts futile against the overwhelming Treasury influence in the court. Since Rockingham did not appear in Parliament until 22 Apr., it is most unlikely that he was in town for the balloting.

Goodwood April the 8th, 1774

My Dear Lord,

I find our Friends in London have at last settled a Proprietors' List. I confess I have no great hopes of carrying many of our new men, and if we should, I am far from answering for their conduct. I shall always suspect Sullivan

---

[1] It was alleged during the debates that not all the directors seemed to be supporting their own instructions. Twelve of them, including the chairman, later voted against the government on the appointment of a Commander-in-Chief, and quite probably the same ones opposed the directors' instructions.

and I dont know the others except Johnstone,[1] Lushington[2] Dempster[3] and Yorke.[4] on them I think I can depend.

But however faint my expectation of success may be, or of good from success in carrying our new men, I think we are bound to exert ourselves to the utmost to support our old friends who now are in the Direction and who are all left out of the Government List call'd the House List amended, merely because they dared to have an opinion of their own in Clavering's Business,[5] and who by this means will be thrown out, if not strongly supported by us.

I therefore recommend it to you most strongly to vote and use your interest to support the Proprietors' List. You know how much may be done by a little activity in Time. I am sensible of your particular objection to vote for Sullivan.[6] I have already said I have not a much better opinion of him than you can have, but in the present Instance he will be of use by supporting our friends, and in return I think it but fair to vote for him. You may besides have this Comfort that it is impossible for him to carry his Point. If you *will* strike him out, dont put a Government man in his place, but some old director from another class, such as Wheeler[7] who is on the 3 years class. If you put him on the 4 years class instead of Sullivan, you will satisfy your desire of doing Sullivan no good, but at the same time you will do the Enemy no good.[8]

I am detained here till the very day of Election viz (?): the 13th. Adieu my Dear Lord, I am ever

Your most sincere and faithfull humble servant,

RICHMOND, etc.

[1] See p. 161, n. 1.

[2] Stephen Lushington, of Boldero, Adey, Boldero, and Lushington, Richmond's bankers. As a candidate of the independent proprietors he had been defeated in the previous election of directors.

[3] See p. 160, n. 1.

[4] Martin Yorke, also a candidate for the independent proprietors, defeated in the previous election.

[5] Hall, Sparkes, Boddom, Chambers, Fletcher, Hurlock, Wier, Cumming, DuCane, and Manship were defeated.

[6] Rockingham feared that Sulivan would use the office purely for his own financial needs, particularly in securing jobs for his relatives.

[7] Edward Wheeler, deputy chairman of the company, elected chairman in April.

[8] Under the Regulating Act one-fourth of the directors were to be elected annually for a term of four years. To inaugurate the scheme one-fourth of the

Richmond to Rockingham

Fitzwilliam MS. R1–867   17 February 1775

A friendly letter written the day after Richmond's departure from
London, and reviving two suggestions which he had pressed unsuccessfully before—a conference with Chatham and attendance on certain
issues in the East India Company. Neither suggestion was taken
(though Rockingham did hold a meeting with Chatham's followers on
7 March). Rockingham remained in town throughout the month; his
answer to Richmond was probably one of three communications mentioned in a letter of thanks from Richmond on 12 March.[1]

                                     Goodwood Friday, Feb. 17th, 1775
My Dear Lord,
      As I found there was not any likelyhood of Business
immediately in the House, I have ventured to leave London
and politicks to your Lordship's care, and have come here to
sweeten myself for a few days. I shall return on Thursday
next the 23rd instant in the morning, time enough to attend
a general Court at the India House. Don't think I am again
going to plunge myself into squabbles in Leaden Hall Street.
I shall attend only out of Compliment to Lord Pigot who
has about a year ago offer'd His Services to return to
Madrass; but the Directors have at Lord North's Request
appointed Mr. Rumbold. Lord Pigot calls a general Court
to set aside this appointment. He has been with Lord North
and asked him if he means to oppose him who never voted
against Government in his Life, except on India affairs,
when he thought himself bound to support that Company
which gave him bread? Lord North told him that as he had
opposed Government about Clavering, and as Rumbold had
supported them, he had promised assistance to Rumbold
and should give it him in the general Court where he hoped
he had some weight. Lord Pigot is with Reason much
nettled that all his former Services, both the real ones in
India, and those which have some claim to favor in England, should be sacrificed, (because he once dares to be grate-
full) to such a creature as Rumbold![2] He seems determin'd

directors were to be elected for the full term, and one-fourth for one-, two-, and
three-year terms.   [1] Fitzwilliam MS. R1–871.
      [2] Lord Pigot (retired as Governor of Fort St. George in 1769) had asked to
return to company service in 1774. Subsequently when the directors appointed

to try his strength. He expects to be beat, as all his old friends, even his Indians whom he has made, desert him. But still he will try, and I think it due to him to support him. For the same Reason that I think I ought, I think your Lordship and Lord John ought to appear in his favor on Thursday next. Your appearing at the general Court is much more material than the Ballot for it is shewing him Countenance. I am sure he will be flatter'd and pleased by it. Pray therefore talk to Lord John about it.

I see we are not likely to have Business in the House till the Bill about the fishing comes to us,[1] or till Lord Chatham can attend.[2] Whatever may be settled between you and his Lordship, if any day is fixed for Business between you, I could wish it were to be Friday, or the Monday following.[3] Would it not be right that you should go to Hayes and talk over matters with his Lordship?[4] Pray, is not it material that the state of the Commerce with N.A. and its Dependencies should be made known to the world? I conceive it would have a good Effect, if Mr. Glover[5] would go into this matter before our House; and the Result might be printed. If you approve of this, you should speak to Mr. Baker[6] and Glover about it then communicate it to Lord Chatham and move a day to hear Glover.

Adieu My Dearest Lord

I am ever most sincerely yours,

RICHMOND, etc.

Thomas Rumbold (formerly Hastings's second in Bengal, M.P. for New Shoreham in 1770 and Shaftesbury in 1774, director of the company 1772) as Governor of Ft. St. George, Pigot complained to the General Court. A ballot was taken on 28 Feb., in which Pigot unexpectedly defeated Rumbold by four votes (see Sutherland, *East India Company*, p. 289; *St. James Chronicle*, 24 Feb. 1775).

[1] The bill to restrain four New England colonies (Virginia, New Jersey, and South Carolina were added on 9 Mar.) from using the Newfoundland fisheries, came up to the Lords on 15 Mar. and was passed on 21 Mar.

[2] Chatham did not attend for the rest of the session.

[3] No business was brought on at all during the following week.

[4] A considerably more positive attitude than Richmond had expressed in his letter of 25 Jan., possibly inspired by Chatham's plan of conciliation presented in Parliament on 1 Feb. The plan was in many ways a conciliatory gesture to the Rockingham Whigs. Rockingham did not visit Hayes.

[5] Richard Glover (1710–85), M.P. for Weymouth, was a London merchant and poet (see *Gentleman's Magazine*, 1785, pp. 922–3).

[6] William Baker (1743-1824), M.P. for Aldborough, York, was a London merchant, one-time follower of Chatham.

Richmond to Rockingham

Fitzwilliam MS. R1–897   11 December 1775

On 12 December the government's bill prohibiting trade with the thirteen colonies during a state of rebellion was first read in the House of Lords. Rockingham had been keeping up the appearance of opposition in the House of Lords; 'The Duke of Richmond, whose health was bad, disgusted with ill success, had gone . . . into the country'[1] a month before. Rockingham must have written asking Richmond to attend the bill.[2] Despite the reluctance expressed in the letter, Richmond did come up to oppose and sign a protest on the second reading, 15 December,[3] but he did not stay for the third reading on 20 December.

Goodwood, Monday Morn:
December the 11th, 1775

My Dear Lord,

    Your express arrived here this morning as soon as I was awake. You know my Readiness at all Times to obey your summons when I can hope to be of any use to you or the Cause, but indeed in the present Moment I see so little chance of either, that I hope you will allow the particular Inconveniency which it would be to me to leave my House full of Company, to be a sufficient Excuse for my staying here. It is not laziness, nor yet fox-hunting (for it is a hard frost) that keeps me from attending you, but it is the desire of not leaving the Dutchess of Richmond alone to do the Honors to 20 people in the House. As it is, I suppose we Peers are obliged to attend the Trial on the 20th[4] and I must therefore go to London for that one day, which will be disagreable enough, but to add four or five days more to my absence would be much worse. However I think it not impossible but that the last Stage of this Bill may be put off till Monday or Tuesday. If it is, I shall be in Town and will certainly attend. If it is decided sooner, I must beg of you to take my Proxy and give it against the Bill to prohibit all Trade and intercourse with the Colonies and for this purpose

---

[1] *Walpole Last Journals*, i. 498.

[2] He also asked Manchester. He received Richmond's letter on the evening of 12 Dec. (Rockingham to Grafton, 12 Dec. 1775, *Grafton Autobiography*, p. 275).

[3] See *Annual Register*, 1776, pp. 119–20 (Eur. Hist.).

[4] The trial of the Duchess of Kingston for bigamy was scheduled to come on 20 Dec., but was put off until 28 Feb. because of the Duchess's illness.

I beg you would send me a Proxy by this night's post otherwise I cannot return it sign'd till Friday, but if you send it
tonight you can get it on Thursday evening by the post, and
then may use it on Friday. If you are full you may make me
give it to any other Friend. I confess that I feel very languid,
about this American Business. The merchants and others
stirring upon a particular bill only when it pinches them will
do no good. They must be made to see that the measures on
the whole are good or bad, if good, a particular measure is
scarce worth opposing, but if upon the whole they are
ruinous, the whole System must be opposed. Will they come
forth and give general opposition to men they feel are ruin-
ing them and the Country? Till they will, no good can be
done, I see none in making now and then an Effort sometimes more, sometimes less strong for men who three times
out of four support that very Government which oppresses
them. The only thing that can restore common sense to this
Country, is feeling the dreadfull consequences which must
soon follow such diabolical measures.

I much approve of your Lordship's opposing the Land
tax[1] and Militia Bill[2] and throwing out the Indemnity Bill,[3]
nor have I the least objection to your opposing this prohibition Bill, but I would not make a great struggle for it, and
you may tell the Merchants that you cannot get an attendance of Lords unless they will take a more decided part, and
firmly stand by them in their general System of politicks.

Pray return my best thanks to the fair Hand[4] that copied
your Letter. I do not wonder at your not having sat for your
Picture during this Bustling time. I know the ninety nine
grains of Friendship are very strong. The one grain of
Vanity will not do much, but if it arises from having one
most devoted Friend it is not ill founded.

---

[1] A bill raising the land tax from 3s. to 4s. reached the Lords on 27 Nov. and
passed on 30 Nov.

[2] A bill enabling the King to call out militia in all cases of rebellion in the kingdom of Great Britain or any dominion was first read on 27 Nov. and passed on
30 Nov.

[3] A bill indemnifying the ministers for sending Hannoverian troops to Gibraltar
and Minorca passed the Commons on 24 Nov. but was thrown out by the Lords on
30 Nov. It had been strenuously opposed by Rockingham (*Annual Register*, 1776,
pp. 115–17. Hist. Eur.).

[4] Lady Rockingham's.

I most sincerely wish you success in your Election for Mr. Watson.[1] The loss of poor Sir Charles Saunders[2] is irreparable. The publick will feel it as well as his private Friends, but most of all my Dear Admiral Keppel, for whom I feel most excessively. I have not yet the Heart to write to him about it. Adieu My Dear Lord.

I am ever your most affectionate and faithfull
humble servant,

RICHMOND, etc.

Richmond to Rockingham

Fitzwilliam MS. R2–147   8 December 1776

Early in November the Rockingham party had seceded from Parliament. They intended to meet privately in town to maintain the appearance of unity, but this letter indicates they took advantage of the opportunity to disperse to the country. Rockingham left for Yorkshire some time after 27 November, while Richmond probably went to Goodwood during the first week of November and was currently entertaining his annual fox-hunting party. His letter consists of comments on Rockingham's two letters and speculations inspired by the newspapers, probably the *London Gazette* in particular.

Goodwood December 8th, 1776

My Dear Lord,

I am to acknowledge and thank you for your two letters of the 24th and 27th of last month. I have already sent you the order you desired for the Cupid and Psyche, but had not at that moment, time to write to you. I suppose this letter will find you in Yorkshire. I dare say you feel there as I do here, wishing never to quit it, but trembling hourly for the bursting of the dreadfull storm that is gathering all around, and which must desolate this beautifull and still happy spot!

News from America grows to be daily expected and must

[1] Lewis T. Watson, eldest son of Rockingham's cousin, Lord Sondes, was elected for Heydon, Yorkshire, in Dec. 1775, to replace Sir Charles Saunders.

[2] Sir Charles Saunders, K.B. (1713–75), M.P. for Heydon and Admiral of the Blue, was a close friend of Keppel and Albemarle. He had commanded the St. Lawrence fleet at the battle of Quebec, and was installed K.B. *in absentia* in 1761 while commanding the Mediterranean Fleet. He was a Lord of the Admiralty in the first Rockingham ministry, First Lord (until Nov. 1766) under Chatham, and a full Admiral in Oct. 1770. Saunders died on 7 Dec. of gout in the stomach.

now be very interesting. Nothing immediately material can be done this year on the side of the Lakes, but the King's Bridge[1] Business seems to be of Importance. If Mr. Washington is attack'd and beat, it may possibly produce some negotiation during the Winter. If he returns to the Highlands all will still remain in suspence. If he maintains his post, it will shew that Mr. Howe's superiority is not so great nor the American spirit so low as is given out, and the Events of next Campaign may not be so successfull as this. If General Howe attacks King's Bridge and is repulsed with any great loss, all chance of future success will be over and our Ministers will run away. But amidst these various Events I see none that can save us from the impending Ruin that in my Eyes is unavoidable. It is impossible to guess what alterations the change in the Spanish Ministry may make.[2] We have more than once owed our safety to the Blunders of our Neighbours, tis the only chance we now have.

You rather surprise me by telling me that another Gentleman[3] was *in very good Humour* tho' your conversation was only on *general matters*. for I am much deceived if you will not find that unless particulars are agreed upon he will fly off. Remember I warned you of it.

Pray give my best Respects to Lady Rockingham. I hope she is quite well again, and that to remain so she will learn again in Yorkshire what restored her to Health some time ago. *Early Hours* and *Constant Exercise* tis the only means to preserve it.

The Dss of Richmond sends her Compliments to your Lordship. I think *the Paper*[4] will require some alterations

[1] On 13 Nov. General Knyphausen had taken possession of King's Bridge from the colonists without opposition (*Annual Register*, 1776, p. 178. Eur. Hist.). For the capture of Fort Washington three days later part of the Hessian troops operated from King's Bridge (F. V. Greene, *The Revolutionary War and the Military Policy of the United States*, 1911, pp. 56–60).

[2] On 6 Nov. the Marquis de Grimaldo had resigned as Minister of Foreign Affairs after the defeat of the Spanish Navy by the Moors. His resignation was considered fortunate for England. In Feb. 1777 he was replaced by the Count de Florida Blanca.

[3] Probably Camden. It would not have been Chatham, who was too ill in November and early December to see even his closest friends.

[4] Possibly a paper on 'Secession with Reasons' (author unknown) circulated among the party in January. Richmond may have seen an early copy (Burke to Rockingham, 6 Jan. 1777, Burke MS. iii. 2/583).

and additions. I will be in Town some days before the meeting[1] but 8 are a great many.

Adieu My Dear Lord I am ever your most faithfull and sincere humble servant,

RICHMOND, etc.

Richmond to Rockingham

Fitzwilliam MS. R1–983   15 March 1778

On Sunday, 15 March, Richmond and Fox held meetings of opposition leaders in the Lords and Commons respectively. Fox's meeting concerned a resolution to be proposed the following day for papers presented to the British court on 14 March concerning the French Treaty of Alliance and Commerce with the North American colonists in revolt. Richmond's may have concerned his own motion, made on 7 April, to withdraw troops from America.

In February Richmond had expressed his support for a continuation of the attempt to win back the American colonies,[2] and as late as 1781 he was willing to grant them full independence only as a last resort.[3] The French-American treaty made no immediate difference in his American policy; this letter is only an outburst against Chatham, for whom Richmond had been developing an intense personal hatred since the preceding autumn.

My Dear Lord,

You will remember that Lord Shelburne[4] and Lord Camden are to be here to night at 8 o'clock. I beg you would not be later. I have not asked any Members of the House of Commons as Charles Fox told me He was to have a Meeting to night upon His Business of to morrow.

I have before shewn my Draft[5] to the Duke of Manchester,

[1] Parliament opened on 20 Jan. The party remained in secession, but Rockingham hoped to continue the original plan of keeping his friends in town (Rockingham to Burke, 6 Jan. 1777, *Burke Correspondence*, ii. 134).

[2] Fitzmaurice, *Shelburne*, ii. 12.

[3] Granville Sharp Diary, Book G, June–July 1781, pp. 118–20, 128.

[4] Judging from William Eden's Memorandum (*Memorials and Correspondence of C. J. Fox*, i. 179–82) which is undated but must refer to 15 Mar., Shelburne did not get to the meeting, but after claiming to have a meeting, spent the evening talking to Eden.

[5] The draft may have concerned either Richmond's motion for withdrawing troops from America or a motion of censure on the ministers, moved 17 Mar. Camden, and later Shelburne, gave tentative assent and referred the matter to Chatham. (For Camden, see *Chatham Correspondence*, iv. 509–10; for Shelburne, P.R.O. 30/8/56, no. 177.)

and as Lord Shelburne wished to have our Meeting as
confined as possible I have asked no Body but himself Lord
Camden and Your Lordship. if you would have any more,
either send to them or let me know.

I have just seen Wm. Keppel[1] who has told me the news
of the French Ambassador's having informed our Court of
the Treaty and that His Master was resolved to protect his
Flag.[2] This Event makes it the more necessary to come out
with the Proposition of declaring the Independency of
America. This being done instantly, and publickly, declaring
against a War with France notwithstanding this Treaty, is
the only means to keep America from joining France as
allies. it is the only Chance we have for preventing such a
Measure which must be our Ruin.

I dare say Lord Chatham will be for instant war without
ever considering the Means. This must be resisted early, or
rather let us be before hand with him and by declaring
against war shew him that he cannot draw us with him into
such Madness. I think these two points should be spoke to,
tomorrow.[3]

I am ever
Yours
RICHMOND, etc.

Richmond to Portland

Nottingham MS.   2 October 1778

At the end of July Admiral Keppel had returned to Plymouth after an
indecisive engagement off Ushant where the French fleet, superior
in number to the estimate which the Admiralty had given Keppel,
had avoided combat by fleeing in the night.[4] Immediately upon his
return he had written Rockingham a description of the encounter,
which the Marquis forwarded to Portland, Burke, and probably Richmond;[5] at that time Richmond, who had strongly opposed Keppel's
taking the Channel Command at all, had sent the Admiral a letter of
affectionate encouragement.[6]

[1] See p. 6, n. 5.
[2] Fox, through Grafton, seems to have had the information earlier than 14 Mar.,
but not to have told Richmond.
[3] Nothing was brought up in the House of Lords on the following day.
[4] See *Keppel Life*, ii, ch. ii, and *Sandwich Papers*, ii. 3–13.
[5] Portland to Rockingham, 1 Aug. 1778, and Burke to Keppel (Aug.) 1778,
Keppel Life, ii. 56–57.   [6] (21 Aug. 1778), ibid. ii. 61–64.

On 9 September Keppel wrote Portland (this time from the *Victory* at sea chasing the French fleet off Brest[1]) including a message of commendation he had received from Admiral Hawke and his reply to Hawke's message, and giving Portland permission to forward the enclosures to Richmond and Rockingham.[2] Richmond's acknowledgement to Portland echoed the fears expressed in a letter to Rockingham of 2 August,[3] as a letter he wrote to Keppel the same day echoed the applause of his previous salutation.[4]

Goodwood October the 2nd, 1778.

My Dear Lord,

The Letter Your Grace did me the Honor to write to me on the 13th of last month was a considerable Time in reaching me. My Porter being directed not to send it by the Post, waited some days for an opportunity & then sent it by the Coach to Brighthelmston, where I did not arrive of a few days so soon as I intended. This will I hope plead my excuse for not answering it sooner.

I am exceedingly obliged to Your Grace for the accounts you was so good as to send me of that most excellent Man, Friend & Officer Admiral Keppel; nothing can be more interesting to me than his situation, from the Importance of His Trust at this Moment and from the Love & Veneration I have for him. I have corresponded with him I believe since Your Grace saw him, but the account you are so good as to give me is much more detail'd than his Letter. Your Grace may depend on the Copy of Lord Hawkes' Letter remaining safe in my hands, to say the Truth, tho' very flattering to Keppel, it is not a Letter to be shewn.

I am not surprised at anything that wears the appearance of Treachery in the Conduct of Administration towards Admiral Keppel.[5] If they can save themselves from the least Blame, they will not scruple throwing it on him tho' it should cost him His Life & Character. Such is the Misfortune attending those who act under an Administration

---

[1] *Sandwich Papers*, ii. 156–86.
[2] Portland to Keppel, 6 Sept. 1778, *Keppel Life*, ii. 70–71.
[3] Fitzwilliam MS. R1–993.
[4] *Keppel Life*, ii. 71–74.
[5] Possibly referring to a letter Keppel had written on 4 Aug. to Philip Stephens, Secretary to the Admiralty. Keppel's friends claimed that the contents of the letter were publicized in distorted form by the government (*Public Advertiser*, 4 Aug. 1778).

they cannot confide in. I am not surprized that the Admiral's spirits should be worked and His Body fatigued with the Continual Exertions which both are put to and neither are in that State of Health to bear. I cannot say I fear any Imputation being justly thrown on Mr. Keppel for returning to Spithead when contrary to the Information Ministers had given him,[1] He found the French fleet so greatly superior to him; nor am I under any Apprehensions that if His Conduct on the 27th of July is examined into by good Naval officers, it will turn out otherwise than to his Credit. But I fear that the Vexation of not having been able to bring about a compleat Victory will wear him down, and the more so as now that the Brest Fleet have a second Time escaped him & got safe into Port, He will again be blamed by an unfeeling Publick whom nothing but success often more due to good Luck than good Conduct, can satisfy.

I very much agree with Your Grace that in such Circumstances tho' he cannot doubt the Affection of His Friends, every fresh mark of their Attention is pleasing. I have therefore wrote to him as friendly a Letter as I could pen, and as Your Grace is in the Neighbourhood of Plymouth (where He will probably put in) and may have safe opportunities of conveying it to him, I take the Liberty of inclosing it to You. I have ventured to tell the Admiral that whatever he may owe His Country He does not owe it the Risk of His Reputation which must ever be in Danger if He acts with discretionary Powers under a Ministry he knows he cannot trust. I have therefore advised him to be firm not to return to Sea without positive, clear & direct orders what to do in all probable & almost possible cases, and either an approbation or Censure of his past Conduct.

I much regret the Return of the Brest Fleet because I trust Mr. Keppel, had he met them would have given a good Account of them: I fear a Junction of the Spaniards & that Mr. Keppel's Health will either oblige him to give up the Command on a Winter's Cruize, or greatly suffer in attempting it.

Our Fate seems long in Suspence and I fear we do not profit of the Time in making proper Preparations. Lord

[1] The French fleet had 32 ships of one line instead of 17 as Keppel had been told.

Amherst[1] is Asleep, or dares not act, & it looks as if the same Man who has lost 13 provinces intended by equal bad Management to risk the Loss of 3 Kingdoms. We are to meet next Month. Your Grace, Lord Rockingham & Lord Shelburne would do well to meet before and to think on what is to be done. I can only offer the assistance of a willing mind, too often check'd both in the Military & in the civil Line by bad health to be of that Service I could wish. Indeed I am often in great Doubt whether it is best to be satisfied with doing the little good one can, or not to attempt things in which one is sure to disappoint one's own wish, and the Expectation of others. I hope Your Grace has had your Health. It is with the most sincere Respect & Regard that I am My Dear Lord

ever Your Grace's faithfull & obedient

Servant

RICHMOND, etc.

Richmond to Shelburne

Lansdowne MSS. 16 January 1780

In December 1779 the city of London voted thanks to Richmond for presenting a vague motion for reduction of the civil list, and to Shelburne for a motion to check increases in military expenditure granted for extraordinary reasons beyond the supplies voted by Parliament for department estimates.[2] To all Lords who supported the motions the city sent letters of thanks, receiving in response some thirty-two replies, a number of which were from conservative whigs like Portland.[3]

Early in January the city also adopted a general resolution against the undue influence of the crown.[4] Richmond's letter concerns both the later resolution and the letter of thanks about which Shelburne must have written him from Bowood. Shelburne must also have

---

[1] Jeffrey Amherst (1717–97), first Baron Amherst, was Commander-in-Chief and Lt.-General of the Ordnance. He had previously been Commander-in-Chief in North America, 1758–64, served as Governor of Guernsey, 1770–97, P.C., and had been created Baron Amherst in 1776. He was Commander-in-Chief, 1793–5, and Field Marshal, 1796.

[2] Significantly, the Sussex petition for economic reform in Jan. 1780 singled out extraordinaries as symptomatic of a corrupt economy. Two years later Richmond, as Master-General of the Ordnance, revised the Ordnance budget with an eye to eliminating the need for extraordinaries.

[3] Maccoby, *English Radicalism, 1762–1785*, p. 296.

[4] *Annual Register*, 1780, pp. 81–82 (Eur. Hist.).

written complaining of Rockingham's renewed hostility to him as a result of a rumour that Shelburne had entered a coalition with the Bedfords.

Goodwood, Jan. the 16, 1780

My Dear Lord,

You forgot to send me the List you mention of Lords who have sent you their Thanks to the City. I have delay'd Mine from not knowing whether they were expected or would be thought impertinent.[1] I was also under some difficulty to know by what Channel to send them. I received the copy of the Resolution sign'd I presume by the Town Clerk but without any Letter, and I should not have guessed from whom it came had not the order of the Resolution informed me that Mr. Remembrancer was to deliver it. I have now written an answer and sent it to Mr. Remembrancer.

Your Lordship is very kind to me on all occasions, but indeed I am not sensible of more Cordiality in our Union than is felt, I believe, by all my Friends and believe me you have no Reason for supposing you have little weight with them: all I have conversed with speak highly of the direct and fair part you have taken this Session and I know they are men who will not say differently from what they think, and will act up to what they say.

I did not intend being in London till the 5th or 6th of February, and should hope that unless you have any very particular Commands for me I might keep my Intentions. I have not been idle since I have been here. Our Meeting is the 20th and I have hopes of great success.

From what I see, a general Spirit is rising.[2] I do not expect such immediate effects as some do but I think it will be gradual only to become more formidable, if commonly well managed. I am with sincere Regard and Esteem My Dear Lord

Your faithfull and obedient Servant

RICHMOND etc.

I can wait on you in Berkeley Square on the 6th in the Morning if that will suit you.

[1] Richmond presumably replied, but there is no record of his letter.

[2] The sentence is mistakenly quoted in Fitzmaurice, *Shelburne* (ii. 46) as being from a letter of 7 Dec. 1779.

Richmond to Shelburne

Lansdowne MSS.   15 March 1780

A letter concerning a motion Richmond had prepared for an inquiry into the defenceless state of Devon and Cornwall, charging that Lord Amherst, the Commander-in-Chief and Lt.-General of the Ordnance,[1] had been inattentive to the demands of Sir David Lindsay, military commander at Plymouth,[2] for more adequate fortification at Plymouth during the previous summer. The motion was put off until 25 April,[3] and on 17 March Richmond left to spend the Easter holidays at Goodwood.

Temporarily Rockingham and Shelburne had settled their differences. On 12 March Rockingham, Richmond, and Shelburne had conferred for several hours; shortly afterwards new rumours were circulating about a Rockingham–Shelburne coalition.[4]

Whitehall, Wednesday night
March 15th, 1780

My Dear Lord,

I went today to the House of Lords intending to give notice for Friday of Sr. David Lindsay's Business. As Lord Amherst was in the House I thought it fair to give him Notice and I read to him the Paper I shewed Your Lordship this Morning. I think he was struck with it and felt how necessary it would be to give it some answer. He said the Time was very short and that he could not be prepared by Friday. I thought I could not hurry him in such a Business and therefore told Him that altho' I certainly thought it my Duty to bring to Light Matters I thought wrong, yet He should never Complain of unfairness in me as to the Manner and therefore I would put it off till after the Holidays.[5] He was sensible of the fair part I acted and thanked me. In this situation not having anything ready to bring on for Friday I did not give any notice; but as the House sits tomorrow it may then be summon'd if Your Lordship can think of anything.

[1] See Richmond to Portland, p. 176, n. 1.

[2] Lt.-General Sir David Lindsay, Bart. (1732–97), Custos Brevium of the King's Bench, was promoted to General in 1796.

[3] *Parl. Hist.* xxi, 25 Apr. 1780.

[4] *Public Advertiser*, 14 Mar. 1780.

[5] The Easter holidays were from 17 Mar. to 10 Apr.

I have not seen any of the Delegates and know nothing of their Proceedings to Day.[1] Your Lordship knows my decided opinions on the Subject of today's Debate among them and therefore I have nothing to add to it but that I shall ever be ready to support and assist it in any way I can.

If You are at Leisure tomorrow at 12 o'clock I will call on You to see if You wish any Business for Friday and in what way You think of introducing it.[2] I am ever My Dear Lord

Your most sincere humble Servant,

RICHMOND, etc.

Richmond to Shelburne

Lansdowne MSS.   24 March 1780

During debates on 6 March concerning the removal of Lords Carmarthen and Pembroke from their respective lord lieutenancies Richmond and Shelburne had strayed off the subject to attack the granting of temporary Army commissions to men without military experience. As an example of such patronage they cited William Fullarton, M.P. for Plympton and temporarily appointed Lt.-Colonel of a new regiment he had raised himself. On 20 March Fullarton attacked Shelburne in the House of Commons in a speech he published in the *Public Advertiser*, and the following day he sent a personal letter to Shelburne demanding redress.[3] A duel was fought on 22 March in which Shelburne was slightly wounded;[4] by the end of the Easter recess he was entirely recovered.

[1] From 11 to 20 Mar. delegates of thirteen counties (including Sussex) in the Yorkshire Association were meeting to draw up an association platform. The platform adopted on 15 Mar. advocated an examination into public expenditure, the addition to Parliament of one hundred Knights of the Shire, and annual parliaments (*Wyvill Pol. Papers*, i. 119–21).

[2] There was nothing except routine business on Friday, 17 Mar.

[3] Fullarton, who had been Stormont's secretary at the Paris embassy, accused Richmond of calling him 'clerk', though Lord George Lennox had been Richmond's secretary when Richmond was Ambassador. He accused Shelburne of calling him 'Commis' to Stormont and of warning the Lords that his regiment would be used for buccaneering (*Walpole Last Journals*, ii. 290–1; *Public Advertiser*, 23 Mar. 1780; Fitzmaurice, *Shelburne*, ii. 52–54).

[4] On 22 Mar. the city of London sent a message inquiring after Shelburne's health. The same day Sir James Lowther moved an investigation into duelling and was defeated. Burke praised Shelburne highly in the debate (*Parl. Hist.* xxi, 22 Mar. 1780).

Goodwood Friday 24th March 1780

My Dear Lord,

I most sincerely rejoice at Your Escape from the wicked attempt which has, I fear, been made on Your Life. The account I had last night was very short but such as did you justice, for to say that You have acted with perfect Propriety is doing you no more than Justice; but that which I am most anxious for because the only possible doubtful Point, is Your recovery. I hear the Bullet has been extracted and that You are in no Danger. God Grant it may be so, for indeed Your Life is of great Consequence. Pray do not take the trouble to answer this Letter, but order a Servant, or Your Surgeon to let me have a Line to know how you go on. I am ever with the most sincere Regard

My Dear Lord Your faithfull humble Servant,

RICHMOND, etc.

Richmond to Shelburne

Lansdowne MSS.   (20 April 1780)

The letter concerns first, the collaboration over the debate of 25 April on Richmond's motion for an inquiry into the defenceless state of Devon and Cornwall, and second, the resolutions passed on 15 March by the Chamber of Deputies of the Yorkshire Association. The resolutions advocated political as well as economic reform: Richmond and Shelburne supported the platform, and on 13 April the Sussex Association under Richmond's personal direction had approved the resolutions; but Burke, Rockingham, Portland, and the Cavendishes wavered and finally boycotted a second Yorkshire meeting at which the resolutions were to be discussed.[1]

Whitehall Thursday night

My Dear Lord.

I am very sorry I missed of the pleasure of seeing Your Lordship when you did me the honor of calling on me yesterday and when I was at Your door this morning.

The notice I have given for Tuesday is on the Plymouth Business and I wish to see you on that subject. If you are at leisure between twelve and one tomorrow I will beg leave to wait upon you and will bring the narrative with me.

All I can say on other affairs is that whatever Lord

---

[1] Butterfield, *George III, Lord North and the People*, pp. 289–90.

Rockingham determines on is I am sure from the conviction
of his Mind; I shall much regret if it does not go so far as
Your Lordship's Ideas and my own lead us and it will certainly not prevent me from submitting to the public my
Notions of the only Remedy for all our Ills and it will be
great Satisfaction to me if they meet with your approbation.
I am ever My Dear Lord

Most sincerely Yours

RICHMOND, etc.

Richmond to Rockingham

Fitzwilliam MS. R166–27–1 and 2   9 July 1780

On 28 June North, through Fred Montague, asked Rockingham to
draw up terms for a possible coalition.[1] Among other conditions
Rockingham insisted upon the appointment of Richmond as Secretary
of State, but when the King learned of the demand he wrote North on
4 July refusing to have Richmond in the cabinet first, because of his
support for parliamentary reform and second, because of his refusal to
appear at court for several years.[2] In conversations with Montagu on
7 July North modified the King's words by omitting all reference to
parliamentary reform and suggesting that 'by some conduct . . . the
Duke of Richmond . . . may wipe off what the King has conceived to
have been meant as a personal affront'.[3] Apparently Rockingham
described Montagu's conversations in a letter to Keppel, which the
Admiral forwarded to Richmond.

It is clear from Richmond's tactless answer that his pride was hurt
by the stipulation, which both he and Keppel[4] considered a trick to
reduce Rockingham's number in any proposed coalition cabinet. By
the time he wrote Rockingham the negotiations had broken off.

Ranmer Camp, July the 9th, 1780

My Dear Lord,

You need make no Excuse for not writing to me. Your
very kind Visit here[5] and the whole Tenor of Your Conduct

---

[1] For a complete discussion of the negotiations see Christie, 'Rockingham and
Lord North's offer of a Coalition, 1780', *E.H.R.* 1954, pp. 388–407.

[2] *Corr. Geo. III*, v. 96–97. The King said seven or eight years, but it is clear from
Richmond's letter to Rockingham of 20 Mar. 1782, that he had not appeared at
court since Oct. 1770 (the letter is printed in Albemarle, *Rockingham*, ii. 467–8,
dated incorrectly as 24 Mar.).   [3] Ibid., p. 99.

[4] Keppel to Rockingham, 9 July 1780, *Keppel Life*, ii. 278.

[5] On Sunday, 2 July. Rockingham had already submitted his terms to North, but
he wanted to consult Richmond about the Treasury and about military appointments

towards me will never leave a Doubt in my Mind of Your
Friendship. The whole of this Transaction has been so much
against my opinion that it would have been only misspending
Your Time to have informed me of the Particulars as it went
on. Its conclusion, for I hope it is concluded, neither sur-
prises, nor grieves me; for I think the manner of its beginning foretold its End, and I confess I should have felt very
uneasy for You, if You had undertaken a share in Government, Circumstanced as Things are at St. James's and in
England. My Belief is, not that the Sentiments of His
Majesty and His Advisers are changed, but that from the
beginning there was no real Intention of taking you in, still
less of giving You the lead in Administration. It was guessed,
if not known, that You had differ'd with Lord Shelburne.[1]
This Negotiation was probably set on Foot to sound whether
that was so or not. If You was drawn in to talk of Measures
and Persons and did not say You must consult with Lord
Shelburne the Duke of Grafton and Lord Camden, it was
evident You had broke with them. This Point they have
ascertain'd and You may be sure they will take Care to let
Lord Shelburne and the others know that You have negotiated without naming them. If by this they keep up the
Disunion their great Point is gain'd. I have already heard
from more quarters than one that every Thing but one Place
has been offer'd You. But they have got more. They have
got an insight into Your Plans and can now tell People,
Lord Rockingham made no Stipulation for this, He never
mention'd that, and so on.

But I thank God this is now at an End, and as I see no
good to be done, I at least rejoice that You are not the Man
to do Harm. As to myself, I told you here my sincere opinion
of publick Affairs and my Resolution to have no Concern
with them till they bore a very different Complexion from
what They do at present. I do not mean as to the Difficulties
of foreign affairs, for, altho' God knows they are bad enough,

(Christie, 'Rockingham and Lord North's Offer of a Coalition, 1870', *E.H.R.* 1954,
p. 395).

[1] Mr. Christie (loc. cit.) suggests that Rockingham and Shelburne had differed
over parliamentary reform in Apr. 1780. It is clear from Richmond's correspondence with Shelburne that a drift had begun in March but that no formal breaks
had ever occurred.

yet I should not despair of recovering them by Good Sense, Activity, and Honesty, but I mean the Temper and Disposition at Home both in the Cabinet and in the Publick. While They remain as they are, I am sure I will not meddle. With these Intentions in respect to myself, and a feeling more of Contempt than of Anger towards the Court I am not much interested in the Sentiments that were entertain'd concerning me. However as the Expression was 'that there should be some Appearance of my being at Court etc., and Conciliation before any Thing could be settled about my being in high Employment', which seems to indicate as if I had shewn some such wish, I must beg the Favor of Your Lordship to write me a short Letter on this subject alone that it may be ostensible in answer to that which I inclose, in which you will do me the justice to say that you mention'd my Name without my Knowledge, and that I never gave you any Reason to believe that I had the smallest Inclination to take any Share in Government while the present System prevails. I would wish to send this Letter of Yours with one of my own to Lord North, not to insult, but in the most affectedly decent Terms to explain the Truth.

But now My Dear Lord I must come to a more difficult Point. When we were *well* with Lord Shelburne, etc., the D. of Grafton did *inform* acquaint us with a Negotiation.[1] You did the same towards them and it was then *agreed* amongst us to communicate any overtures that might hereafter be made. I know and lament, that Circumstances are changed, but still there has been no formal declaring off, and till then it seems to me that You may be accused of not keeping to our Agreement if you do not mention what has now passed. This seems to me necessary and yet it will be awkward to tell them that You have negotiated and never named them. Still any Thing is better in my opinion than appearing to act secretly till our Union is in due form dissolved.

If I could prevail, it should not be dissolved, it should be cemented stronger than ever. I am sure the late Transaction shews how little you can expect acting seperate. No Treasury,[2]

[1] 3 Feb. 1779.
[2] Rockingham had not demanded the Treasury for himself, but North had said that personally he would be glad to leave the office.

Keppel unfit for the Admiralty,[1] Ch. Fox treated like a Child,[2] and Your humble Servant like a man begging for Employment. Be assured My Dear Lord Rockingham that nothing is to be expected from Court than tends to change the System by good will. Nothing but necessity will make it reasonable. That necessity can arise but from a Union of all Parts of Opposition and upon strong popular Ground. But alas such are the Violences of private Animosities that I see no Prospect of such a Union. I can therefore only say that I lament and retire from publick Business.

I must be at the Sessions at Horsham on Tuesday but do not think I shall proceed to Goodwood. I shall be happy to see Your Lordship here or to wait on You at Wimbledon or in London any Day You please.

Pray present my best Respects to Lady Rockingham and believe me ever My Dear Lord

Your Sincere and faithfull humble Servant

RICHMOND, etc.

In an answer written on 11 July[3] Rockingham urged Richmond not to take precipitate action before having a 'quiet conversation' at Wimbledon with him the following weekend. Insisting that Richmond had been considered not as 'a man begging for employment' but as one very reluctant to enter office, he reassured the Duke of his intention to consult all parts of opposition, Lord Shelburne alone excepted because of personal rudeness to Rockingham during the London Riots.

Richmond to Thomas Conolly

MS. of Prof. G. H. Guttridge   23 November 1780

In the spring of 1780 Richmond's brother-in-law Thomas Conolly[4] had retired from English politics in order to concentrate his political activity entirely in Ireland. At the close of the Irish session, on 2 September 1780, Lady Louisa, always solicitous of Richmond's approbation of Conolly, sent Richmond a summary of Conolly's record,[5] which was so consistently pro-government that the Lord

---

[1] The King had complained that no man was as fit for the Admiralty as Sandwich (Christie, *E.H.R.*, p. 399).

[2] The King had approved of a 'lucrative not ministerial office' for Fox (loc. cit.).

[3] Fitzwilliam MS. R166-26.

[4] See p. 6, n. 2. Conolly had not been in England since April.

[5] See L. S. Gwynn, *Grattan and his Time*, 1939; also Henry Grattan, *Memoirs of*

Lieutenant considered him a supporter[1] and the Irish Volunteer Association passed him by for Charlemont as reviewing officer for their meeting in October.[2] Conolly had supported both the Mutiny Act brought over from England and a motion on 24 August for punishment of several publishers who printed irresponsible attacks on the act.

Richmond's letter indicates that Lady Louisa had distorted Conolly's record into one of moderation rather than government support.

Goodwood Nov. 23rd, 1780

My Dear Conolly,

I am much obliged to Louisa for the detail'd History she has been so good as to send me of your Parliamentary Conduct. My sincere Affection and Regard for you, must ever make me anxious for Information on any subject You are engaged in, and that of the Affairs of Ireland is by no means uninteresting in such times as these.

It is impossible for any one at the Distance I am at, to form decided opinions upon Matters which consist of such a Variety of detail, and knowing so little as I do of Your Country: but from Louisa's account I think You judged truely for the benefit of Ireland and that of the two Kingdoms, in taking Advantage of the weakness of our Ministry and of Your own Strength, to secure to Yourselves those Benefits which I will say, God and Nature has given you, and to free Yourselves from those shackles which were preserved, not for any real Good to England, but merely to enable an English ministry to corrupt an Irish Parliament, and to enrich their own Dependants, at the same time endeavouring to preserve the Connection between the two Countries. My opinion is that a Connection is necessary for our mutual Safety. I confess that that which is established is founded upon Absurdity and Injustice and whenever examin'd must fall, but still as *a connection* is necessary, I would not pull that down which does exist before I erected another to stand in its Place. This I am sensible is a very arduous

the Life and Times of the Rt. Hon. Henry Grattan, 1839, i. 395–403; *Journals of the Irish House of Commons; H. M. C. Stopford-Sackville*, i. 267–76. Memoirs of the period are extremely sketchy: formal records of the debates do not begin until 1784, and reports appear only sporadically in English newspapers before that date.
  [1] Buckinghamshire to Lord George Germaine, 5 Feb. 1780, *H. M. C. Stopford-Sackville*, p. 267.
  [2] Gwynn, *Grattan and his Time*, p. 107.

Task and perhaps impossible to execute with a Ministry so incapable to Act, to think, or to plan any Thing, as that which now governs us both. However I would not discourage those who have a Head Assiduity sufficient for undertaking such a work. The more it is discussed, weigh'd and consider'd, the better. It will tend to open men's Minds and induce them to think for themselves which is always a good. The only Point I would never give up in all these considerations is that a Connection is necessary. Let men differ as they always must, about the mode; let them even adopt a wrong one; any is better than none; and example has shewn us that a very imperfect one may still preserve the two Kingdoms united. Whenever a better Bond of Union can be framed and meet with the concurrence of the two Kingdoms, I think it ought to be adopted, and the more liberal it is, the more it is likely to be of general Benefit and to last. But I should in Your Place earnestly Beseech my Countrymen not to pull down this Party wall, which tho' it keeps us separate, still connects us and gives us mutual strength, until they can substitute a better in its stead, to lead them to do this you must preserve the weight which Your Fortune and Character naturally gives you among them. And I think You and the Duke of Leinster judged very right to take a Part in the Associations to put Yourselves at the Head of them and thereby be enabled more easily to lead them to good and to prevent them from doing Mischief. The only Point in which perhaps I differ from You is the means of checking them when You found them going too far. I would have remonstrated in private, have prayed and beseech'd them not to go so far, but I would not have publickly censur'd and attempted to Punish them. And for this plain Reason, that they will never yield to Punishment; that the attempt, only makes them more obstinate, and loses You the Influence which you might still possess of preventing further Mischief. Now I fear they will get into other Hands who having no good publick views will encourage them to every act of Violence to further their own Consequence. The Result of which can be no other than Civil War. I certainly would never have agreed to act with them on a Point I thought wrong, but there is great difference between acting with

them and not acting against them. And there is a Medium
of holding back without taking a Part against them, which
might have equally check'd them, still have preserved Your
Influence over them. Men like Your Associations having
taken up arms for their Liberty and feeling themselves
powerfull and successful will not brook Censure and Punishment. They must be treated with much Gentleness. Your
Country is not in a state of regular Government, and you
cannot think of enforcing upon all occasions those Restraints
which in ordinary Times may be proper. For God's Sake get
over as soon as You can this disagreeable Business, and get
as soon as you can on good Terms again with Your Associations. I think you may lead them from wrong but you will
never drive them. I can say nothing good of this Country or
its politick and therefore shall say nothing about it. I am
endeavouring to preserve my Health here and to become as
quiet a spectator of Our approaching Miseries as I can be
without divesting myself of feeling for a Country so wretch-
edly lost.

I have order'd two Hundred and twenty five Pounds to
be paid according to Your Desire to Mess. Drummond and
Co, Charing Cross.[1] I had only paid £25 to the Chichester
Associated Company. Adieu. Give my best Love to Louisa
and believe me my Dearest Conolly ever
Your faithfull and Affectionate
humble servant,
RICHMOND, etc.

Richmond to Lord Mahon[2]

Chevening MSS. 12 March 1781
From 3 March to 11 April occurred the second annual meeting of the
Chamber of Deputies of the Yorkshire Association. Eight counties

[1] For a brief history of the banking house of George Drummond and Sons see
Gentleman's Magazine, 1794, p. 676. There is no evidence of the reason for
Richmond's deposit.

[2] The present Earl Stanhope has kindly provided a copy of this letter. Though
Richmond and Mahon were not close friends, they apparently corresponded fre-
quently; but the majority of the letters were alienated from the family estate by the
present Earl's grandfather and cannot be located. At the time Richmond wrote,
Mahon was on his honeymoon with his second wife, Louisa, d. of Henry Grenville,
Ambassador at Constantinople. He had returned to London by 24 Mar. (*Stanhope
Life*, p. 47).

(including Lord Mahon's county of Kent) and the cities of London[1]
and Westminster were represented—a total drop of eight groups from
the previous year—and interest was so low that the meeting resolved
that a platform on political reform would be 'inexpedient' at the time.[2]
Realizing the extent of public apathy, Richmond kept Sussex representatives from the meeting, although the county had been represented
the previous year and had ratified the resolutions then.[3]

Richmond had been at Goodwood since the beginning of February;
he returned to Parliament on 26 March.

Goodwood

My Lord,   March the 12th, 1781
    I am very sorry that Your Lordship should have taken
the trouble of writing to me on the subject of the Sussex
Association. I have not endeavour'd to assemble the County
again because I have not had any application for that purpose, and because my own mind leads me strongly to believe
that no good can arise from any such steps while men's minds
are so much divided upon what is proper to be recommended, and that instead of any previous meetings to concert
unanimity, every Day produces greater marks of dissagree-
ment between those who must be united before any good
can be done. I have the Honor to be with great Esteem
                My Lord
                    Your Lordship's most obedient and
                        most humble Servant,
                            RICHMOND, etc.

Richmond to Rockingham

Fitzwilliam MS. R2   12 March 1782

In the election for a successor to General William Keppel, M.P. for
Chichester, deceased, Richmond put up Percy Wyndham, brother of
the Earl of Egremont, Richmond's close friend and supporter at the
county meeting on parliamentary reform, while the 'independents' of
the city, backed by government and the Pelham-Ashburnham interest,
put up a Bryan Edwards. When Richmond wrote to Rockingham he
had only the news from 10 March; on 13 March Wyndham was

----

1 London withdrew from the meeting.
2 *Wyvill Pol. Papers*, i. 395; *Sound Reason*, p. 81.
3 13 Apr. 1780, *Wyvill Pol. Papers*, i. 180–4. Wyvill listed Sussex in 1781 (i. 382)
as favouring the Yorkshire Association but not a member of it.

declared victor by 247 votes to 239,[1] an unexpectedly close margin
which materially damaged Richmond's prestige in the city.[2] Edwards
later petitioned against the results on the grounds that the mayor of the
city, whose election was controlled by Richmond, had admitted non-
residents to vote illegally; two years later the King's Bench decided in
Wyndham's favour.

My Dear Lord,
    As you may wish to hear of Chichester, I find they polled
alternately and concluded equal, each having one Hundred
and Eleven Votes. Ministry interferes and have sent their
orders to the Custom House officers to vote against Wyndham and Mr. Edwards has been detected in sending a
Messenger to Mr. Robinson[3] on which circumstances alone
7 or 8 doubtfull People at once polled for Mr. Wyndham.
Mr. Steele[4] assures me that He thinks Mr. Wyndham safe
if those who have promised keep their word, but I fear
corruption at the pinch. At all Events it will be a near run
Heat.

                                        Ever Yours,
                                        RICHMOND, etc.

Whitehall Tuesday Morn:
    March 12th, 1782.

    I doubt this news of Sir Sam'l Hood's[5] will tell against us

    [1] See T. W. Horsfield, *The History, Antiquities, and Topography of the County of
Sussex*, 1835, ii. 37–39; *Victoria History of the County of Sussex*, ed. L. F. Salzman, 1935, iii. 100; *Journals of the House of Commons*, xxxviii. 25 Mar., 22 and
27 Apr. 1782; Minutes of Chichester Court of Common Council, 13 Mar. 1782.
Richmond's account books at Goodwood indicate that he spent no money on the
campaign outside newspaper advertisements.
    [2] John Robinson estimated Chichester as 'uncertain' in his calculations for the
election of 1784 (*Robinson Parliamentary Papers*, p. 78). In the election of 1790
Richmond was forced to compromise with the independents and concede them
one seat permanently (Horsfield, *Sussex*, ii. 37). There is no evidence to support
Richmond's claim that in 1782 the government was behind the independents.
    [3] John Robinson (1727–1802), M.P. for Harwich, Secretary of the Treasury,
and chief electioneering agent for the government. See *Robinson Parliamentary
Papers*, pp. v–xx.
    [4] Thomas Steele, the other M.P. for Chichester, See p. 6, n. 3.
    [5] Sir Samuel Hood, Bart. (1724–1816), Rear-Admiral of the Blue, was in com-
mand of a squadron in the West Indies. On 25 Jan. Hood had outwitted the French
Commander de Grasse by luring him out of port at St. Christopher's and slipping
into the same port in an attempt to relieve a British garrison on the island.

on Friday. We should therefore be prepared for being best
and for a strong but decent Remonstrance.[1]

Richmond to Shelburne

Lansdowne MSS.   20 March 1782

Richmond to Shelburne

Lansdowne MSS.   (21 March 1782)

After North's resignation on 18 March and the failure of Thurlow's
negotiations with Rockingham the same day, Thurlow was sent to
sound Shelburne on 19 March. Shelburne refused to consider office
without Rockingham and also refused further negotiations except
directly with the King. The King saw Shelburne on 21 March and
authorized him then to treat with Rockingham.[2]

There is no evidence that Shelburne saw Rockingham himself
concerning the negotiations until 24 March.[3] Richmond, then, was
acting as go-between in the later stages of negotiation. His metaphoric
style, always indicative of familiarity, here illustrates the peak of
Richmond's friendship with Shelburne.

The second letter, which is incorrectly dated 'Thursday, March 20',
could be either Wednesday evening, 20 March, or Thursday morning,
21 March. Internally it looks as if it were written the same day as the
first letter; on the other hand, Richmond would have been more likely
to know the correct day than the correct date, and since his handwriting on the date is nearly illegible, he may have written a 1 which
looked like an 0.

My Dear Lord,

I was set out to wait on You and had got half way when
I was again attacked with the Pain I have had so much of
lately in my Teeth which obliged me to return and will I
trust plead my excuse for not waiting on Your Lordship.
Indeed I had nothing more to say than to tell you from Lord

---

[1] Nothing material occurred in the House of Lords on Friday, 15 Mar.;
Richmond did not attend for the rest of the week.

[2] Robinson to Jenkinson, 20 Mar. 1782, *Corr. Geo. III*, v. 402; *Memorials and
Correspondence of C. J. Fox*, i. 290–8; Fitzmaurice, *Shelburne*, ii. 87; *Grafton Autobiography*, p. 316; Rockingham to Shelburne, 24 Mar. 1782, Albemarle, *Rockingham*,
ii. 463.

[3] Shelburne saw Rockingham at a party at Devonshire House after his audience
with the King, but did not talk politics with him.

Rockingham that He had again seen the Chancellor but it was only to explain and understand one another right which they found they had done from the beginning, and matters rested yesterday (since when I had not heard anything), precisely as they were with however one additional and important circumstance. The Chancellor ask'd Lord Rockingham whether supposing the Measures He proposed were granted more would not be proposed? to which I understand Lord Rockingham answered that such a Question might be asked with a view to create disunion where there was none, but He would answer it distinctly, if He meant a Parliamentary Reform it was what we all had equally at Heart although we might differ as to the practical Means, but that we differed fairly and honestly as men may do about an End they wish to accomplish and that if we could amongst us settle some Plan that should unite the opinions of the Publick, He should by no means hold himself bound to resist it, but on the Contrary should give it every assistance in His Power. But if You see Lord Rockingham He will tell you this himself.

I am My Dear Lord
Ever Most truely
Yours RICHMOND, etc.

Whitehall, Wednesday, 3 o'clock.

Whitehall, Thursday
March 20th 1782, 10 o'clock

My Dear Lord,

I will not give you the trouble of calling here but will wait on Your Lordship in about an Hour. My Pain in my Tooth has left me for the present but I fear like the Ministry will require a radical Cure by (Extirpation), and what is worse, I doubt whether like the nation I have not already suffer'd so many (losses) that I shall never be able to bite a hard Crust again. Your Lordship is very kind in Your Friendship for me and I can safely assure You that as far as sincerity goes I am not unworthy of it. I am ever

most truely and sincerely yours
RICHMOND, etc.

Richmond to Shelburne

Lansdowne MSS.   22 January 1783

In a cabinet meeting held on 5 December to discuss the treaties of
peace, Shelburne announced his intention to acquiesce in French
demands for Newfoundland and Spanish demands for Gibraltar.
Richmond, leader of a 'war party' within the cabinet, objected to both
terms and complained to the King of his own unimportance in the
ministry.[1] Early in January, when he discovered that Shelburne had
authorized still further concessions to France and Spain without consulting any other ministers except Grantham, Richmond definitely
decided to leave the cabinet, but promised the King he would wait until
the preliminary articles of peace were signed.[2] The signing took place
on 20 January;[3] two days later Richmond officially stopped attending
the cabinet.

He remained at the Ordnance because he had just completed preliminary plans for the fortification of Portsmouth and Plymouth and
for a newly reorganized Ordnance budget,[4] and because he realized
that if he resigned office, Camden and Grafton would join him and the
ministry would fail immediately.[5] Richmond's first public acknowledgement of his split with Shelburne occurred in his disavowal of the
peace terms during the parliamentary debates of 17 February.

                                   Whitehall, Wednesday night
                                        January 22nd, 1783

My Dear Lord,
      Having laid before the King to Day my Reasons for
begging not to attend Cabinet Council, any more, and His
Majesty having been so good as grant my Request, I have
to make my excuses to Your Lordship for not attending You
tonight. The King was exceedingly King an [sic] Good to

      1 George III to Shelburne, 5 Dec. 1782, Add. MS. 34,523, f. 369. Richmond had
frequently complained of a lack of cordiality and communication in Shelburne's
ministry. See Harlow, *Second British Empire*, pp. 389, 293, 349, 355, 379.
      2 George III to Shelburne, 12 Jan. 1783, Add. MS. 34,523, f. 340.
      3 Fitzmaurice, *Shelburne*, ii. 448–52.
      4 Richmond to Shelburne, 30 Jan. 1783, W.O. Out letters 46/18/11 (O.B.).
      5 *Grafton Autobiography*, pp. 354–67. Walpole (*Last Journals*, ii. 479–80) sug-
gested with some justification that Richmond was attempting a coalition of Shelburne and Fox. He certainly wished to avoid a coalition of North with either faction,
but there is no actual proof for Walpole's statement.

me and I was happy to find that the manner in which I took this Step was well receiv'd by His Majesty.

I have the Honor to be

Your Lordships' Very sincere and
obedient Servant,
RICHMOND, etc.

Richmond to the Bishop of Exeter[1]

Add. MS. 34,523, ff. 373–4   27 January 1783

A letter explaining to the Bishop of Exeter Richmond's reasons for leaving the cabinet. The address must be assumed to be correct, since it is in the same hand as the body of the letter, but the Bishop of Exeter, contrary to Richmond's assumption in writing the letter, was actually in town on 27 January and in fact never missed a meeting of Parliament in January–February 1783. The fact that he offered to give his proxy to Richmond, and that Richmond told only his close friends of his decision not to attend cabinet meetings, indicates a fairly close personal acquaintance. These two letters, however, are the only extant indications of such acquaintance; it can only be surmised that Richmond knew the Bishop through Fox and through Weymouth, his early patron.

Whitehall, Jan. 27th, 1783

My Dear Lord,

I was very sorry to miss the opportunity of speaking to you the other day in the House of Lords, when I wished to have informed you that not being able to approve the terms of the Peace I had withdrawn myself from His Majesty's Councils. I well know that this Country wants Peace and that after the waste of Men and Money we have had, that further Exertions must be difficult to make; but as by the Treaty with America we had in fact agreed with Her, there was little doubt but we should soon have detached her from France or at least have had in her a very cool Enemy. I am persuaded that this circumstance must have operated on France, and that her Fleet & that of Spain were in a very bad condition, whilst ours was more numerous and in better

---

[1] John Ross (1719–92), F.R.S., was a classical scholar and Fellow of St. John's College, Cambridge, 1743–70. In 1757 he was appointed preacher at the Rolls, in 1769, Canon at Durham, and in 1778, through Weymouth's influence, Bishop of Exeter (see particularly *Gentleman's Magazine*, 1792, ii. 774, 864–5).

order than it had ever been at any period. Under these circumstances I think that if we had stuck to our first and better terms we should have had them, or that if our Enemies had been obstinate we had the fairest prospect in the course of next Summer of striking some essential blow against their Fleet besides attacking the weak Possessions of Spain already much distressed by the Rebellion in Her Provinces. Instead of which we after having already made great sacrifices, have made still more and have given up Tobago to the French,[1] and Trincomali a place of the greatest importance in the East Indies to the Dutch.[2] I would not consent to be involved in these Measures & have therefore quitted the Cabinet where besides my situation had been for some time not very pleasant. I have not resigned the Ordnance because I consider it as a Military Employment totally separate from Administration & because I have begun a variety of reforms of great Importance which I wish to see compleated, and therefore wish to remain in this Employment for sometime longer if I can do it with consistency.

Your Lordship sees that under these Circumstances I must object to the Peace altho' I shall do it with as much Moderation as possible, for altho' I cannot approve of the present Measures in respect of Peace yet I do not see that the great Measures of Parliamentary Reform & publick Economy are abandoned by Ministry, or adopted by our late Friends. My future conduct will therefore be determined by the Measures I see pursued.

In Your Lordships situation you will judge what is right for yourself to do. If from the Confidence you are pleased to place in me, and for which I am much obliged to you, I might venture to advise, I should think that being out of Town Your Lordship is not absolutely called upon to give your Proxy at all, & that you might with great propriety

[1] Tobago was ceded to the French on 3 Jan., in partial exchange for Britain's retention of Dominica. See Harlow, *Second British Empire*, pp. 377-9.

[2] Trincomali, the only good harbour on the west side of the Bay of Bengal, had been captured from the Dutch by Sir Edward Hughes in Jan. 1782, and was recaptured by de Suffren in August, too late for news to reach England before the peace negotiations were terminated. With great reluctance Shelburne yielded Trincomali, when it became apparent that British insistence on retention of the harbour would jeopardize the peace settlement. See ibid., pp. 384-90.

stay away and not Vote on a question which after all requires a complete knowledge of all the negotiations to decide properly upon. But Your Lordship will judge best for Yourself & I can only assure you that on this as on all occasions I shall be most happy to obey your Commands as it is ever with the most sincere esteem & perfect regard that

I have the Honor to be My Dear Lord, Your Lordship's
Most obedient and most humble Servant,
RICHMOND, etc.

Richmond to the Bishop of Exeter

Add. MS. 34,523, f. 377   25 February 1783

On 24 February Shelburne resigned; the following day Portland asked Richmond to keep the Ordnance and return to the cabinet.[1] Richmond remained undecided until Portland pressed him for a decision on 4 April, the day after the coalition ministry was actually settled; then he resigned the Ordnance in anger.[2] Far more than his remaining with Shelburne in July 1782, the decision not to join Portland in 1783 alienated Richmond from the 'Old Whigs'.[3]

Though frequently at the Ordnance office in February and March Richmond attended Parliament only twice. The Bishop of Exeter attended regularly.

Whitehall, Feb. 25, 1783

My dear Lord,
I would not enter your Proxy, thinking it best not to make you Vote as I did, when you had not the same Information, and considering your situation, I judged there was no necessity for producing your Proxy.[4] Ld. Shelburne is now out with all his Cabinet, tho' all do not follow him. The new Arrangement will be formed immediately and I understand that the Duke of Portland is to have the Treasury with the 2 Secretaries the Admiralty and Commander in Chief

[1] *Walpole Last Journals*, ii. 487.
[2] Ibid., pp. 509–10. See Lady Sarah Lennox to Lady Susan O'Brien, 25 Mar. 1783, *Life and Letters of Lady Sarah Lennox*, ii. 33. Portland was considering Richmond alternatively as Secretary at War (Fox to Portland, 4 Apr. 1783. Nottingham MSS.). See also Sackville to Irwin, 4 Apr. 1783, *H. M. C. Stopford-Sackville*, p. 144.
[3] In 1795 after Portland's union with Pitt, it was the 'Old Whigs' who demanded Richmond's removal.
[4] The only date to which Richmond might refer would be 24 Feb., when the Bishop of Exeter did not attend Parliament.

amongst his Friends, in short the efficient Offices, leaving
to Lord North the Presidency of the Council, Privy Seal,
and other Lucrative Employments.[1] In support of this
arrangement they are beating up for Volunteers and wish
to get as many of the Old Whigs to support them as they
can but they are daily loosing some of the best and steadiest
of their old Friends. You have doubtless heard that Mr.
Powis, Mr. Masham, Sir Harbord Harbord, Sir Edwd.
Astley, Mr. Parker of Devonshire, Sir—Skipwick, Mr.
Honeywood, Mr. Duncombe, Charles Turner[2] and many
others have declared against supporting Mr. Fox in this
Coalition with Lord North, and I find that in Westminster
it creates such a ferment as to make it certain He will lose
his Election if any body opposes him.

The goodness Your Lordship has always shown me & the
Friendship you have honor'd me with makes me desirous to
communicating to you the part I mean to take. The D. of
Portland was with me this Morning and very politely desired
my assistance and support. I told His Grace that I would do
anything to unite the Whigs and to keep out Lord North,
but that I must resign the moment He comes in, which after
much very friendly conversation is what I must adhere to.
I doubt it will be indispensable for your Lordship to come to
Town, for unpleasant as the division is you must take your
part for things are now come to that crisis, that we must all
decide. Your Lordship's own judgment will of course decide
you, but indeed you should be on the spot and see what is
doing and converse with different People to be able to judge
of the Effect these events have on the publick. I confess I

1 Portland had the Treasury, Fox and North were Secretaries of State, Keppel, a
Portland supporter, had the Admiralty, and Conway was Commander-in-Chief,
while Stormont, a North supporter, had the presidency of the Council and Carlisle,
whose personal loyalties appear to have been divided equally between Fox and
North, had the Privy Seal. The other 'Lucrative Employments' seem to have been
divided fairly equally between the followers of Fox and North.

2 Of the nine names mentioned, five (Thomas Powis, M.P. for Northampton-
shire, Henry Duncombe, M.P. for York, John Parker, M.P. for Devonshire, and
Filmer Honeywood and Charles Marsham, M.P.s for Kent) were definite opponents
of the Fox–North coalition; so probably was Sir C. Turner, M.P. for the city of
York. Sir Edward Astley, M.P. for Norfolk, opposed Fox's India Bill, and was
expected by John Robinson to be a fairly consistent supporter of Pitt. But Sir
Thomas Skipwith, M.P. for Steyning, supported the coalition, and Sir Harbord
Harbord, M.P. for the city of Norwich, probably gave it moderate support.

feel more hurt than I can describe at the Whigs losing themselves so entirely as this will do in the opinion of the Publick; for you have no conception how it is resented. I told the D. of P. that I feared his would be the weakest of Ministrys, without the support of the King, having lost that of the People and depending on Lord North for his Majorities in Parliament.

Lord North too has taken care to declare that he is against any Parliamentary Reform and I am sure he will have the power to prevent any Measure he may not like. But indeed my dear Lord you must judge of all this on the spot. I therefore hope you will come to Town soon.

You will I hope do me the Justice to believe me ever with the Sincerest esteem & regard

My dear Lord

Your most obedient & faithful Servant,

RICHMOND, &c.

Richmond to Shelburne

Lansdowne MSS. 28 May 1783

Richmond to Camden

Camden MSS. 2 June 1783

On 1 April Thurlow resigned and the Great Seal was put into commission to Baron Loughborough,[1] Sir William Henry Ashurst,[2] and Sir Beaumont Hotham.[3] On 3 June, when copies of their patents for holding the Seal were presented to the House of Lords, Richmond moved to establish a committee 'to consider further regulations to secure the independency of the judges'. Camden, who had absented himself since March, did not appear; Shelburne was present, but not in support of Richmond. The motion, which Loughborough took personally,[4] was rejected, and the Seal remained in commission until December.

[1] Alexander Wedderburne (1733–1805), created Baron Loughborough in 1780, was Attorney-General, 1778–80, Chief Justice of the Court of Common Pleas, 1780–92, and Lord Chancellor, 1793–1801. In 1801 he was created Earl of Rosslyn.

[2] Sir William Henry Ashurst, Bart. (1725–1807), Sergeant-at-Law and Judge of the King's Bench, was on the Commission for the Great Seal again from June 1792 to Jan. 1793.

[3] Sir Beaumont Hotham, Knt. (1737–1814), Sergeant-at-Law, and Baron of the Exchequer Court, 1775–1805. [4] *Parl. Hist.* xxiii, 3 June 1783.

Richmond had attended Parliament only occasionally since April; he retired to Goodwood immediately after the debate on 3 June. His letter to Camden shows the void in leadership of Shelburne's party left between the fall of Shelburne—who had dismissed his adherents and retired to the country—and the rise of William Pitt. Richmond was aware that he himself might try to fill the gap but that age, temperament, and personality would prevent his doing so successfully.

Whitehall, Wednesday morning
May the 28th, 1783

My Dear Lord,

As Your Lordship wished to be acquainted with the Time I meant to bring on any Business in the House of Lords I have the Honor to inform you that I mean to move to Day that the Lords should be summon'd for Tuesday next the 3rd a[s I] shell (sic) give notice that the subject I mean to bring forward is the appointment of Three Judges to hold the Great Seal, conceiving that chosen by Favor as they are, and holding this commission with the considerable salary annexed to it at the will of the Crown, is inconsistent with that Species of Independency which was attempted to be established by the act of King William[1] and that of His present Majesty[2] which give them their commission of Judges & their Salaries quam diu se bene gesserint. This Position I believe will not be denied me, or at least will not be difficult to maintain but the Difficulty will be to find the proper Remedy. To say the Seals must *never* be put in Commission may be too much. And if they ever are, into what Hands shall they go? If the Judges are altogether excluded from being Commissioners on account of its affecting their Independency which is one Idea, on whom must it fall? If the commissioners are taken from the Bar, they cannot return to it again & of course must have floating Pensions or some Provision which will cost the Country a great deal. The Master of the Rolls only could accept of such an office

---

[1] By the Act of Settlement (12 and 13 William III, c. 2) when the House of Hanover came to the throne, judges' commissions were to be made *quam diu se bene gesserint,* and their salaries were to be fixed. Judges could be dismissed only for conviction for some offence, or on an address of both Houses.

[2] In 1760 Parliament passed a bill which provided that judges' commissions were not to be determined by a demise of the crown, and that salaries were to be duly paid (1 Geo. III, c. 23).

without other Provision. Another Thought is to make the Judges when they become Commissioners act as such only, and not as Judges at the same Time, and receive no additional salary; so that on the same Pay they would only sit in Chancery instead of their own Court, whence it is said one might be spared without Inconveniency. but then it is said they would not accept of being commissioners. if the House seems inclined to come into any of these Remedies or to propose any other I shall be glad to adopt any provided the Evil is cured. If I find no disposition to any remedy I shall I think barely state the Fact in a Resolution & take the sense of the House upon it meaning to follow it up with a Reference to a Committee to consider if some means of remedying the Evil. I have mention'd the subject to Lord Thurlow, who feels himself under some personal Difficulties but, I believe will not be against it. I shall write today to communicate it to Lord Camden, altho' I hear he is out of Town & does not mean to attend any more this session. I shall be obliged to Your Lordship if you will acquaint Lord Ashburton with my Intentions.[1] Inclosed I send the Resolution I think of moving.

I beg Leave to return Your Lordship my very best thanks for the very fine fish you was so good as to send me which proved the best I ever tasted & were much admired. I am also much obliged to Your Lordship for the Champaign You was so good as to let me have and as You said You had a great Quantity, shall be glad to know if You can spare me any more & what Quantity. You will further oblige me if You will trust Your servant to let mine know what it cost. I am ever very sincerely my Dear Lord

Your most obedient & faithfull Servant,

RICHMOND, etc.

To a similar letter Camden sent an undated reply[2] excusing himself from attendance at Parliament because of a dinner engagement with Thomas Conolly and Lady Louisa. He urged Richmond to accept the commission as a temporary expedient of far less assistance to the ministry than the immediate appointment of a chancellor; if passed, Richmond's motion would give the ministry a chance to defend any appointment, however unpopular, by claiming that their decision was

---

[1] Ashburton did not attend Parliament on 3 June.   [2] Camden MSS.

forced prematurely. Camden concluded his letter with a melancholy comment on the aimless state of Shelburne's former friends.

(Richmond to Camden)   Whitehall, Monday June 2d 1783

My Lord,

I do assure your Lordship that I feel very particularly flatter'd by your goodness in condescending to enter so fully into the subject of my motion for to morrow, and I cannot but look on your fairness in stating your objections as the best proof your Lordship can give of the friendship you are pleased to honor me with.

I, in return, shall not disguise that I agree with the greater part of your Lordship's observations, and yet I think that if I had the honor of some conversation with you, I might be able to convince your Lordship that I ought not totally to abandon this subject. It is certainly far more extensive than the words of my motion convey, for if the idea of rendering the Judges independent by Commissions during good behaviour, and by fixed salaries, is a right one, there are a thousand ways by which the present regulation may be defeated; and the present commission tho' legal & not new, is evidently an effective way of rendering the act of Wm. the 3d of little or no effect, for nothing can be more opposite to its principles. Lord Loughborough's pension is another instance of the same kind. Lord Mansfield's being Speaker is a farther example, and these considerations naturally lead to others respecting the Judges sitting in the H. of Lords any more than they do in the H. of Commons. Their attendance in the H. of Lords which is the reason given 200 years ago for their not sitting in the H. of Commons would equally apply to Masters in Chancery, & does apply to the Att: & Solicitor General, but is not observed in their case, and in fact such a reason is too bad a one for such a regulation which however stands as yet on no other foundation than that ridiculous resolution. The true ground, and that which is felt, but no where expressed by Law, seems to be that the judicial & legislative power should be kept as distinct as possible, & this reason goes as well to keep judges out of the H. of Lords as Commons. In truth Judges should

not be politicians; for whenever they become so that alone
deprives them of their independency, and altho' I perfectly
agree with your Lordship that there has been no intention
of corrupting Baron Hotham or Mr. Justice Ashurst, I
believe Your Lordship will as readily agree with me that the
two Chief Justices are more of politicians than quite becomes
the character of judges & that a variety of court favors
may in some degree have put their independency in danger.

I am very sensible that the publick may not feel all the
danger I do from the situation of the Judges which appears
to me to stand in need of attention; and I know that more
pointed and personal attacks on subjects more immediately
affecting the present passions of mankind would be more
popular both within & without doors. But in the present
unsystematick state of politicks when one knows not whether
one is doing harm or good by stirring, I wish to be as quiet
as possible, and yet as a total abandonment of politicks has
also its objections, I wished to steer a middle way, and this
business seem'd to me worthy being stirred [sic]. I mean to
open the whole of it, perhaps to move only for a Committee
to consider of the subject, or perhaps only to bespeak the
attention of Lords to it for another year. In short I would
follow the temper of the House. I cannot but regret Your
Lordship's absence as I must always do, on all occasions,
and I am very sorry that my having this business prevents
my accepting your Lordship's kind invitation to Camden
Place, when otherwise I should be particularly happy to
wait on you to morrow.

I mean soon after the Birth Day to go to Paris for a short
time, and am meditating for next year a much longer absence, the Tour of Europe with my nephew. For perfectly
unsettled in all my old connections & unwilling to form new
ones unless it can be on Whig principles & with such men
as I can confide in, which at present I see no appearance of,
I mean to turn my mind to what I hope will answer better
than politicks, the education of my nephew, who perhaps
may reap more advantage from travelling with one who has
seen too much of the world, than with one who knows
nothing of it, which is the case of common tutors. I shall
however always be ready when I see I can do any good in

publick to sacrifice private considerations for such an end, and do most sincerely assure your Lordship that there is no man with whom I could act with more pleasure than your Lordship for whose publick principles & private virtues I have so sincere a veneration. I have the honor to be My Lord,

Your Lordship's most obedient and most humble servant,

RICHMOND, etc.

Richmond to Lord Sydney[1]

Brotherton MSS.   27 March 1784

Richmond to Lord Sydney

Brotherton MSS.   29 March 1784

On 21 March Pitt's cabinet had decided to leave on the government's recommended list of Scottish representative peers Viscount Stormont,[2] Secretary of State under North, supporter of the Fox–North Coalition, and a Scottish representative peer since 1754. Stormont was recommended on the assumption that the King wished him returned. When the King proved lukewarm, Richmond insisted that the less influential Lord Roseberry, friend of the Duke of Argyll, be included instead. Against the wishes of the majority of the cabinet who thought it better to support Stormont than risk defeat, Roseberry was left in,[3] only to be defeated by Stormont.

Richmond had come to Goodwood only two days before writing Sydney. On the day before he left London Pitt had offered Richmond the Home Department, in place of Sydney who would have the Privy Seal.[4]

Goodwood, March 27th, 1784
Saturday Morning

My Dear Lord,

I was last night honor'd with Your Lordship's Letter the

[1] Thomas Townshend (1733–1800), first Baron Sydney, was a Lord of the Treasury in Rockingham's first administration, Joint Postmaster under Chatham (until June 1768), Secretary at War in the second Rockingham ministry, and Secretary of State for the Home Office under Shelburne and Pitt until 1789.

[2] David Murray (1727–96), Viscount Stormont, was Ambassador to Vienna, 1763–72, and to Paris, 1772–8, Lord Justice General of Scotland, 1778–95, Secretary of State for the South, 1779–82, President of the Council in the Fox–North Coalition and again, 1794–6. In 1794 he succeeded his uncle as Earl of Mansfield.

[3] *Leeds Pol. Mem.*, p. 100.   [4] Ibid., p. 102.

contents of which give me much Concern. I will not trouble
Your Lordship with the Many Objections I have to Lord
Stormont's receiving the Countenance of an Administration
in which I have any share but merely state to Your Lordship
that in Consequence of the authority I receiv'd from the
Cabinet on Tuesday, and the Doubt that was afterwards
entertain'd being given up I wrote on Wednesday to the
Duke of Buccleugh to desire His Grace to accept of my
Proxy for *the List* which I sent Him, and have taken Pains to
have it known that the List I sent was the List of Government and that Method agreed upon as the proper Means of
circulating it. After this step I hope I shall not be disavowed
and that the List I had the authority of the Ministry to pledge
myself for will be supported.

Your Lordship's saying that this Measure was to be taken
without any Communication makes me Hope that no Difficulties will occur but I must repeat that I trust at all events I
shall not be given up in a Measure undertaken by Your
Desire. I have written to Mr. Pitt more fully on this Subject
and have the Honor to be with great Esteem Your Lordship's

most obedient humble Servant,

RICHMOND, etc.

P.S. I have thought it necessary to trouble Your Lordship
with this answer by Express.

Goodwood Monday 29th March, 1784

My Dear Lord,

I am much concern'd to find by Your Lordship's Letter
of last night, which Your Messenger has just brought me,
that the entire Rejection of Lord Stormont from our List
can still admit of Doubt, after all that has passed, and after
the assurances given me by Mr. Pitt in His Letter written
Yesterday Morning that He would do every Thing in His
Power to let it be fully understood that the List sent by me
was that to which Government wished well. That Your
Lordship was gone to take every Step You could, and had
recalled Your Letters of the night before.

It is with great Sincerity I assure Your Lordship that I
am exceedingly sorry to occasion You any Embarrassment

and that if this was a Subject in which a private wish of my own only was concerned, I should be happy to give every Facility I could in smoothing the Difficulties Your Lordship has been drawn into; But Lord Stormont's receiving the Countenance of Government is a Measure which appears to me so much to affect our Characters that, for one, I cannot consent to it; and after the Steps I have taken, I fear any alteration in the List I have circulated as that of Government can be construed in no other way than a disavowal of me.

If these Steps were taken officiously, precipitately, or without authority, I deserve, and shall submit to be disowned. It is to this Fact that I venture to appeal to Your Lordship and those before whom the Transaction passed. I beg leave to call to Your Recollections that the Proposal of my sending our List with my Proxy was universally approv'd and that not a syllable passed desiring me to wait for further Discussion about Lord Stormont's name. Your Lordship will also remember the Surprise I expressed the same Day to You in the House of Lords on hearing that there was any More Thought about Lord Stormont and that upon my objecting Lord Gower and Your Lordship gave way, and Lord Mansfield was not spoken to. Even then not a word was said to desire me to suspend till further consideration the sending my List. I waited however 24 Hours afterwards without hearing of any objection, before I sent it; and it was not till the Day after that, that Your Lordship did me the Honor of enquiring whether I was in Town in order to Communicate the Alteration then wished to be adopted. Your Lordship does me but Justice in believing that I enter fully with You into the Hardness of the reversing what has been done, in considering it not very practicable consistently with the Credit of Government, and in not wishing to have that *risked*, but I submit it to Your Lordship whether this Reasoning does not apply more properly to the reversing what I had first done at the Desire of the Cabinet, than to the Alteration Your Lordship was induced to make without calling another. I am thoroughly sensible that Your Lordship's situation is a difficult one. I am sure I was not desirous of taking this Business out of Your Lordship's Hands to which it properly belongs, and meant only to relieve You from the Embarrassment of Conveying the wishes of Government without offense, which my Situation enabled me to do; and if Your Lordship finds it a Difficulty to be absolutely tied down by a conversation in Cabinet You will I hope feel that it is no less a Difficulty for those who act by its Instructions to find alterations made after they have committed themselves.

I should be happy to suggest, as Your Lordship desires, any Expedient upon this occasion; the only one that occurs to me is that which generally turns out the best viz: to avow the Truth. That it was originally agreed in Cabinet not to support Lord Stormont; that it was afterwards the wish of some to put Him on the List which government wished well to; and that in consequence of that wish and of Your Lordship's Belief that you should find no Difficulty in prevailing on others to consent to this alteration You had take(n) some Steps: But, that you found Lord Stormont's political Conduct so much objected to by those who have the Honor of acting with You, and the good wishes of Government towards Lord Roseberry already so fully expressed, that it was impossible to make the alteration. I have not the smallest objection to be quoted as one who adhered to the Rejection of Lord Stormont, and I cannot think that any Scotch Lord that wishes well to Mr. Pitt and the present Government will be inclined to favor so decided an enemy to it as His Lordship undoubtedly is.

I do assure You with great Truth that I never entertained a Thought of Your Lordship's meaning any Thing unfriendly to me in this Business. It is very far from my wish to shew any Difference at this Critical Time, and if I did not think that our now taking up Lord Stormont would be highly disgracefull to us, infinitely prejudicial to our Cause, and give more appearance of Instability than adhering to His Rejection, I should be happy in giving way to any Wish of Yours; But I must correct myself in calling this so, for I was sure, before you informed me of it that You had as little Predelection for his Lordship's Political Character as I have. Do then let us act consistently with our opinions, and never let us attempt that wretched Policy of keeping Terms with our decided Enemies; it never succeeds and only gives them strength. There is no Disgrace in being Beaten, but I do confess I should feel much in having given any Countenance to Lord North's most efficient Colleague in the Disgraces of the American and Dutch War.

It is with the greatest Esteem and Regard that I have the Honor to be Your Lordship's

most obedient and Sincere humble Servant,

RICHMOND, etc.

Richmond to Pitt

P.R.O. 30/8/171, ff. 95–96   (5 April 1786)

This letter must have been written some time between 27 February 1786, when Richmond's bill for coastal fortification was defeated in the Commons, and 16 May 1786, when a revised bill was presented again. Probably the letter was written some time before 12 April, for it contains a suggestion that Pitt canvass his House of Commons friends who had opposed the initial bill, and in a letter of 12 April the Duke inquired whether Pitt had found time to follow up this suggestion.[1] March, however, would seem too early for the letter, since it was then uncertain whether a second bill would be presented at all.

Behind this letter is Richmond's unwritten acknowledgement that the initial bill was defeated for reasons of personal hostility rather than financial policy, and his assumption that a second presentation of the bill, with only token revisions, would allow not only a chance for better canvassing but also an opportunity for would-be ministerial supporters, having once vented their dislike of the Master-General, to vote on the financial and military merits of the bill alone. But the government's second bill was thrown out without a vote after angry charges that repeated presentation of a bill previously defeated was an insult to the House. The ministers were forced to limit fortifications to minor works at Portsmouth and Plymouth which could be financed from the normal ordnance budgets for the next six years.

My dear Sir,

The difficulties we must be under in making any proposals short of our original, are very great, and I see the opposition mean to put us in this Dilemma. if we propose a great deal they will say it is trying the former question over again and not submitting to the decision of the House. And if we propose but little, they will say, how preposterous it was to propose so much more as we did.

[1] P.R.O. 30/8/171, ff. 92–94.

I confess myself inclined to propose largely. little or no objection has been started to the works for Portsmouth, I would therefore propose all that were intended for that Place and this would rid us of the difficulty of the reduction of £70,000 for finishing the works round the Common on the *reduced Plan*. I would also propose the work on Mather, and leave out of the whole Plan only the work at Merrifield which with the ground to be purchased for it, will make a reduction of 115,964 in the expense.

I should think it very dangerous in point of responsibility for us to offer any Thing less, but if the House does not approve of the offer we make, it may still curtail it. But I would wish to have that alteration appear an act of the House and not an act of ours.

If however you think some further Reduction necessary in the proposal, I should be for confining that reduction to the work at Frater Lake which with the Land to be purchased for it would further

diminish the expense in the sum of £121,278. 11. 8.
which with the first diminution of 115,964
would make the Difference of £237,242. 11. 8.
from our first Proposal.[1]

I would very much wish to preserve the work at Hilsea Lines, as then at least we should have Portsea Island compleat and as I said get rid of the Difficulty of the Reduction of £70,000 for finishing the works near the Common on the reduced Plan.

Inclosed I send You a Draft of some words which I have put down for the Title of our new Proposal which I have found very difficult to arrange, but I think these would do. It also appears to me very desirable that this Proposal altho' arranged and presented by Government should originate in a call from the House for that Purpose and that a Motion should be made in the House for an address to H.M. for this account.[2] Our Responsibility would then

[1] Subtracting this amount from £760,097, the original estimate, would leave a total of £422,854. 8s. 4d. In the debate of 16 May Pitt estimated the total to be about £400,000.

[2] Pitt presented the budgetary motion himself. There was no mention of an address to the King.

Stand on the safest Ground, and I am really so much convinced that it will be ere long put to the Test upon this Subject that I cannot recommend too much Caution in our Proceedings.

I should also think that if you was to make a Point of seeing all your Friends who voted against You on the former Question, and very seriously explain to them the infinite Difficulties they have put Government under, that you would get them almost all by a proper language, to support you in this motion for an address and afterwards in support of the several Parts. for I am persuaded that many of them repent of the vote they have given and will be glad of an opportunity, when you have seriously talked to them of the distresses they drive you to, to get off by having the Question stated to them in Another Form, and surely so considerable a Reduction as even the first proposed of £115,964 will give them good Ground & as Mr. Carew's Land[1] will not be touched it may operate on some of the western Gentlemen.

I should think that Mr. Macbride Himself, if You was to talk to Him, might be induced to be less busy, at least out of the House.

At all Events if the Question can by any means be brought to a Vote on any particular work or works, I am persuaded many who voted against a general system of Fortifications will not like to vote against a particular work. This I think will give as great advantage and probably enable us to carry our Question; but if we lose it, it will be much more satisfactory to know precisely what we must not or cannot do than to be thrown at large by general words to the Responsibility of proposing something less without having any Rule or Line to direct us in a measure which our own Conviction is so much against.

Ever Yours
RICHMOND, etc.

---

[1] One of the Carews of Devon; possibly Thomas of Haccomb, John of Moverton, or William of Exeter. See *Alumni Oxoniensis*, on the debate of 27 Feb. Courtenay had cited the experience of a Mr. Carey as a warning that, if the Fortification Bill passed no man's house and domain would be safe from seizure. The editor of the *Cornwallis Correspondence* has estimated that a large part of opposition came from members whose constituents thought their property to be threatened. *Cornwallis Corr.* i. 188–9.

Richmond to Pitt

P.R.O. 30/8/171, ff. 143-5   29 August 1788

The main part of this letter probably refers to offers Richmond had received of electoral assistance in the boroughs of Seaford, Queenborough, and Shoreham, three places in which he successfully prosecuted Ordnance interests in the general election of 1790. Pitt replied immediately to Richmond's letter, asking the Duke to come straight to town for discussions. Probably he mentioned the election; certainly he was more concerned with foreign policy and the advisability of offering mediation jointly with Prussia and Holland in a Baltic war which Sweden was losing to Russia and Denmark.

Since 'My attendance in town upon the affairs of the North could in my present uninformed state be of little use' Richmond declined to come up in a letter of 1 September.[1] He did not return to London until the week of 15-21 September and apparently even then saw Pitt only on the last day of his visit.[2]

Goodwood August 29th 1788

My Dear Sir,

I am much obliged to you for the Communication of Mr. Ewarts Letter which I return; I am glad the Treaty is signed,[3] but think it very material now to concert with Prussia what steps should be taken, in the various possible Cases that may arise in the present critical situation of the North. Pray how have you got over with Sr James Harris the very awkward Proposition He chose to make.[4] for I trust you have not been persuaded to give way to it, and I should

1 P.R.O. 30/8/171, ff. 131-3.

2 Richmond to Carmarthen, 21 Sept. 1788, Add. MS. 28,063, f. 257.

3 Probably Ewart's dispatch of 14 Aug. (F.O. 64/14, no. 63). On 13 Aug. the British had concluded a defensive alliance with Prussia providing for joint protection of Holland and stipulating that either power would provide a force of 20,000 men if the other was attacked. (Prussian soldiers were not to be used outside Europe.)

4 That Great Britain voluntarily relinquish to the Dutch two concessions incorporated in the peace treaty of 1783—Negapatam and the free navigation of the eastern sea in India. Harris had urged in a letter to Pitt of 19 Oct. 1787 (P.R.O. 30/8/155, ff. 63-64) that such concessions would raise the shareholder's prestige in Holland and increase British popularity there. Richmond supported the restoration of Negapatam only in trade for Trincomalee, a port whose cession he had strongly opposed in 1783. Apparently he was ignorant of rumours currently being circulated of a French attack on Trincomalee (W. Lindsay to Pitt, 22 Aug. 1788, P.R.O. 30/8/336, ff. 34-35). Harris was in London during August (Harris to Pitt, 3 Aug. 1788, P.R.O. 30/8/155, f. 79) and doubtless talked to Pitt.

hope that this business will be pushed now that the Dutch are in a Good Disposition and other Circumstances are favourable for our getting possession of Trincomale.

Patronage requests: a promotion for Lord Edward Fitzgerald; the secretaryship to the Madrid embassy for Lord Robert Fitzgerald.[1]

I have much to say to You on other Subjects. You once mentioned an intention of favouring me with your company here. I trust I need not assure you how happy I should be to see you, but should that not be convenient pray let me know when you are likely to be in Town and will allow me an Hour's Conversation with you there, and I will go to London. I should be glad to take the same opportunity of going to a Levé and Drawing Room. My Business is not very immediate, and yet is such as I must soon come to some determination upon. It is relative to various Plans I have to submit to you concerning the next general Election upon which I have had offers, but cannot engage in any of them without feeling that I have the means of undertaking them with a reasonable Prospect of success, and that depends so much upon my own situation that I must have some determination upon that subject, before I can persuade myself to embark in a business of much Trouble, & not a little expence. I mean to lay before you every particular, and of the means I conceive necessary to success. You will judge whether on the whole the object is worth seeking by the means I shall propose. I can assure you that I shall feel perfectly satisfied with whatever your determination may be, either to give me the means or to give up the Thing, or to try to effect it by other means. All I have to request is that you would not expect me to engage in a Business without those means that appear to me necessary to give success.

I am ever most sincerely Yours

RICHMOND, etc.

[1] In September Lord Robert Fitzgerald obtained the secretaryship of the Paris embassy through Carmarthen (Richmond to Carmarthen, 21 Sept. 1788, Add. MS. 28,063, f. 257). Richmond was trying unsuccessfully to obtain a lieutenant-colonelcy for Lord Edward Fitzgerald; Lord Edward, then in Canada with the 54th Regiment, did not want the promotion as it would necessitate his active support of the government. P. Byrne, *Lord Edward Fitzgerald* (1955), pp. 50–58.

Richmond to Pitt

P.R.O. 30/8/171, ff. 143–5 (18 February 1789)

By the end of November 1788 the King's mental derangement had become serious enough to necessitate a regency. Should the Prince of Wales have been given full powers as regent, including the power of forming a government, Pitt's cabinet would certainly have been dismissed in favour of Fox and Portland; Richmond therefore favoured a joint regency including both the Prince of Wales and the Queen, and a cabinet coalition with Portland, the initiative to be taken by Pitt.

The ministerial bill drawn up instead made the Prince of Wales regent but with powers circumscribed by the clause to which Richmond refers in this letter, giving to the Queen the care of the King's person and the power of appointing and dismissing officers of the royal household. The bill was first presented to the Lords on Wednesday, 18 February, but the Committee of the Whole, scheduled to discuss it on the following day, was postponed when indications appeared of the King's recovery. On 10 March the King's complete recovery was announced; on the same day the Regency Bill was discharged.

Whitehall Wednesday night
½ past ten

My Dear Sir,

I am just returned from the House of Lords where Lord Loughborough has suggested some Difficulties upon the Household clause which we could not solve & must have recourse to you. He stated that the Queen was to appoint in her own Name & not in the Kings & that under the Description in the Bill there were several offices for Life or usually granted for several Lives & in reversions. He quoted the Clerk of Parliament, the Gentleman Usher of the Black Rod & the Master of the Ceremonies and asked whether we meant the Queen should have those Powers of granting places for Life & in Reversion which we desired to the Regent. He said He would not propose any amendment as none could make this Bill meet with His Concurrence but thought it fair to state the Consequences. The Chancellor said He could not directly & on a sudden say anything positive except as to the Clerk of Parliament which was not in the Recommendation of the Lord Chamberlain, but he believed the others would be found not to fall within the objection, However we would enquire. I also said that if such was the Case as supposed no doubt the Clause must be amended to make it correspond with the Intentions of the Bill which certainly were not to give the Queen any such Powers.

Now My Dear Sir I understand You are gone out of Town & meant to remain out of Town to morrow. Indeed in such a moment as this you cannot be spared for so long, as every Instant some thing occurs that you must be consulted upon. I have therefore at the Desire of all the Cabinet I could speak to, undertaken to send this to Your House with Directions that it should be sent to wherever You are, to desire you will come to Town to morrow & have a meeting for 12 o'clock which I will in the mean Time desire Lord Sydney to summon. I say at 12 because the Chancellor wished it and we agreed to begin business early to morrow in the Committee[1] which is adjourned for we could finish only one clause to night. The opposition contended strongly for going on, & abused us for Delay. We must also see you tomorrow to consider of our further Proceedings. I am sorry to disturb you, but indeed in time of action our general must not have a furlough.

Ever Yours most sincerely,

RICHMOND, etc.

Richmond to Pitt

P.R.O. 30/8/171, ff. 153–6   16 October 1790

This letter is in answer to one Pitt had written on 13 October requesting papers concerning Lord Edward Fitzgerald.[2] Richmond used the opportunity to present a long argument on the importance of a well-planned campaign against Trinidad in the event of war, and to make an undisguised offer to accept leadership of a war effort. Pitt did not acknowledge the letter.

By 'a certain Quarter' where he was out of favour, Richmond could have meant either the King or Pitt's political friends. It is unlikely that he meant the King, whose favour Richmond's nephew had received in rapid military promotion the year before; and of Pitt's

---

[1] The Committee of the Whole.

[2] Possibly concerning Lord Edward's refusal of the command of an expedition to Cadiz which Richmond had procured for him earlier in the year.

friends it is unlikely that he anticipated Grenville's promotion to the Lords, which Pitt did not discuss with him until 25 or 26 October. More probably Richmond referred to Dundas, already an intimate advisor of Pitt's and strongly critical of the Duke's plan for West Indian fortifications.

Goodwood Oct. 16, 1790

My Dear Sir,

. . . .

And believe me my Dear Sir the success may attend operations taken up hastily and undigested, yet the Chances are much against them. and I confess I do not as yet see any System formed for the Conduct of this war, if it is to be one, that at all promices that forethought of every consequence & that attention to every preparation that is necessary to give one a reasonable confidence in success.

I do not say this with any view to myself, for every Days' Experience convinces me that if there were not a thousand other insuperable objections to my taking the Lead in such a Business, the want of Health would be alone sufficient to prevent my taking it. I really am fit for nothing but attending my Farm here; and recommend it to You to put Lord Dorchester[1] at once at the Head of the Army, and in the Cabinet. I shall always be ready to give any assistance I can, and from the being now in the Habits of the affairs of the Ordnance may be able to prevent Your meeting with Disappointment in that Branch of the Service. But while Prejudices are entertain'd of me in a certain Quarter I could not if I had the best Health be of the use I ought to be in any Situation that requires Confidence. I have therefore only to offer my best wishes for success and the small assistance that I can be of in my Department.

But whatever my Feelings may be as to publick matters believe me I shall ever feel the warmest attachment & gratitude for the Friendship you have ever shown me.

I am ever most
truely & sincerely Yours
RICHMOND, etc.

---

[1] Guy Carleton, created Baron Dorchester in Oct. 1786, and appointed Governor of Quebec, Nova Scotia, and New Brunswick in April of that year as repayment for friendly services on the Fortifications Board.

Richmond to Pitt

P.R.O. 30/8/171, ff. 157–63   24 November 1790

Some time in October Thurlow had put in the name of a friend to fill
a Scottish vacancy which was instead filled by a nominee of Dundas.
In a bitter letter to Pitt and a conversation with Dundas, the Chancellor refused further close association with the ministers in the House of
Lords; and since Thurlow was the only competent ministerial speaker
in the Lords, and the ministry possessed no other supporters either
disciplined enough to attend the Lords regularly or fast enough to
anticipate the Chancellor's forensic attacks, Grenville was promoted,
over the heads of Richmond and Carmarthen (the current lead) to be
the ministerial lead in the House of Lords. The promotion was sought
and received in letters between Pitt and the King on 21 November;[1]
on 6 December Grenville, created Baron Grenville, was sworn into
the House of Lords. Thereafter, until Thurlow's dismissal in 1792,
Grenville never missed a meeting that the Chancellor attended.

It is evident from this letter that Richmond knew Dundas to be
involved in the patronage quarrel, but that he mistakenly thought
Grenville's promotion an attempt, however misdirected, to please the
Chancellor. Richmond had probably discussed the appointment with
Pitt when he was in town on 25 and 26 October, but Pitt waited three
days after the King's approval had been given to inform Richmond of
the actual promotion. The duke refused to attend the opening of Parliament or Grenville's swearing in, and from the day of Grenville's
appointment he never again attended Parliament regularly.

Goodwood Nov. 24th, 1790

My Dear Sir,

I cannot but very much regret that Mr. Grenvilles being
called up to the House of Lords, appeared to you to press
for such an immediate Decision, as to prevent the wish you
had of conversing with me upon the subject from taking
Place; because I should at least have had an opportunity of
previously giving you my most serious advice not to adopt
a Plan which to me seems likely to be attended with many
bad consequences.

I must conclude from your Letter as well as from all the
Circumstances attending this Measure, that it will have been

---

[1] P.R.O. 30/8/101, ff. 23–28, and P.R.O. 30/8/103, ff. 401–2. See also Grenville
to Buckingham, 22 Nov. 1790, Buckingham and Chandos, *Courts and Cabinets of
George III*, ii. 179–81.

carried into Execution before my answer can reach you, but
I will take my chance of the Possibility of a Delay, and state
to you fairly some of the principal objections that strike me.

In the first Place I think it Ruin to Mr. Grenville. He
has in the space of a very few years gone thro many great
offices, and now holds the second political Situation in the
House of Commons. In case of any accident happening to
You or Your Brother he would naturally become the first
Servant of the Crown in that House; and the Circumstances
of the Time join'd to his own abilities justify in the Eyes of
the Publick His being where He is. But by removing him
from the House of Commons You deprive Him of all the
Prospects of future advantages which Talents can make their
way to in that place. He now stands in every Light in an
advantageous Situation born for Himself and for His
Friends; is it then wise to risk a Change? He has succeeded
admirably well hitherto; but it may be very uncertain
whether He will succeed so well in another Situation, certainly a very different one from that which He is now in. To
call up a Younger Brother to the House of Peers for the
evident Purpose of giving him the Lead there is a Degree of
Reflexion upon the whole House of Lords, that there is no
one there fit for such a Situation, which will be felt and may
cause him to fail in that for which alone you place him there.

If this should be the case or by any other means a Change
happen a Lord Grenville without a fortune would be but a
poor Situation!

But of all this to be sure Mr. Grenville must be the best
Judge, and I must suppose that He likes the risking all this
for the sake of being made a Peer & having the Lead in the
House of Lords rather than remain Second in the House of
Commons, for whatever His attachment may be to You no
man with that laudable Degree of ambition which Mr. Gren-
ville has, can be supposed to Hazard such an entire political
Sacrifice of Himself as he is exposing himself to without He
saw some considerable Gratification to Himself in so doing.
But the wisest men have their weaknesses and I fear this is
a very fatal one in Mr. Grenville. However since it is His
Choice there is nothing more to be said upon His account.
But on Your account and that of the Permanency of the

present Government in which the King's Happiness and the Prosperity of the Kingdom are I think deeply interested, I do apprehend the worst Consequences.

It would be inconsistent with the Friendship I trust I have upon all occasions shewn You and with the Fairness I will always act with, not to say that I believe this country will not be satisfied to see You two Younger Brothers take the Lead of the two Houses of Parliament and by Yourselves govern the Country. With Your abilities, which without a Compliment are very transcending, You may take that Lead in the House of Commons; But Mr. Grenville, whose Parts, however solid and usefull, are certainly not upon a level with Yours, cannot as I conceive succeed in taking one Lead in the House of Lords, where something of higher Rank and more Fortune and Dignity is required and I do apprehend that both of You being in such Situations, so nearly related with Lord Chatham at the Admiralty, will be thought engrossing too much in one Family. You will consider too that at the same Time that You deprive Yourself of Mr. Grenville's support and that of a Cabinet Minister in the House of Commons which was the Reason for which You made Him Secretary of State and thereby remain almost singly there as to Speakers of any weight, You will place Mr. Grenville as singly in the House of Lords. The Duke of Leeds who never took a very active Part in Debates will probably not be very desirous of standing forward when he is so evidently set aside. Lord Chatham has never yet spoke. Lord Camden is idle & grows old, Lord Stafford will seldom speak and but a few words. Your account of the Chancellor makes it more likely that He will be adverse than otherwise. and as to myself I must confess that I do not see how I can be of any Use. It is not therefore from Your Cabinet that Mr. Grenville can derive much Support, and I do not imagine that Lord Hawkesbury will feel much disposed to act under Him. there remains Lord Walsingham and the Chance of What the Duke of Montrose may turn out [   ] as a Speaker in the House of Lords.

This, against the present Speakers in opposition and possibly the Chancellor will form but a poor Line of Debates to defend the Errors of Government that from the present way of carrying on Business unavoidably arise, and which it falls to the Lot of the House of Lords to be afterwards obliged to support.

I have said that I could be of little use. perhaps in no Situation could I have been of much, but to be of any as a Speaker a man must feel some thing for Himself and not appear to the World in an unbecoming Situation. I trust I have not shewn myself a difficult man, when after having had for many years a considerable share in the Debates in the House of Lords, I first wished to support Your Government as an Individual, and afterwards defended Your Measures as a Minister under Lord Sidney & the Duke of Leeds. But to continue to act a second part under every change and particularly under one which is avowedly made for the sole purpose of giving the House of Lords another Leader would be depriving myself of every sort of Consideration which I may hope to have in that House and rendering myself totally useless there.

I must say too that after having been of late so particularly called upon to take a very active part in a Business of some Consequence where it was thought I could be usefull,[1] and having shewn a Disposition to accomodate as far as it was possible my situation to Your wishes, I cannot but feel myself somewhat neglected by Your deciding upon this Measure without my Consent or even Knowledge, for when we conversed on this Subject some Time ago I had expressed my objections to it, and afterwards understood You had entirely dropped the Idea.

You will also recollect my having often expressed that altho' I feel very little Interest in the Disposal of Employments or the making of Peers yet I could not think it right that Your Colleagues of the Cabinet should never hear of what is doing in these Respects till the Things were done. Those with whom I have formerly been connected in Politicks and in Friendship used to treat me with more attention, and indifferent as I am upon those Subjects in general, I cannot be entirely so when they tend to prevent me from being of that use, tho' small which otherwise I might possibly be of in the House of Lords to the King's Administration of which I have the Honor to form a Part.

[1] Richmond must refer to the general election in June.

If I had any political ambition I might feel disappointed and hurt at such a Conduct, but having none it only adds to that Desire of retiring from publick Business which you know I have long had in view. In so doing I shall endeavour not to give it the appearance of any Dissatisfaction with You, for in Truth I feel none, believing as I do that Your Conduct does not proceed from any intentional want of Kindness towards me, but from (you must forgive me for saying so) an Idleness in Your Disposition that too often makes You neglect to cultivate the Friendship of those who are most attached to You; and which makes You expose Your Judgment to be biased by the opinion of the narrow circle to which You confine Your Intimacy.

I have before observed that I think Mr. Grenville must have some strong Predilection for this Measure, and perhaps Mr. Dundas whom you mention to have had some Concern, at least in what has led to it, may not be sorry to have Mr. Grenville out of His way in the House of Commons. The Hurry and Manner in which this Business has been conducted, not allowing twelve Hours for the Return of Your Messenger, lead me to these Suspicions, and as the French say I doubt Your Religion and Good Sense have been surprized. But of all Things this is a measure the least calculated to conciliate the Chancellor who is not fond of Mr. Grenville and who with some Reason will think He ought to have been consulted as to the Person who is to have the Lead in the House of Lords.

But perhaps Mr. Grenville & Mr. Dundas who know that the Chancellor does not like either of them may not be sorry to force him out. I wish this may not end in breaking up that administration on which they both depend.

With every sincere wish for Your Prosperity I am My Dear Sir

> Your most obedient & faithfull humble
> Servant
> RICHMOND, etc.

Richmond to Pitt

P.R.O. 30/8/171, ff. 163-4   7 December 1790
Richmond ostentatiously remained away from the opening of Parlia-

ment on 25 November and Grenville's swearing in on 6 December, eventually coming to town only for the debate on the presentation of an address of thanks to the King for negotiating a convention with Spain restoring British settlements at Nootka Sound and arranging Spanish reparation after an attack on the Sound in April 1789. In the debate on the address Grenville made his maiden speech in the Lords; Richmond did not speak at all. Apparently he returned to Goodwood immediately afterwards.

The main part of Richmond's letter refers to taxes on liquor, requested by the government for one year with the announcement of some intended renewals, and a tax on malt, requested with the anticipation of one renewal. The taxes were first presented on 5 December to the Commons sitting as a Committee of the Whole House to Consider Ways and Means of Increasing the Supply. Richmond must refer to the debate on Thursday, 16 December, when the resolutions were reported out of committee. Either Pitt was dissuaded from taxing beer or Richmond was wrong in supposing that he intended to include beer in the category of spirits; the government resolutions provided for increased allowances on beer.

My Dear Sir,   Goodwood Tuesday Dec 7th 1790

The Duke of Leeds' Letter informing me that the Business in the H. of Lords was put off till Monday was so comfortable a reprieve that I really cannot help availing myself of it during this fine hunting weather, and especially if we may judge from the two good runs we have had yesterday and today, of the good sport we may expect. We killed both Days after a tollerable run yesterday, and one of the best I ever saw of the two Hours and a quarter today.

I shall therefore leave You to resolve on your own Destruction on Thursday. but remember that now that You have sent Grenville to the H. of Lords it would be extremely ·nconvenient to the Party that you should be knocked at Head.

I seriously do think that the Beer Tax is a very hazardous Measure & not necessary but if you who must be the best judge and who are most concerned think otherwise, I shall submit to your Decision & trust to Your Good Luck tho I think you will try it rather too much.

Amongst the variety of things that have occurred to me on this Subject one is that it is a pity to risk the unpopularity of the Measure for one Year's Profit, and that if it is to be urged it would be better to make it permanent, applying the whole of it after it has paid for the armements [*sic*] in addition to the sinking Fund which would then begin to operate very rapidly indeed.

However I leave this all to You. I would attend the meeting on Thursday if I did not think the Subject has been already pretty fully discussed & if I had any new Lights to throw upon it, but not having any & the whole of the matter being a Consideration of Prudence I trust my Conscience to You.

I am ever most truly
& sincerely Yours
RICHMOND, etc.

Richmond to Pitt

P.R.O. 30/8/171, ff. 167–8   27 March 1791

On 21, 22, 27, and 31 March the cabinet met to discuss a Prussian request for aid (in accordance with terms of Triple Alliance) in forcing Russia to give up acquisitions she was gaining in war with the Porte. Leeds, Chatham, and the Chancellor favoured discussing in general terms a plan to send arms to the Baltic and the Black Sea, while Richmond, Stafford, and Grenville, insisting that Parliament would not support war preparations, argued against any general discussion before specific details had been settled.[1]

Richmond's letter refers to the meeting on 27 March at which it was agreed to send an ultimatum jointly with Prussia demanding that the Tzarina give reasonable terms to the Porte and threatening to enter hostilities if a favourable answer to the demand was not received within ten days. Apparently at the insistence of Grenville, not Richmond, Pitt agreed four days later to send a messenger to Berlin postponing the ultimatum; by the middle of April Pitt had modified his original position to allow for some concessions to Russian territorial expansion.

Although on 7 January Richmond had extended to Pitt his customary invitation to go fox hunting at Goodwood,[2] this letter of 27 March is markedly formal. Pitt apparently did not acknowledge its contents; four days after writing it Richmond spoke to Leeds of resigning since his opinions carried no weight in the cabinet.

---

[1] *Leeds Pol. Mem.*, pp. 151–6.
[2] P.R.O. 30/8/171, ff. 165–6.

Whitehall Sunday night
March 27th 1791

My Dear Sir,

Altho' it is next to impossible for two Persons in the Course of a variety of Events always to see the same Things in the same Point of View, yet I cannot but feel hurt when I happen to differ from You in any essential Point. At the same Time I am sure that in one of such Importance as that we discussed this morning in Cabinet, You would not wish me to keep back my real Sentiments; and the more I think of the Subject the more I am confirmed in my opinion that unless we have Holland, in some ostensible shape at least, with us; and the Swedish Ports open to our Fleet; with an accession of Poland to our Alliance, we risk too much in pledging this country to Prussia to make war against Russia in order to compel Her to make Peace with the Porte upon the status quo.

I have duely weighed all the arguments you made use of, which undoubtedly have great Force, but I cannot say they have convinced me.

I have not the Presumption to wish that my Ideas should preponderate against Yours and the Majority of the Cabinet, and I by no means wish to enter any formal dissent to the Measure, but merely to be understood by You that my opinion does not go with it.

When once it is adopted, I shall contribute the little I can towards its success.

I am ever most truely and Sincerely Yours.

RICHMOND, etc.

Richmond to Charles Lennox

Dublin MS. 1274   6 June 1804

Richmond to Charles Lennox

Dublin MS. 1273   12 June 1804

Two letters concerning Pitt's Additional Force Bill, reducing the militia from 70,000 to 48,000, raising the Army of Reserve to 79,000, of whom 13,000 would be transferred to the Regular Army each year and hence replaced by new recruits, and making parish officers responsible for the filling of the quotas.[1] The bill was presented to the Commons on 5 June, passed on 19 June, and the following day carried to the Lords where Richmond spoke against it on 25 June. Richmond's pamphlet on the subject of recruitment, entitled *Thoughts on the National Defense* was published later in the same year.[2]

Richmond had entered the Prince of Wales London circle in May after spending the early part of the spring in Sussex with his militia, and had dined at least once with the Prince, who solicited his political advice. The letter is significant for Richmond's misplaced optimism that in a ministry of the Prince's he would be considered for a cabinet office.

Whitehall, Wednesday, 6th of
June 1804

My Dear Charles,

I was very sorry at the Report I heard that you was come to Town to vote with Mr Pitt yesterday in His proposals for the Defense of the Country. I sent a note to You (to) day to desire to see you wishing to have some Conversation with You on that subject but Your note was returned with an account that You was this morning set out for Brighton and supposed I was at Earl's Court. I cannot help thinking that going to or returning from the House you might as well have taken the trouble of enquiring, and at all Events not have left me to pick up from Common Report that you was come to Town on Purpose to vote differently from what you knew would be my wishes.

I earnestly hope that Your return to Brighton is from Your own Recollection, or the Suggestion of some real Friend of You who has had the Good Sense to see that it would be full as creditable for you to abstain from taking a Part so different from Your Uncle as to be forward in supporting Measures you know he cannot approve. I do therefore trust that you do not mean to return to vote on Friday for Mr Pitt's Plan.

You may say that I have told You I did not mean to direct your Vote in Parliament, nor do I wish You to be like some who because they owe their seat to a man think they must

---

[1] The exact provisions of the act are summarized in Fortescue, *The County Lieutenancies and the Army, 1803–1814*, pp. 132–3.

[2] The pamphlet is listed in the *Dictionary of Anonymous and Pseudonymous English Literature*, ed. James Kennedy (1926), vi. 39. Apparently no copies are extant.

implicitly follow him. But surely there is a difference between that extreme and paying no sort of attention to the sentiment and Inclinations of a person to whom You owe not only Your Seat, but to an Uncle who has adopted You as his Child, bred you up, and to whom You owe every Thing. I grant that in all matters, the opinion & vote of a Member of Parlt ought to be free. But if he suffers it to be biassed by a Minister He may as well let His Uncle have some influence over it. If without considering the Question you vote with a view of one Man or another, being minister, that destroys all Pretense of acting as a free Member of Parliament conscientiously upon the Merit of each Question, and launching out into General Politicks; in which case, I do maintain that a man should not make use of the Situation another has put him into contrary to what He knows His Politicks to be. And as to the Question to be decided on Friday relative to the Defense of the Country, you know that I am publishing a Plan of my own for that Purpose, I have shewn it to you, and you appeared to think it a good one, but you would be voting directly against [?] to support Mr Pitt's.

I cannot help also recalling to You what Mr Pitt's Conduct towards me has been. After owing me a great deal at a Time He stood in much need of my assistance, & being served by me with all the Fidelity of the Warmest Friendship, He turned me out of office, and in the most shuffling manner, without alledging any cause for it, but evidently to sacrifice me to the Duke of York & Mr Dundas' jealousy. & You was yourself included in the Consequences which had he cared for either could never have allowed him with one grain of feeling of real Friendship to have occasioned.[1]

Whatever I might feel at such Treatment I shewed no Resentment, nor enter'd into any opposition against him and very lately you know that I desired You to mention to him the Plan I had formed for the Defense of the Country and when he desired to see it you sent it to him.

Wanting the Manuscript to shew to others while I know He was too much engaged in His Politicks to attend to it, I desired to have it back and in returning it He begged to

[1] Charles Lennox resigned his secretaryship to the Master-General when Richmond was dismissed from the Ordnance.

have it again when I could spare it. I accordingly sent it to him near 3 weeks ago with a note saying that if he wished for any explanations I should be ready to attend him. But to this, not one word of an answer has he sent, & now has brought forth His Plan without condescending to inform me even what his opinion was of mine. This is wanting even in that Civility that is due from one Gentleman to another, But is easily accounted for by the same principles that before guided him. Now connected again with the D. of York & under Lord Melville's Influence, He dares not take any notice of me. Be it so. But is this the Man my nephew & Child is to be eager in supporting against me! for in the present Question it is against my plans.

As to Politick in general I have much to say that I have not time or (chance) to commit to Paper. But convinced as I am that the partial and illegal Part Mr Pitt is now acting, I feel it my Duty, altho I should wish to remain retired from all Politick, to oppose with what means remain to me. Not wishing, however to preclude him in the *proper* share He has a just claim to from His abilities in the Government of the Country. but determined as far as I can to resist that inordinate ambition of his that will make him expect to be sole and only Minister to the Exclusion of that just share of Influence & Power which others have to the full as much & in some cases more claim to than he has.

At the same Time I say do as You please but you cannot expect that I should not feel hurt at a Conduct I so much disapprove and at the Blame you will incur in the eyes of all but your own little Party, in the world.

I send this by the Coach in Hopes it may not miss you.

Yours.

RICHMOND, etc.

Lennox answered[1] pleading ignorance of Richmond's opposition to Pitt and defending his support of the bill for two reasons. First, he saw no need to choose between the defence plans of Richmond and Pitt since Richmond was not presenting his to Parliament. More important; 'I cannot, however, but consider the question before the House to be a trial of whether Mr Pitt is to remain in power or not. Should

[1] Richmond's following letter acknowledges the receipt of two letters from Charles Lennox. The draft of one, undated, is in the Dublin MSS. 12749.

he be turned out, who are we to look to? Mr Addington cannot return. The Grenvilles have in my opinion proved themselves unfit to be in power. They have for a Length of time said Addn. ought to quit and an administration formed on the broadest basis. Yet the moment they succeed in their first object they because one individual is objected to do all they can to narrow the administration they have assisted in bringing in.'

Rather than oppose Pitt, Lennox did not attend Parliament, pleading his militia as his excuse. His reply to Richmond's letter acknowledged Dundas's steadiness since joining Pitt, expressed doubts as to the firmness of Grenville's alliance with Fox, as well as astonishment that Richmond would knowingly support an advocate of peace at any price.

'I believe it would do harm to you . . . in the eyes of the Country if they saw you joined in Administration with a man whose political conduct you have disapproved of since the death of Lord Rockingham, that is to say for about 22 years. I am far from saying a man may not see the bad effect of Plans & Schemes he may have approved of, & may not then be taken into confidence, but I see nothing in Mr Fox's conduct to make me suppose he is less partial to French Revolutionary principles than he formerly avowed himself to be.'

As Lord Lieutenant of Sussex Richmond refused either to co-operate in raising the county quota for the Army of Reserve or to allow inspectors to visit his militia, as required in the act. By the beginning of the following year it had become clear that opposition would force Pitt to devise a new plan of recruitment.

Whitehall Tuesday
June 12th 1804

My Dear Charles,

I was very glad to find by your first short letter that you did not come to Town, and only waited for the more detailed one it promised me to thank you for attending to my wishes. I shall now reply to that letter which I got yesterday; but must first assure you, that however hurt I must feel at any neglect from one I love so much as I do you, yet I ever felt inclined to attribute it to some excusable cause rather than want of affection in you. I know the warmth of your heart, and the eagerness of your temper to be zealous in a cause you undertake and however I may lament that you should have retained an attachment to a man who has behaved so ill to me and to you as Mr Pitt, and whose publick conduct has in many respects appeared to be reprehensible, yet I was willing to find a good motive in the zeal of your friendship, however misplaced, even for neglecting me. But I will now reply to the arguments of your letter.

You begin by saying that you did not know that your supporting Mr Pitt was contrary to my wishes. That ignorance was the first of my complaints. Why did not you enquire? Why have you never open'd to me your mind and confidentially talk'd to me on a subject now so interesting since the fate of the country depends upon it, and on which you know, as well as all others, I should have no reserve to you but freely have given you my opinion and advice. When you did come to town why did you not call on me to know what I thought, and twice pass my door, relying upon vague information that I was not in town when had you been desirous of seeing me you might so easily have yourself enquired if I was at home or not.

You next say that you knew I had a plan for National Defence, but did not know that I meant to propose it to Parliament or to oppose any other that might be brought forward. I certainly did not, nor do I mean to propose my plan on my legs in the House of Lords. But you know that I meant to print it, tho' without my name, and in that way to propose the matter of it to the publick. Nor in so doing, did I mean to oppose *every* other plan that might be brought forward. But when I see one not only different but if it is carried, setting mine quite aside, and in itself full of objections, diminishing instead of increasing the Militia, enveighling men by art and low tricks to enlist in the army after telling them that they are engaged only for Home Service, and oppressing the landed Property with heavy fines if the parish officers do not turn recruiting officers and succeed in getting men. A scheme which Mr Pitt had himself before tried and abandoned from its absurdity and total failure of success, I am surely justified in opposing it & had you allowed yourself to think about it, you must have thought I should oppose such a measure.

You seem to think that Mr Pitt's plan and mine differ only as to species of men we mean to raise, mine only for defence his for offence as well as defence. But you are mistaken in the object of mine, and in the success of his. Mine certainly considers defence as the first object, but while it is pursuing that so far from impeding greatly forwards the means of obtaining a large force for offence whenever circumstances may make offence by land forces adviseable. Mine filling up the militia ballots in one month every year, leaves during the other eleven no competition with the army for getting recruits. It permits the army to recruit from the unembodied militia, and suggests means of rendering the army service less disgustfull than we now find it to be so generally. In my plan I require 30000 regulars for the defence of England and Wales alone and these with whatever more we may get form a body with which offensive operations may be pursued whenever a proper object presents itself, and the probabilities of invasion from a great force are so reduced as to make it prudent for us to send part of ours out of the country, indeed my plan rather facilitates than impedes the means of our sending troops abroad. Because it leaves a great militia at home even if all the 30000 regulars wanted to repell a great invasion were sent abroad, whereas if by Mr Pitts plan our militia is reduced to 50,000, such an ignorant Minister as Lord Melville, for it is he that still governs Mr Pitt, may fancy we are secure with such a force, send all the army abroad upon some such wild scheme as that of his to the Helder and we may be caught at home with very inadequate means of defence.

But you say that our force consisting of army instead of militia will oblige France to keep a large force on every part of her continent lest we should attack it, and consequently can afford a less army for the purpose of invading us, whereas if we have nothing but militia, and thereby cannot attack her she may draw down her whole force to invade us. This I take to be the ji[s]t of your argument, understanding that you do not mean our having no militia, nor I our having no army, but in which species our chief forces should consist, and I do not think that your argument is good. Because with the immense armies that France has, and can raise, she has abundant for all her purposes of invasion and security for her coasts. The idea that we can be on a footing with France both for defence and offence, both having armies for each, is contending with her by means which we do not possess, our small population compared with that of the French territory and influence cannot find numbers to equal her in extent of armies. We must be content with defence, at least for the present, and by rendering that secure, wear her out in the vain and numerous attempts she may make, and the loss her commerce must feel from our naval superiority, the maintenance of which our finances had better be applied than in idle expeditions for in finance too as well as in men, we must be governed by our means. If we waste our money as Mr Dundas did in the last war, it will not hold out, and Mr Pitt will be obliged to beg for a bad peace as he did at Lisle. We must not fancy ourselves what we were, equal to France as she was and having alliances on the continent. The bad management of the war by Lord Melville lost us all our allies, and the peace of Amiens which Mr Pitt approved gave up all we had got and left France double in power to what she ever was. It is therefore these two little islands alone and without any assistance that have to contend with France doubled and influencing all Europe. In such a contest we must feel that we have the weaker side and be content to parry at least for a time till our great adversary has got out of breath and weakened himself in vain efforts. Then if opportunities offer we may begin to thrust. My plan goes first to make our parrys effectual, but still getting on in the means of reposting. Mr Pitt's plan abandons the first, and from its bad contrivance will fail in the latter, for he will not get his army.

But I have said enough about our plans. You will read mine which in a few days I hope to send you, and you will hear enough of his in the papers.

It is not however the plan itself, but whether Mr Pitt should remain Minister that you considered to be the question to be decided by the votes on this occasion, and you ask, if he is turned out who is to succeed him? You say certainly not Mr Addington, and I agree with you that as sole Minister he was very unfit for it. Then you turn to the Grenvilles and object to them both for want of power and their conduct. They too I agree with you ought not to be sole Ministers. But I cannot see their conduct especially if compared with that of Mr Pitt to be half so exceptionable as his. You say that after opposing Mr Addington to substitute in his place on administration on the broadest base yet because one man is objected to, they do all they can to narrow the administration they have assisted in bringing in. But surely if you consider these very words of your own statement you will find that instead of blame they fully justify the Grenvilles in the part they have taken. They did oppose Mr Addington in order to have an administration formed on the *broadest* basis, it is not therefore consistent in them not to join in one on a *narrow basis?* But you say only one man is objected to, and that it would have been on administration on a *broad basis* if they would have come in with Mr Pitt. But this I deny because it was very natural to suppose that Mr Fox's old friends would not consent to abandon him and suffer him to be proscribed; and therefore without him and his Party the new administration even if the Grenvilles had joined it, would not have been upon the *broadest basis*. But you seem to think that it was right in the King to proscribe Mr. Fox. For argument's sake let us admit that it was. But I dont think you have yet said that it would have been right in his friends to have abandoned him. Nor do I think that in their situation you would have done so, merely because the King had some years ago struck him out of the privy Council. If that measure was justifyable on account of his principles, his friends should then have abandoned him. But they did not perhaps from thinking that from living in intimacy with him they could judge of his principles, full as well as the King could from the reports of his Ministers or speeches delivered at the Whig Club, and it is possible that notwithstanding some imprudences they may have still considered him as a real friend to the true Constitution of this country and altho often hurried into indiscretions by the eagerness of his temper yet in reality a sound character, and no one will deny his abilities. But perhaps you will say that their principles are as bad as his. Be it so again, but then this is a stronger reason for their not abandoning him now, so that either way, having hitherto stuck to him, you must agree that his friends could not leave him now. Will you then say no but we are better without them. You may say so if you please, but the Grenvilles cannot say so after having joined with Mr Fox. Nor can Mr Pitt say so, after having said that he had urged as strongly as he could to the King (except by refusing to take place without him) the great advantage if not necessity there was to include him in the new administration. If Mr Pitt thought the King was right in persevering to object to Mr Fox because he had before by Mr Pitt's advice turned Mr Fox out of his privy council, he should not have urged as he says he did his being joined to him in the new administration, and Mr Pitt's accepting office without Mr Fox was evidently departing from the original plan in which all Parties had joined to turn out Mr Addington in order to form an administration on the *broadest basis*. Without Mr Fox and his friends it became one on a *narrow basis*, as such the Grenvilles had a right to say they would not depart from the original plan. By their refusal they certainly narrowed it still more. But Mr Pitt had first begun to narrow it by leaving out Mr Fox and his friends, and altho Mr Pitt might consent to leave behind him those by whose support he had obtained the means of getting into power yet I cannot but think the conduct of the Grenvilles far more honourable in sticking to those with whom they had joined and in refusing to take office unless they were included.

The Kings refusal of Mr Fox on account of his principles is at all events what cannot be maintained by Mr Pitt after his having as he says recommended and urged his being joined in the same administration with himself.

On what grounds therefore can Mr Pitt justify his taking office without Mr Fox assisted as he had been by him to get into power, and contrary to the original plan of an administration on the *broadest* basis? None as I conceive that can be maintained. Will his friends say, I think he will not say himself that the Kings prerogative of chusing his own Ministers must not be infringed, and that if he has conceived a prejudice right or wrong against any individual, his consent ought not to be forced nor the Government of the Country be impeded on account of any one man. I say that I do not believe Mr Pitt holds such language because he must be sensible that his own coming into place now, is a force upon the King's consent. He knows that the King is as averse to him as to Mr Fox, that if the King were allowed to use his prerogative of nominating a Minister after his own choice it would be Mr Addington not Mr Pitt, that the King strongly objected to Lord Melville and yet Mr Pitt would not give way to that objection and consequently did force the King in that respect. Mr Pitt cannot therefore pretend that to have stood out for Mr Fox as he did for Lord Melville would have been more an infringement on the King's Choice of Ministers in one case than in the other. He also knows that he himself has not the influence with the King and the Power without which no Minister can serve the country as he ought, since not only he could not carry Mr Fox's appointment, but meets with perpetual contradictions and slights in his other recommendations, and even his friend Lord Amherst turned out for voting with him, and it is well known that the King declares that all the arrangements made are political matters that he has no concern with, and that in all his household arrangements he will have his own way. So that in fact Mr Pitt is acting as Minister forced upon the King by the votes of Parliament against Mr Addington's measures in which the Grenvilles and Mr Fox and his friends had a considerable share, and remains so without their support and without the confidence or good will of the King. Is that right?

If it is not, is it not right in those who think such a situation unconstitutional and tending to no good but to gratify the personal ambition of one man, to oppose him?

But you ask who is to succeed him? I answer I hope no one in that stile that Mr Pitt has assumed to himself of a dictatorial Minister. What I wish for, is the principle upon which all agreed being carried into effect of an administration on the *broadest basis* in which all the real talents of the country shall be united, and no one shall take such an ascendency as to make all the rest cyphers, and I by no means wish to exclude Mr Pitt whose talents I acknowledge to be very great. I wish him to have his just and proper share, but not to engross the whole power, which I fear he is bent upon, and knowing that that cannot be when united with those who are his equals makes him prefer to be at the Head of His party whom he can lead as he pleases, than to join with those to whose opinions he would be obliged to pay some deference. But you may again ask what hopes I have that such a plan can succeed, and I own there are a thousand difficulties, but the greatest is in Mr Pitt himself. Tho' he truckles to back stair influence to obtain the appear(an)ce of being sole Minister yet I fear his ambition is such as will never permit him fairly to join with and put himself on an equal footing with any one. He will be *Cesor aut nullus* and if we are unfortunately driven to the choice of the two I must say *nullus* for usurped as this situation of first Minister has sometimes been and soon abused into being *sole Minister*, our Constitution knows of no such place. The King is advised by a Committee of the privy council that he choses to select and which are nick-named the Cabinet, in which no man has a right to assume and direct. Great talents and knowledge of business will undoubtedly give a preponderance to the opinions of those who possess them. But if to prevent opposition which will necessarily arise amongst those who cannot brook such a partial Government and to assist the country with all the abilities it possesses in a crisis like the present an administration upon the broadest basis, has been thought desirable by all Parties and the sense of the nation, surely every man meaning well to such a Plan ought to be content with a share in it and not engross the whole to himself.

Another very material circumstance cannot be passed by, which is the situation of the Prince of Wales. Whatever different opinions may be entertained of him, he is heir apparent to the crown, 42 years of age, with a great following and his father is 66 and in bad health both in body and mind. These circumstances cannot be altered, they exist, and must be attended to. To countenance and support the King's Prejudices against the Prince and against Mr Fox, is leaving as it is found to be, a minority so formidable in Parliament that no Minister can carry on business against it, aware as he must be that the King's declining health and age will make many in such a precarious state of things fly to pay early court to the rising sun.

What then shall the King be forced? No otherwise certainly than by that refusal which every man has a right to

make of taking any share in so weak and ineffective an
administration as the present and in addresses and petitions
to the King to form one more effective. The King may still
refuse, but if he is so ill advised, or rather of his own head
suffers the country to go to ruin rather than give up his
personal aversions, we must suppose that his illness is the
cause of it. But I have no such apprehension and upon the
same ground the publick necessity that induced the King
to give up Mr Addington and submit to Mr Pitt, I am con-
fident that if Mr Pitt tells him as Mr Addington honestly
did, that he cannot go on, the King will form a new administration that can have more weight with the country and
nothing can in my opinion be more likely to produce that
effect in the present moment all things considered as a union
of all parties in some shape or other under the Prince of
Wales influence. For his situation would prevent any party
from feeling the mortification of submitting to another.
None need be ashamed of admitting a lead in the heir apparent when whether from sickness or convalescence the King
himself find less business conducive to his recovery. But
even if Mr Pitt should refuse to take his proper share in
such a Government I am persuaded that without him the
Prince and Mr Fox would in the present state of things
form a stronger Government than Mr Pitt now exhibits
without them. If therefore we were only to consider the
strongest Government as the best for the country we should
oppose Mr Pitt to introduce that of Mr Fox under the Protection of the Prince. But I am for neither. I am for an Union
of the whole, but if Mr Pitt persists in preventing that, I am
for the best choice that remains, that of the strongest Government and that which has no unreasonable pretensions and
would have yielded much for the general good. You see
that notwithstanding Mr Pitt's former and present conduct
to me, I am no otherwise adverse to him than as he stands
in the way of that very broad basis, he professed he was for,
and upon which ground alone he has got into power. This I
say upon publick grounds, for willing as my temper is to
forget injuries, yet when they, or slights are persevered in,
I cannot remain indifferent, and surely Mr Pitt can have
no claims upon me from private friendship which he has

sacrificed, and when instead of making the smallest attempt at reconciliation he continues ever deficient in those attentions that one gentleman has a right to expect from another. You say that you never knew the cause of his former conduct or why I was turned out. Nor I either. You saw the shuffling letter he wrote to me on that occasion in which he assigned no reason and was ashamed to own the true one, which was that the Duke of York thought I in some sort stood in his way while I remained the friend of Mr Pitt who as such could not give me up, that Mr Dundas was afraid that from the friendship Mr Pitt proffessed towards me and which he had before really felt, I might prevent his getting the entire ascendency which he has since obtained over Mr Pitts mind. An excuse was therefore laid hold of, that being against our plunging so deep in the ruinous war as we were then getting deeper and deeper entangled with, I had for some time avoided attending Cabinets, and Mr Pitt having already allowed Mr Dundas to get so much power and interest with the Duke of York by coming into all his plans dared not oppose the wishes of both, and sacrificed his friend to them. Nor did he mind your being involved in my being turned out tho' to you there was not the same political objections as to me, and you lived in the utmost intimacy with him. You then lost a place worth I believe 7 or 800 a year to you in one way or other. But Mr Pitt in the many years he afterwards remained Minister nor on his present return to power has, that I have heard of, [n]ever thought of making you any compensation which subject to my consent, surely he might at least have offered you.

You say that altho' not pledged by any speech in Parliament you had thought I meant to support Mr Pitt, you say provided Lord Melville was not war Minister, and I certainly was inclined to support Mr Pitt, not because he might make so slight an alteration as to transfer Lord Melville from one important place to another, but on account of the system in which we had all joined in opposing Mr Addington and I trust I have sufficiently evinced that disposition in the communication I made to Mr Pitt thro you of my plan of defence; but had I on my legs in Parliament declared that I had meant to support him, I should have considered myself acting consistently in withdrawing it when Mr Pitt withdrew from the grounds on which I had promised it.

I must revert to the state of the King's health which causes great embarrasment. To the state of mind he has been in must be imputed his conduct to Mr Pitt, but now his physicians declare that he is at any time competent to any business that may be laid before him, but that it is expedient still to keep him from a free intercourse with his family and under the control of the people that Dr. Simmonds has put about him. Such an arrangement may be very proper for preventing as they say a relapse, and for establishing his perfect recovery. But it is a strange circumstance to have a King shut up from his family and subjects except his Ministers exercising the Royal functions and yet under the control of Dr. Simmonds and his people. But this is the state that his physicians own to! and it would seem that Mr Pitt intends to let this state of things go on, and Parliament be prorogued as soon as the business is over, leaving it impossible to assemble it again in less than 40 days during which time should any relapse take place the Government must be without a head, or if the King continues as he is, it must remain effective from the acts of the King but still under control of keepers for many months, and we know not by whose authority this control while the King can act as King is or can be imposed. For a short time such a question may be blinked, but it would be a most dangerous precedent to be avowed and acted upon. God grant that the King may soon compleatly recover and be himself again and get rid of these keepers, but remaining under their control and yet acting as King is a strange situation for Parliament to submit to.

When I mentioned Mr Pitt's acting illegally it was to this situation I meant to allude of suffering any control to continue over the King when he is well enough to exercise the Royal Function, for either the King is well or he is ill, if ill enough to be under control and that be necessary he is not well enough to act as King, if he is well enough, it is no less than high treason to keep the Kings person under control and confinement. As to your exposing yourself to blame except by your own little party, I meant in acting directly contrary to the part it is well known I am now taking because it must be thought by every impartial man that I deserved more of your attention than Mr Pitt. If I mentioned your obligations to me, it was not to reproach you with them, but to remind you of what would be the general opinion if you suffered them to have no weight in your political conduct. It vexes me much that your inclinations should be different from mine on this subject, but I cannot help it and you must judge for yourself how far you will follow your own or attend to mine. It is very true that for many years I have declined all interference with politicks, and during that time there was no reason on my account why you should not support Mr Pitt tho' I see no reason why you should. But no inference is from the support you then gave to be drawn why you should continue it under very different circumstances and when the times obliged me as I thought to take a public part again, and altho' I shall probably never be a Minister again yet I must feel anxious to give my support to what I think the best cause. Unwilling however to distress your feelings tho' I lament them I feel content in your remaining where another duty calls you. Be assured my dear Charles that I ever feel the utmost affection for you and am as anxious as you can be that you should upon all occasions act in a manner that the thinking part of the world will approve of, and I think that if we could see a little more of each other and you would communicate your thoughts to me with more confidence than you have hitherto done, that we might not differ on so many points as we have done. For I cannot but think that most of the errors you have fallen into, have been from the company you keep and that a little friendly advice from one who loves you so much as I do and to whom I flatter myself you would attend to if opportunities offered, might have prevented them. Believe me ever your most affectionate uncle.

RICHMOND, &c.

BIBLIOGRAPHY

I. MANUSCRIPT SOURCES

A. *Official papers concerning Richmond's activities as Ambassador to France, Secretary of State, or Master-General of the Ordnance, and his efforts to register his French peerage*

Archives du Ministère des Affaires Étranges:
 Correspondence Politique avec Angleterre, 466, 468, 469, 470, 472.
 Papers concerning Richmond's Embassy to France.
Archives Nationales, Douzième Volume des Ordonnances du Roy Louis Seize:
 Registration of Richmond's Dukedom of Aubigny.
British Museum, Additional Manuscripts:
 Secretary of State:
  Papers of Sir William Hamilton. Add. MS. 41,197.
  Papers of Sir H. Moore. Add. MS. 12,440.
  Newcastle Papers. Add. MS. 33,056.
 Master General of the Ordnance:
  Nelson Papers. Add. MSS. 34,902 and 34,933.
  Windham Papers. Add. MS. 37,874.
  Papers of General Haldemand. Add MS. 21,709.
  Carmarthen Papers. Add. MSS. 28,060–3 and 26,066.
  Dundas Papers. Add. MS. 38,734.
  Liverpool Papers. Add. MSS. 38,211, 38,223, 38,301, 38,306, 38,472.
Public Record Office:
 Correspondence concerning the Embassy to France.
 State Papers 78/268 and 9.
 Ordnance Board, Outletters General, 1782–1795. War Office 46/14–24.
 Ordnance Board Minutes, 1782–1786. War Office 47/99–107 (Irregular collection).
 Extracts of Ordnance Board Minutes and Reports by the Surveyor General. War Office, 46/2557.
 Foreign Office: Dispatches to France (27), the United Provinces (37), Prussia (64), and Austria (7).
William L. Clements Library:
 Sydney Papers (Ordnance).
 Sir Henry Clinton Papers (Ordnance).
 Gage Papers (Secretaryship of State).
 Shelburne Papers (Secretaryship of State).
Cirencester: MSS. of the Earl of Bathurst.
 Lord George Lennox's copies of Richmond's correspondence as Ambassador to France.
Goodwood:
 Miscellaneous Collection of Ordnance Board Letters. Box 29, Bundle XI.

B. *Manuscripts concerning Chichester*

Chichester Cathedral Chapter Account Books D and E.
Minute Books, Court of Common Council, Chichester, 1751–1806.
Minutes of Quarter Sessions held at Chichester, 1751–1806.

C. *Sources of non-official manuscripts*

British Museum. Additional Manuscripts:
MSS. of Sir Peter Collinson. Add. MS. 28,727.
MSS. of J. Caryll. Add. MS. 28,233.
MSS. of Duchess Dowager of Leinster. Add. MS. 30,990.
Newcastle Papers. Add. MSS. 32,723 to 33,072.
MSS. of Sir Philip Francis. Add. MS. 40,763.
McIntosh MSS. Add. MS. 34,523.
Hardwicke MSS. Add. MS. 35,607 and 35,662.
C. J. Fox MSS. Add. MS. 47,568.
Egerton Manuscripts:
MSS. of Count Bentinck. Eg. MSS. 1722, 1731, and 1862.
Public Record Office:
Chatham MSS.
Pitt MSS. including fourteen letters from Richmond to Pitt, 1786–98.
Typescripts and Microfilms consulted through the History of Parliament Trust:
Lansdowne MSS.
Camden MSS.
Dowdeswell MSS.
Albemarle MSS.
Bute MSS.
Devonshire MSS., (Valuable information concerning Richmond's resignation of the Bedchamber in 1760.)
Sheffield: Wentworth-Woodhouse MSS. of the Marquis of Rockingham, Edmund Burke.
Also collected typescripts of Burke manuscripts.
Nottingham: MSS. of the Duke of Portland. Useful for 1770–84 and again, 1795, concerning Portland's coalition with Pitt.
Goodwood:
General Wolfe to Richmond. Fifteen letters on military subjects, 1755–7.
Duchess of Richmond to Richmond, approximately thirty-five personal letters, 1793–6. Valuable for events surrounding Richmond's dismissal from the Ordnance, 1795.
Miscellaneous letters to Conway, James Adair, the Earl of Loudoun, and Richmond's bankers, and from Conway and the Earl of Bute.
Richmond's Diary, 1761.
Richmond's Journal, June–July 1766.
Miscellaneous account books, 1755–1806.
Miscellaneous military exercises, Embassy instructions, &c.
Leeds: Brotherton MSS.
Papers of Thomas Townshend, Baron Sydney. Useful for early years (1784–5) of the ministry of the younger Pitt.

Bury St. Edmunds:
    Grafton MSS. Several letters from Horace Walpole to Grafton, 1766–7; one personal letter from Richmond to Grafton, 1788.
    Conolly MSS. One valuable letter, Thomas Conolly to Richmond, 1786, concerning Irish politics. Copy book of Lady Louisa Conolly's letters; forty-five personal letters to Richmond, 1761–1799.
Dublin, Fitzgerald MSS.
    Valuable letters of the Lennox family including Emily, Duchess of Leinster, Lady Louisa Conolly, &c., with particularly interesting political correspondence between Richmond and his nephew, Charles Lennox, 1804–6.
Ann Arbor, Michigan, William L. Clement's Library:
    Dowdeswell MSS.
    Lacaita MSS. A few miscellaneous letters, 1779–84.
Hardwicke Court, Gloucester: Granville Sharp MSS.
San Marino, California. Huntington Library: Grenville MSS.
    Letters concerning Chichester patronage, 1764.
Cirencester: MSS. of the Earl Bathurst.
    Correspondence of Lord George Lennox.
Manuscript sources of single Richmond letters.
    Autograph letter of Prof. G. H. Guttridge (to Thomas Conolly).
    Belfast, Northern Ireland Record Office (to the Earl of Buchan).
    Chevening: MS. of the Earl of Stanhope (to Lord Mahon).
    Edinburgh, National Library of Scotland (to Walker King. Also Dundas memoranda of 1801).

D. *Historical Manuscripts Commission Reports*

Carlisle MSS.
Abergavenny MSS.
Eglintoun MSS.
Bathurst MSS.
Buckingham MSS.
Savile Foljambe MSS.
Stopford-Sackville MSS.
Fortescue MSS.
Dropmore MSS.
Various collections.
Rutland MSS.
Charlemont MSS.

II. REFERENCE WORKS
MOST FREQUENTLY CONSULTED

A. *Parliamentary Reference Works*

Journals of the House of Lords, 1760–84.
Journals of the House of Commons, 1760–84.
Journals of the Irish House of Commons, 1780–4.

Cobbett's Parliamentary History, 1765–85.

ROGERS, THOROLD. *A Complete Collection of Protests of the House of Lords.* Oxford, 1875. Vol. ii.

Return of Members of Parliament. Part II. London, 1879.

An Account of the Sussex Election held at Chichester, 1820. Chichester, 1820. (Compares the elections of 1774 and 1820.)

The Poll for Knights of the Shire to Represent the County of Sussex. Taken at Chichester in 1774 by George Peckham, Esq., Sheriff. Lewes, 1775.

B. *General Reference Works*

Alumni Cantabrigienses
    Part I. Comp. by John Venn and J. A. Venn. Cambridge, 1922.
    Part II. Comp. by J. A. Venn. Cambridge, 1940.

Alumni Oxonienses, 1715–1886. Arr. Joseph Foster. London, 1887.

AUSTEN-LEIGH, R. A. *The Eton College Register.* Eton: Vol. 2 (1698–1752), 1927; Vol. 3 (1753–1790), 1921.

COCKAYNE, G. E. *The Complete Baronetage.* Exeter, 1900–6.

—— *The Complete Peerage.* New edn. Revised. London, 1910–52.

The Commissioned Sea Officers of the Royal Navy, 1660–1815. Greenwich, 1954.

LA CHENAYE-DESBOIS et BADIER. *Dictionnaire de la Noblesse.* 3rd edn. Paris, 1863–76.

Dictionary of Anonymous and Pseudonymous English Literature. Ed. James Kennedy. London, 1926.

Dictionary of National Biography. Ed. Sydney Lee and Leslie Stephen. London, 1908–9.

The Knights of England. Comp. W. A. Shaw. London, 1906.

LENEVE, JOHN. *Fasti Ecclesiae Anglicanae.* Oxford, 1854.

MUSGRAVE, SIR WILLIAM. *Obituary, Prior to 1800.* Ed. Sir George J. Armytage. London, 1899–1901.

The Record of Old Westminster. Compiled by G. F. Russell Barker and Alan H. Stenning. London, 1928.

III. CONTEMPORARY PERIODICALS

A. *Newspapers*

London Chronicle.
London Gazette.
Morning Chronicle.
Public Advertiser.
St. James' Chronicle.
Westminster Gazette.

B. *Magazines*

Annual Register.
Gentleman's Magazine.
The Political Magazine.

IV. CONTEMPORARY PAMPHLETS, AUTOBIOGRAPHIES, AND PUBLISHED CORRESPONDENCE

Editions of the *Letter to Colonel Sharman:*
London, 1783, 1792 (identical editions in 1795 and 1797), 1817, 1824, 1859.
Dublin, 1783.
Sheffield, 1792.

ABINGDON, THE EARL OF. *Thoughts on the Letter of Edmund Burke to the Sheriffs of Bristol.* London, 1777.

The Journal and Correspondence of William, Lord Auckland. London, 1861.

Correspondence of John, Fourth Duke of Bedford. London, 1842–6.

BELSHAM, W. *Memoirs of the Reign of George III to 1793.* London, 1795.

THE DUKE OF BUCKINGHAM AND CHANDOS. *Memoirs of the Courts and Cabinets of George III.* London, 1853–5.

BURGH, JAMES. *Political Disquisitions.* London, 1774.

Correspondence of the Right Honourable Edmund Burke, 1744–1797. Ed. Charles, Earl Fitzwilliam and Sir Richard Bourke. London, 1844.

BURKE, EDMUND. *Thoughts on the Cause of the Present Discontents.* Ed. W. Murison: Cambridge, 1913.

The Works of the Right Honourable Edmund Burke. London, 1867.

CARTWRIGHT, MAJOR JOHN. *American Independence: the Interest and Glory of Great Britain.* London, 1774.

—— *Give Us our Rights!* London, [1782].

—— *The People's Barrier against undue Influence and Corruption.* London, 1780.

—— *The Legislative Rights of the Commonality Vindicated, or 'Take Your Choice.'* 2nd edn. London, 1777.

SIR HENRY CAVENDISH's *Debates in the House of Commons.* Ed. John Wright. London, 1840–3.

Correspondence of William Pitt, Earl of Chatham. Ed. W. S. Taylor and Capt. J. H. Pringle. London, 1839.

The Letters of the Earl of Chesterfield to his Son. Ed. C. Strachey. London, 1901.

COLE, REV. WILLIAM. *Journal of my Journey to Paris.* Ed. F. G. Stokes. London, 1931.

Correspondence of Charles, First Marquis Cornwallis. Ed. Chas. Ross. London, 1859. Vol. i.

The Letters of George Dempster to Adam Ferguson. Ed. James Fergusson. London, 1934.

Georgiana, Duchess of Devonshire. Ed. the Earl of Bessborough. London, 1955.

Diary of the late George Bubb Dodington, 1749–1761. Ed. Henry Penruddocke Wyndham. Salisbury, 1784.

The Speech of the Rt. Hon. Charles Jas. Fox . . . in Westminster Hall, July 17, 1782. Taken in shorthand by W. Blanchard. London, 1782.

Memorials and Correspondence of Charles James Fox. Ed. Ld. John Russell. London, 1853.

The Correspondence of King George III, 1760–1783. Ed. Sir John Fortescue. London, 1927.

Letters from George III to the Earl of Bute, 1756–1766. Ed. Romney Sedgewick. London, 1939.

Autobiography and Political Correspondence of Augustus Henry, Third Duke of Grafton. Ed. Sir William Anson. London, 1898.

GRATTAN, HENRY. *Memoirs of the Life and Times of the Rt. Hon. Henry Grattan.* London, 1839–46.

The Grenville Papers. Ed. James Smith. London, 1853.

Memoir of Thomas Hardy, Founder of, and Secretary to, the London Corresponding Society. London, 1832.

The Trial of Thomas Hardy for High Treason. . . . Taken by Joseph Gurney. London, 1794.

An History of the Late Important Period: from the Beginning of His Majesty's Illness to the Settlement of the Executive Government in the Appointment of a Regent. London, 1789.

The Journal of Elizabeth, Lady Holland. Ed. the Earl of Ilchester. London, 1908.

Letters to Henry Fox, Lord Holland. Ed. the Earl of Ilchester. London, 1915.

Letters written by Sir Samuel Hood. Ed. David Hannay. London, Navy Record Society, 1895. Vol. iii.

JEBB, JOHN. *Address to the Freeholders of Middlesex, December 20, 1780.* London, 1782.

The Works of John Jebb. Ed. John Disney. London, 1787.

JONES, WILLIAM. *The Principles of Government, in a Dialogue between a Scholar and a Peasant.* London, 1783.

JUCKER, NINETTA S. *The Jenkinson Papers.* London, 1949.

Political Memoranda of Francis Godolphin Osborne, Fifth Duke of Leeds. Ed. Oscar Browning. Camden Society Publications. New Series XXV, 1884.

Correspondence of Emily, Duchess of Leinster. Ed. Brian Fitzgerald. Dublin, 1949–53.

(LENNOX, CHARLES). *An Answer to 'A Short Essay on the Modes of Defense best Adapted to the Situation and Circumstances of this Island'.* London, 1885.

Life and Letters of Lady Sarah Lennox. Ed. Earl of Ilchester and the Countess Stavordale. London, 1901.

LOFFT, CAPPELL. *Observations on a Late Publication entitled, 'A Dialogue on the Actual State of Parliament.'* London, 1783.

Memoirs and Correspondence of George, Lord Lyttleton. Ed. R. J. Phillimore. London, 1845.

Diaries and Correspondence of James Harris, first Earl of Malmesbury. Ed. the third Earl of Malmesbury. London, 1844.

The Life and Letters of Gilbert Elliot, first Earl of Minto. Ed. the Countess of Minto. London, 1874.

NEWCASTLE, DUKE OF. *Narrative of Changes in the Government, 1765–1767.* Ed. Mary Bateson. London, 1898.

NUGENT, CLAUD. *Memoir of Robert, Earl Nugent.* London, 1898.

Henry, Elizabeth, and George (1734–80). Letters and Diaries of Henry, Tenth Earl of Pembroke and his Circle. Ed. Lord Herbert. London, 1939.

Pembroke Papers (1780–94). *Letters and Diaries of Henry, Tenth Earl of Pembroke and his Circle.* Ed. Lord Herbert. London, 1950.

PRICE, RICHARD. *Observations on the Nature of Civil Liberty.* . . . 9th edn. London, 1776.

—— *Additional Observations on the Nature of Civil Liberty.* Philadelphia, 1778.

PRIESTLEY, DR. J. *Essays on the first Principles of Government, and on the Nature of Political, Civil, and Religious Liberty.* 2nd edn. London, 1771.

The Authentic Correspondence between his Grace the Duke of Richmond and the Rt. Hon. Lord Rawdon. London, 1789.

The Parliamentary Papers of John Robinson. Ed. W. T. LaPrade. London, 1922.

Memoirs of the Marquis of Rockingham and his Contemporaries. Ed. The Earl of Albemarle. London, 1852.

Private Papers of John, Earl of Sandwich, First Lord of the Admiralty, 1771–82. Ed. G. R. Barnes and J. H. Owen. London, Navy Record Society, 1933. Vol. ii.

HOARE, PRINCE. *Memoirs of Granville Sharp.* London, 1820.

SHARP, GRANVILLE. *A Declaration of the People's Natural Right to a Share in the Legislature.* London, 1774.

The Trial of John Horne Tooke for High Treason . . . November 17–22, 1794. Taken by Joseph Gurney. London, 1795.

The Controversial letters of John Wilkes . . . and the Rev. John Horne, and their Principal adherents. London, 1771.

The Correspondence of the Late John Wilkes with his Friends. Ed. John Almon. London, 1805.

WALPOLE, HORACE. *Correspondence.* Ed. W. S. Lewis. London, 1937–56.

—— *Memoirs of the Reign of King George III.* Ed. G. F. Russell Barker. London, 1894.

The Last Journals of Horace Walpole from 1771 to 1783. Ed. Dr. Doran with notes by A. F. Stewart. London, 1910.

The Life and Correspondence of the Right Honorable William Windham, 1750–1810. Ed. the Earl of Rosebery. London, 1913.

History and Posthumous Memoirs of Sir Nathaniel William Wraxall, 1772–84. Ed. Henry B. Wheatley. London, 1884.

WYVILL, REV. CHRISTOPHER. *Political Papers.* . . . York, 1794–1804.

V. LATER WORKS

ADAMS, R. G. *Political Ideas of the American Revolution.* Durham, North Carolina, 1922.

ADOLPHUS, JOHN. *The History of England from the Accession of King George III to the conclusion of Peace.* London, 1802.

ANDERSON, TROYER S. *The Command of the Howe Brothers during the American Revolution.* Oxford, 1936.

ARMSTRONG, SIR WALTER. *Sir Joshua Reynolds, First President of the Royal Academy.* London, 1900.

ASPINALL, A. *Politics and the Press, 1780–1850.* London, 1949.

BAIN, R. NISBET. 'The Hats and Caps and Gustavus III'. *Cambridge Modern History. The Eighteenth Century*, New York, 1908. Ch. xxii, pp. 758–84.

BARROW, SIR JOHN. *The Life of Richard, Earl Howe*. London, 1838.

BECKER, CARL. *The Declaration of Independence*. New York, 1922.

BERRY, WILLIAM. *Sussex Genealogies*. London, 1830.

BLEACKLEY, HORACE. *Life of John Wilkes*. London, 1917.

BLEASE, W. LYON. *A Short History of English Liberalism*. London, 1922. Vol. ii.

BOLTON, ARTHUR T. *The Architecture of Robert and James Adam*. London, 1949.

BROOKE, J. *The Chatham Administration*. London, 1956.

BURNE, A. *The Noble Duke of York*. London, 1949.

BUTTERFIELD, HERBERT. *George III, Lord North, and the People*. London, 1952.

BYRNE, P. *Lord Edward Fitzgerald*. London, 1955.

CARTWRIGHT, F. D. *Life and Correspondence of Major John Cartwright*. London, 1826.

Cassell's Topographical Guides: The County of Sussex, Its History, Antiquities, and Topography. London, 1862.

CHAMBERLAIN, ARTHUR. *George Romney*. London, 1910.

CHRISTIE, IAN R. 'The Marquis of Rockingham and Lord North's Offer of a Coalition, June–July, 1780', *English Historical Review*, July 1954, pp. 388–407.

CLARK, DORA MAE. *British Opinion and the American Revolution*. New Haven, 1930.

COBBAN, A. *Ambassadors and Secret Agents*. London, 1954.

CURTIS, E. R. *Lady Sarah Lennox, An Irrepressible Stuart, 1745–1826*. London, 1948.

DALLAWAY, JAMES. *History of the Western Division of Sussex*. London, 1815.

DAVIDSON, PHILIP. *Propaganda and the American Revolution*. Chapel Hill, North Carolina, 1941.

DE CASTRO, J. P. *The Gordon Riots*. Oxford, 1926.

DRINKWATER, JOHN. *Charles James Fox*. London, 1928.

DUNN, MATTHIAS. *An Historical, Geological, and Descriptive View of the Coal Trade of the North of England*. Newcastle-upon-Tyne, 1844.

ELLIS, W. S. *The Parks and Forests of Sussex, Ancient and Modern*. Lewes, 1885.

EYCK, ERICH. *Pitt vs Fox, Father and Son*. Transl. Eric Northcott. London, 1950.

FINBERG, H. F. *Canaletto in England*. Walpole Society. Oxford, 1920–1. Vol. ix.

FITZGERALD, BRIAN. *Emily, Duchess of Leinster, 1731–1814*. London, 1949.
—— *Lady Louisa Conolly, 1743–1821. An Anglo-Irish Biography*. London, 1950.

FITZMAURICE, LORD. *Life of William, Earl of Shelburne*. London, 1912.

FORBES, A. *A History of the Army Ordnance Services*. London, 1929.

FORTESCUE, THE HON. JOHN. *The County Lieutenancies and the Army, 1803–1814*. London, 1909.

FORTESCUE, THE HON. JOHN. *History of the British Army.* London, 1911. Vol. i.

FURBER, HOLDEN. *Henry Dundas, First Viscount Melville, 1742–1811.* Oxford, 1931.

GALLOWAY, ROBERT L. *A History of Coal Mining in Great Britain.* London, 1882.

GAMLIN, HILDA. *George Romney and his Art.* London, 1894.

GEORGE, MRS. ERIC. 'Fox's Martyrs; the General Election of 1784', *Transactions of the Royal Historical Society* (1939), 4th ser., vol. xxi, pp. 133–68.

GOEBEL, JULIUS. *The Struggle for the Falkland Islands.* New Haven, 1927.

GORE-BROWN, ROBERT. *Chancellor Thurlow, The Life and Times of an XVIIIth Century Lawyer.* London, 1953.

GREEN, F. V. *The Revolutionary War and the Military Policy of the United States.* New York, 1911.

GRENVILLE, C. C. F. *A Journal of the Reigns of King George IV and King William IV.* Ed. H. Reeve. London, 1874.

GUTTRIDGE, G. H. *English Whiggism and the American Revolution.* Berkeley, California, 1942.

—— *The Early Career of Lord Rockingham.* University of California Publications in History, xliv. Berkeley, 1952.

HAMMOND, J. L. LEB. *Charles James Fox. A Political Study.* London, 1903.

HARLOW, VINCENT T. *The Founding of the Second British Empire, 1763–1793.* London, 1952.

HAY, REV. ALEXANDER. *The Chichester Guide and Directory.* Chichester, 1804.

—— *History of Chichester.* Chichester, 1804.

HOBHOUSE, CHRISTOPHER. *Fox.* London, 1947.

HOLDSWORTH, W. S. *A History of English Law.* London, 1903. Vol. vii.

HORSFIELD, T. W. *History, Antiquities, and Topography of the County of Sussex.* Lewes, 1835.

HOVELL, MARK. *The Chartist Movement.* Manchester, 1925.

HUNT, HENRY. *Memoirs.* London, 1820.

HUNT, WILLIAM. *The Irish Parliament in 1775.* Dublin, 1907.

ILCHESTER, EARL OF. *Henry Fox, First Lord Holland.* London, 1920.

JESSE, J. HENEAGE. *Memoirs of the Life and Reign of King George III.* London, 1867. Vols. i and ii used.

JUDD, G. P. *Members of Parliament, 1734–1832.* New Haven, 1955.

KIER, SIR DAVID L. 'Economic Reform, 1779–1787', *Law Quarterly Review,* l (1934), pp. 368–85.

KENT, C. B. R. *The English Radicals, an Historical Sketch.* London, 1899.

KENT, JOHN. *Records and Reminiscences of Goodwood and the Dukes of Richmond.* London, 1896.

KEPPEL, HON. AND REV. THOMAS. *Life of Augustus, Viscount Keppel.* London, 1942.

LASCELLES, EDWARD. *The Life of Charles James Fox.* Oxford, 1936.

LECKY, W. E. H. *History of England.* London, 1892.

LEWIS, G. C. *Essays on the Administrations of Great Britain from 1783 to 1830.* Ed. Sir Edmund Head. London, 1864.

LOVETT, WILLIAM. *The Life and Struggles of William Lovett.* London, 1876.

LOWER, M. A. *The Worthies of Sussex, Sketches of Eminent Natives from the Earliest Period to the Present Time.* Lewes, 1865.

MACCOBY, S. *English Radicalism, 1762–1785.* London, 1955.

MAGNUS, SIR PHILIP. *Edmund Burke, a Life.* London, 1939.

MASON, WILLIAM HAYLEY. *Goodwood, its House, Park and Grounds.* London, 1839.

MORE, THOMAS. *The Life and Death of Lord Edward Fitzgerald.* London, 1831.

MORGAN, WM. *Memoirs of the Life of the Reverend Richard Price, D.D., F.R.S.* London, 1815.

MORLEY, JOHN, VSCT. *Burke.* London, 1923.

MURRAY, REV. ROBERT H. *Edmund Burke, a Biography.* Oxford, 1931.

NAMIER, SIR L. B. *Structure of Politics at the Accession of George III.* London, 1929.

—— *England in the Age of the American Revolution.* London, 1930.

NEF, J. U. *The Rise of the British Coal Industry.* London, 1932.

OLDFIELD, T. H. B. *Representative History of Great Britain, and Ireland.* London, 1816.

PARES, RICHARD. *King George III and the Politicians.* Oxford, 1953.

Public Characters, 1798–1810. First parts ed. by Alexander Stephens. London, 1801–9.

RAMSAY, J. F. *Anglo-French Relations, 1763–70.* University of California Publications in History, xvii, 3. Berkeley, 1939.

Recollections of the Table-Talk of Samuel Rogers. Ed. Rev. Alexander Dyce. London, 1887.

REID, W. HAMILTON. *Memoirs of the Public Life of John Horne Tooke, Esq.* London, 1812.

RIKER, THAD. W. *Henry Fox, first Lord Holland.* Oxford 1911.

ROMNEY, REV. JOHN. *Memoirs of the Life and Works of George Romney.* London, 1830.

ROSE, J. H. 'The Duke of Richmond on the Conduct of the War in 1793', *English Historical Review,* xxv (1910), pp. 553–6.

—— 'Great Britain and the Dutch Question in 1786–7', *American Historical Review,* xiv (1908–9), pp. 262–83.

—— *William Pitt and the National Revival.* London, 1911.

RUSSELL, LORD JOHN. *The Life and Times of Charles James Fox.* London, 1859.

SANDBY, WILLIAM. *The History of the Royal Academy.* London, 1862.

SHERRARD, O. A. *Life of John Wilkes.* London, 1930.

SICHEL, WALTER S. *Sheridan.* London, 1909.

STANHOPE, GHITA, and GOOCH, G. P. *Life of Charles, third Earl Stanhope.* London, 1914.

STANHOPE, THE EARL OF. *Life of William Pitt.* London, 1879.

STEPHENS, ALEXANDER. *Memoirs of John Horne Tooke.* London, 1813.

SUTHERLAND, L. S. 'Edmund Burke and the first Rockingham Ministry', *English Historical Review*, xlvii (1932), pp. 46–72.
—— *The East India Company in Eighteenth Century Politics*. Oxford, 1952.
SYKES, JOHN. *Local Records, or Historical Register of . . . Newcastle-upon-Tyne*. Newcastle, 1833.
THOMAS, ROLAND, M.A. *Richard Price, Philosopher and Apostle of Liberty*. Oxford, 1924.
TREVELYAN, SIR G. O. *The Early History of Charles James Fox*. London, 1908.
VEITCH, G. S. *The Genesis of Parliamentary Reform*. London, 1913.
The Victoria History of the County of Buckinghamshire. Ed. William Page. London, 1905–27.
Victoria County History of Sussex. Ed. L. F. Salzman. Oxford, 1940.
VON RUVILLE, ALBERT. *William Pitt, Earl of Chatham*. Transl. H. J. Chaytor. London, 1907.
WADE, JOHN. *Junius*. London, 1850.
WARD, HUMPHREY and ROBERT W. *Romney, a Biographical and Critical Essay, with a Catalogue Raisonné of his Works*. London, 1904.
WEBB, BEATRICE and SYDNEY. *English Local Government*. London, 1906. Vol. i.
WECTER, DIXON. *Edmund Burke and his Kinsmen*. Boulder, Colorado, 1939.
The History of White's. London, 1892.
WILLIAMS, BASIL. *The Life of William Pitt, Earl of Chatham*. London, 1913.
WINSTANLEY, D. A. *Lord Chatham and the Whig Opposition*. Cambridge, 1912.
—— *Personal and Party Government* (1760–67). Cambridge, 1910.

INDEX

(R. denotes Richmond, third Duke of)

PRINTED IN GREAT BRITAIN
AT THE UNIVERSITY PRESS, OXFORD
BY VIVIAN RIDLER
PRINTER TO THE UNIVERSITY